The
MAYOR
of
MOGADISHU

The
MAYOR
of
MOGADISHU

A Story of Chaos and Redemption in
the Ruins of Somalia

ANDREW HARDING

ST. MARTIN'S PRESS
NEW YORK

www.stmartins.com

Map of Africa and Somalia by Paul Pugliese
Book design by Ellen Cipriano

LIBRARY OF CONGRESS CATALOGING-IN-PUBLICATION DATA

Names: Harding, Andrew.
Title: The mayor of Mogadishu : a story of chaos and redemption in the ruins of
   Somalia / Andrew Harding.
Description: First edition. | New York : St. Martin's Press, 2016.
Identifiers: LCCN 2016012738| ISBN 9781250072344 (U.S. edition) |
   ISBN 9781466883925 (e-book)
Subjects: LCSH: Nur, Mohamud, 1956- | Mayors—Somalia—Mogadishu—
   Biography. | Mogadishu (Somalia)—Politics and government—21st century. |
   Mogadishu (Somalia)—Biography. | Nomads—Somalia—Mogadishu—
   Biography. | Orphans—Somalia—Mogadishu—Biography. | Political
   activists—Somalia—Mogadishu—Biography. | Somalis—England—
   London—Biography. | Immigrants—England—London—Biography.
Classification: LCC DT409.M63 H37 2016 | DDC 967.73—dc23
LC record available at http://lccn.loc.gov/2016012738

First Edition: November 2016

10 9 8 7 6 5 4 3 2 1

To my family

And in memory of
my parents and grandparents

CONTENTS

PART 3
Picking Up the Pieces: 2010–2016

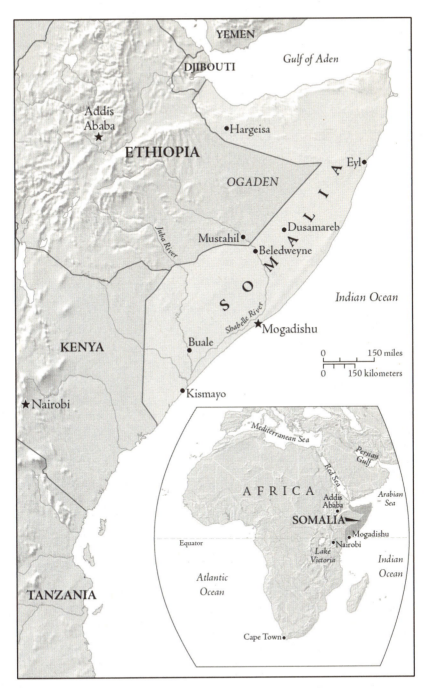

Map of Africa and Somalia. MAP BY PAUL PUGLIESE

Villa Somalia

"We're safe in here. Surely."

—MOHAMUD "TARZAN" NUR

IMAGINE, FOR A MOMENT, THAT you're floating in the cold silence of space, somewhere over the equator, perhaps five thousand miles above the earth. From this height you can see the whole of Africa spread out below you. Pale yellow at the top and bottom. A stripe of avocado green across the middle.

At first glance, the continent resembles nothing in particular.

But if you tilt your head to the right, the shapeless lump below is suddenly transformed into an elegant horse's head, leaning in from the left, and bowing down in a docile manner to sip the waters of the Antarctic Ocean.

The dark blotch of Lake Victoria is the horse's right eye. Cape Town sits placidly on the bottom lip, and the place we're interested in—the place we're now racing toward—is the horse's perky right ear as it juts out and up into the Indian Ocean. From this height the ear, better known as the Horn of Africa, looks almost pink.

As we slip down, a thousand miles above the earth now, we glide toward the northeast, over Mount Kenya and Mount Kilimanjaro—from this height, just white pimples in the savannah. A straight, white coastline appears on the right.

We're over Somalia. Green patches in the south, then a vast, smudged expanse of grays and curdled yellows, with pink and red dabs, and the tiniest veins of dark green.

Now Mogadishu is directly beneath us. Somalia's capital is just a dull smear on the coastline from this height. But we're sinking faster,

---

Mogadishu, 1960s. OFFICIAL MOGADISHU GUIDEBOOK, 1971

and swinging out over the bright blue water to approach the city like the commercial airlines still do—keeping away from the shore until the very last minute to avoid rockets and gunfire.

And then suddenly the city takes shape before us in three dimensions.

The name itself seems forbidding. Like Stalingrad, Kabul, Grozny, and, these days, Syria's Homs, Mogadishu conjures up lurid images of destruction.

But *Mogadishu* covers even more territory. It has become a bloated cliché, not just of war but of famine and piracy, terrorism, warlords, anarchy, exodus . . . All the worst headlines of our time invoked by one lilting, gently poetic, four-syllable word.

And yet today, as we swoop down toward the city center, Mogadishu looks unexpectedly, impossibly, undeniably pretty. A sandy, sunny seaside picture postcard of a city perched on a hill beside a turquoise sea.

Two curving harbor walls reach out into the Indian Ocean like crab claws. The airport runway emerges from the gruff, white waves to the south, to point like a guidebook's arrow toward the city's heart. There's the beautiful old stone lighthouse, the outline of the cathedral, the fish market and a cluster of handsome old buildings around it, then a handful of taller buildings halfway up a gentle, dune-like hill, and the parliament at the top. And there's Lido beach further north, almost at low tide now, and starting to fill up with young bathers, some just visible either in groups on the sand or leaping into the surf in bright orange lifejackets, rented from tiny stalls on the rocky shoreline.

At first, it's hard to see the ruins. The cathedral, for example, seems determined to hide the fact that it's just a roofless shell, one of its twin towers missing. But as we glide inland and up toward the parliament, the rest of the city, tucked behind the first ridge like a guilty secret, comes into view.

The land dips behind the parliament, and we can see a makeshift camp of ragged tents, and beyond it, the slump of a shallow valley where the buildings seem to huddle before rising again toward the Bakara market. An experienced eye might notice the absence of greenery. Where are the trees that once shaded so many streets in this neighborhood? And here, in the middle of the slump, the fierce sunlight ripples sharply along a jagged line of rooftops. It's another clue. Like a bandage on a healing wound, the shiny corrugated iron roofs are evidence of the repair work now underway, as families try to move back into the ruins of what was, until recently, Mogadishu's frontline—a scar that split the city in two.

This aerial view is appropriately perplexing. These are edgy, beguiling, bewildering times for Mogadishu, and indeed for the entire country. There is smug talk of corners being turned, signs of a "failed" nation clawing its way back toward viability, of the diaspora returning after decades in exile, businesses thriving, and stereotypes being shattered. Perhaps the worst is finally over. And if Somalia can breed optimism, what lessons might it hold for those now trying to fix Syria, Iraq, Yemen, and other broken states?

And yet below us, on the dusty streets of Mogadishu, the same beasts still prowl. Terror, corruption, clan conflict, extremism, and, chasing at their tails, the lingering fear that Somalia is merely flirting with stability. That it will soon slide back into old habits. That the only lesson it can teach us is what not to do.

It's almost exactly noon on a hot, cloudless Friday. And suddenly our attention is jerked away from that sunlit line of corrugated roofs. On what now looks like the highest point in the whole city, a large cloud of black smoke is rising like a balloon into the humid air.

It is Friday, February 21, 2014, and in a country where the percussion of violence—gunshots, rockets, mortars, grenades, bombs—has, over the decades, become embedded in people's minds as the background music of an ordinary day, a particularly loud and brazen attack is beginning.

A DEEP, SHARP, BOOM rolls across the contours of the city.

A car bomb has just been detonated by a suicide attacker outside the half-renovated northern gate of Villa Somalia, the hilltop seat of the country's government. Seconds later, a second car explodes nearby. The echoes of the two blasts mingle and separate, like thunder, across Mogadishu.

The explosions have entirely shredded two cars and torn a hole in the compound's wall below a new, half-built watchtower. Seven gunmen, dressed to look more or less like the official security guards patrolling the area, are rushing inside.

Villa Somalia is a fortress. But the attackers surely have inside knowledge. They've picked a weak point. At first they meet no resistance as they run up a wide, empty avenue along the outer wall of a house now occupied by Somalia's new president.

Ahead of them, other large buildings are half-hidden behind trees. There's the prime minister's residence, and the speaker of parliament's. Villa Somalia is an oddity—a swaggering Italian colonial palace, now caught somewhere between a luxury gated compound and a dilapidated college campus. It is home to the latest in a succession of fragile new Somali governments, some of whose authority has extended no further than the walls of Villa Somalia itself.

Mohamud "Tarzan" Nur is halfway through the doors of Villa Somalia's mosque, just opposite the president's quarters, when he hears the first explosion, perhaps a hundred yards away.

"Stay calm," he says to the men nearby, trying to sound nonchalant.

There's a big crowd at the mosque today. Perhaps three hundred shoes and flip-flops sit on the tiled steps outside what seems like a surprisingly modest little white-walled building.

There are nods at the door, and a low murmur of conversation. No one here is a stranger to adrenaline. Indeed, to be a politician or a government official or any public figure in Mogadishu these days is to live, if not in fear, then in an almost constant state of antennae-twitching awareness, masked by a half-competitive, macho struggle to remain composed no matter what.

The daily routine of trying to avoid routine is exhausting. Was that a motorbike in the rearview mirror? A bearded stranger? How to vary your journey to work? Where to sit in a restaurant? And for how long? Which colleagues to trust? Which functions to avoid? In the past few months the high court, parliament, and several hotels have come under attack. Individual assassinations—usually on the street with a bullet to the back of the head—happen almost daily, ratcheting up the tension like the relentless beat of a metronome.

Right now, inside the mosque, two thought sequences are rattling more or less simultaneously through Tarzan's head.

"Sounds like a car exploded outside. The military can take care of it. We're safe in here. Surely. There must be enough soldiers to keep us safe."

The second thought is a reaction to the increasingly nervous, questioning faces around him; to the scrum starting to form at the blue-tinted glass door; and to Tarzan's own sense of himself—as the mayor of Mogadishu—a powerful position, even if he's only clinging to it by his fingertips these days.

He's been in the job for almost four years. That's far longer than anyone expected, not least because of his reckless habit of speaking his mind, bluntly. Caution is considered a survival instinct here, above all for politicians, but Tarzan seems unable to bite his tongue.

"I don't afraid anyone," is the way he's put it to me, in his fluent, self-taught English. "I'm not a person—what do you call it?—an arse-licker."

And the result is that no one in Mogadishu is merely indifferent to the mayor. In a city of grudges, score-settling, and fiercely whispered judgments, everyone has an opinion about Tarzan.

He's a thug, a shallow charmer, the only honest politician in town, a useful whirlwind, a slave to his own clan's interests, a corrupt hypocrite, a cheap populist, Somalia's future president, a media sideshow, the diaspora's darling, the city's savior.

The only thing no one seems inclined to dispute is his courage. Although his critics call it a showy disdain for self-preservation, and his enemies see it as a recklessness he will surely be made to regret.

And so that second thought takes shape in Tarzan's mind, and turns almost instantly into action.

"Let me go over and start to pray. We should all pray. It will help prevent panic. Believe me."

Beckoning briefly to the others, Tarzan walks in his black socks across the faded green and gold carpet toward the front right corner of the mosque—his usual spot—and kneels down, toes peeping out from below black trousers, flecks of gray in his close-cropped black hair.

Outside, the shooting is getting closer.

Tarzan bows his head toward the carpet, and somehow manages to let his mind drift away—or at least half away—into the routine of prayer. He's a man inclined toward brusque certainties, and right now he has decided that the shooting is all "outgoing." The situation is under control.

In his early sixties, Tarzan still looks like he's in good shape. He's stockier than many Somalis. A bulldog, you might say, in a nation of whippets. He has a round, pleasant face, but his bright white teeth seem perpetually exposed in a snarling sort of grin. His oval brown eyes leap and flash in tune to his every thought. High on his forehead, there's a lump left behind from an old fight, and the lobe of his left ear is gone, bitten off years ago. The trimmed beard below his mouth has turned a suave white. It looks like the chin of an aristocrat framing the face of a brawler.

Down the slope perhaps two blocks east of Villa Somalia, Tarzan's wife, Shamis, has heard the explosion and the gunfire and has quickly worked out where the noise must be coming from. It's less than ten minutes since Tarzan left their house; driving past the guards at the end of their short road, then up through the labyrinth of concrete barriers and gates leading into the main entrance of the Villa. Surely he must be the target.

"Oh my God! They've killed him."

Shamis is a confident, talkative woman. She thinks of herself as a worrier, but she's not prone to overreacting. She never wanted Tarzan to come back to Mogadishu after so many years in London, but for years she's tried to bury her fears about his job, and the threats and assassination attempts against him. It's a game they both play.

But now she's standing in the cluttered sitting room of their bungalow, screaming to the walls as the bullets zip overhead. In her heart, she knows her husband has died.

The couple's eldest son, Ahmed—the first of six—comes rushing in. He looks a lot like his father, and he has a reputation—far less admired than Tarzan's—for taking unnecessary risks. He often drives around Mogadishu after dark without security, and his friends have come up with a new nickname for him—"Kill Me." But Friday prayers are not a priority for Ahmed. Rather than accompanying his father to the mosque, he was half-asleep in the neighboring house on their small cul-de-sac, until he was woken by the gunfire and by his mother.

Now the seven gunmen have reached the back of the mosque. This is their target. The president should have strolled over from his villa for prayers by now. Killing him will be straightforward. Except that the president, for no particular reason, is unexpectedly late today. It means he's safe behind high walls.

There's a mixture of security teams guarding Villa Somalia—foreign peacekeepers on the perimeter, Somali government troops inside, along with a chaotic assortment of close protection and national intelligence agents. In the past that's been a recipe for confusion and infighting, but they're edging forward as a group now, firing constantly, some crawling in the dirt, others sheltering behind a small office building just a few yards from the mosque. Beside them, a big satellite dish on a concrete stand has been turned into a bullet-riddled colander.

Inside the mosque, the imam has taken refuge in an alcove just in front of Tarzan. He's a light-hearted, bespectacled man. Suddenly, he sees a figure in army fatigues at the nearest window, to Tarzan's right. A soldier, perhaps? Another man joins him. The imam can see their faces clearly now. One of the men shouts "Allahu Akbar" and starts shooting through the clear glass into the mosque.

Everything is happening at furious speed.

There's an elderly man—once a senior figure in the intelligence service—kneeling beside Tarzan in the front row. Bullets from the gunman at the window rip into him. He is killed on the spot.

It seems hard to believe that Tarzan is still praying beside the dead man. When gunfire is close by—particularly in and around buildings—it can be almost impossible to work out which direction it's coming from. Still, surely he must have noticed what's happening around him.

But the imam is in no doubt. Tarzan has not moved an inch. Months later, it's the one detail in the whole story that makes him chuckle.

"He stayed praying! No one else did. Not even me. He believed in Allah!"

By this point, Abukar Dahir's instincts have finally kicked in. He's been crouching just outside the mosque's entrance, caught in a blur of panic. Now he catches a glimpse of two gunmen, perhaps twenty yards away, and his legs make the decision for him, sprinting south, across the courtyard, and out of danger.

Abukar is a skinny, self-assured twenty-six-year-old; a banker from a well-to-do family who grew up in Mogadishu, then Damascus, Moscow, Stockholm, and finally west London. He's back in Mogadishu trying to do his bit, which in his case means stints at the central bank and the foreign ministry.

Within a couple of minutes, Abukar has talked his way through the security cordon at one of the hotels at the far edge of the compound—a place where any MPs and officials who can afford the rates often camp out for weeks at a time. And here are two of his colleagues, who escaped just ahead of him. They're sitting in a corner, inside, hunched over a mobile phone, trying to get through to a fourth friend.

The missing man is Mohamud Hersi Abdulle. Like the others, he's a member of the spirited, fast-changing pool of diaspora Somalis who've come back to the country to work up at the Villa. He's a rising star—already the chief of staff in the prime minister's office. But when he finally answers his phone, it is to tell his friends that he's pinned down by gunfire, trapped in another building just beside the mosque.

"They came in they came in they came in!" he's shouting down the phone. Abukar is listening with the other two on speakerphone. "They'reshootingthey'reshooting . . ."

The voice stops abruptly, and Abukar feels the air pulled out of his own chest as he hears the gunshots. He can hear them all too clearly through the phone, and a split second earlier—or maybe later—from outside the hotel. And he can hear, or at least he thinks he can hear, the sound of bullets hitting flesh. It's hard to explain, but they sound different, as if he can tell there's no ricochet.

Outside the mosque windows, the attackers don't have much time left. Perhaps a minute or less. They're outnumbered and pinned down. One of the attackers throws a grenade into the mosque, but it fails to explode. One of the officials inside has a gun and finally begins shooting back, hitting an attacker as he approaches the main entrance.

And now a solitary figure makes his way across the carpet, past the tiled pillars, toward Tarzan.

Mohamed Fanah is a gruff, muscular man in a leather jacket. He is Tarzan's cousin, and has remained in Mogadishu through all its wars. Now he's in charge of the mayor's security and somehow he has managed to bring a car up close to the mosque door. In the process, some of the car's tires have been shredded by gunfire.

"They're inside. They're inside. We leave now," says Fanah, grabbing Tarzan's shoulder and pulling him sharply up from the carpet.

Tarzan is jolted out of whatever thoughts or prayers were keeping him on his knees; and only now, as he sees the dead body to his left, does he begin to understand what's been happening. Bullets are still coming into the room as Tarzan and Fanah join the back of the scrum now pushing its way out of the door, trampling barefoot over the shoes still lying on the steps. Out into the harsh sunshine.

≈≈≈◉≈≈

LATER IN THE AFTERNOON, when it's all over, the bodies of seven attackers—all those who entered Villa Somalia—are dragged down the path and out onto the street, near to the wreckage of their car bombs and to an incongruously bright patch of pink bougainvillea blossom.

The rest is predictable: the phone call from a spokesman for the Islamist militant group Al Shabab, claiming responsibility for an attack against "infidels"; and the defiant presidential speech, asserting that Al Shabab remains "on the brink of extinction."

And then a practiced collective shrug.

After all, Mogadishu has been through all this before, so many times.

The seven bodies lie for hours in the dirt. They've been dumped haphazardly, contemptuously. Some have lost their shoes. One is shirtless. Their blood has sunk into the earth around them and been dried by the sun.

Who were these men? The truth is that nobody even tries to find out. It has been years since Somalia's bureaucracy was destroyed, along with all records of births and of identity. Besides, the police have no forensic capability. So the usual rumors begin instead, scratching at the official version of events. Maybe it was an inside job; maybe Al Shabab is everywhere; maybe the attack was more about clans, or business, than religion; maybe the truth doesn't even matter anymore.

And what of Tarzan? The mayor has already sidestepped death

many times in Mogadishu. Can luck reset, like a stopwatch, or does it drain away like a puddle in the sand?

What follows in these pages is Tarzan's life story, or something close to it—the truth can be a hard thing to pin down in Somalia. It's a story of reinvention, defiance, and ambition—of an abandoned child, turned restless teenager, who fled from war and then dared to return home from exile, to a city of ruins, to fight his own battles.

Some Somalis would say Tarzan's life mirrors their country's tumultuous journey, from the optimism of independence through a generation of conflict and despair and now back to a faltering sort of hope. Some would go even further, arguing that Tarzan's story is an eloquent riposte to those foreign politicians outside Somalia who want to build walls and block immigration—that two decades of safety and study in Britain acted like an incubator, providing him, and countless others, with the skills needed to start, eventually, rebuilding Mogadishu.

Others will tell you that Tarzan deserves no such praise. That he's a callow, corrupt survivor. Nothing more. He is, as I mentioned, a divisive figure. But one thing seems clear to me: His story is a thread that weaves its way through decades of upheaval—a glint worth following in a dark maze.

PART 1

The Pearl of
the Indian Ocean

1956–1976

*"Mogadishu was the safest city.
We had the delicacies of life on a plate."*

—NURUDDIN FARAH,
SOMALI NOVELIST

A Constellation of Nomads

"There are no records. So you can claim whatever you want."

—YUSUF NUR

I T ALL STARTS, I SUPPOSE, with a lie. Or perhaps it would be fairer to call it an invention.

"I was born here in Mogadishu. My mother came here when she was about nine months. Then she had baby. This baby was me," says Tarzan.

He has an abrupt, intense way of speaking. His brown eyes dart, as if I'm not enough of an audience and he's sweeping the room for other reactions.

It's just gone dark, and we're sitting on the covered terrace outside his house, just below Villa Somalia, the mosquitoes whining lazily at our ankles. It's the last week of Ramadan—a hot, sluggish time in the city—and Tarzan is breaking his daily fast with some dates and a sip of tea, and waiting for Shamis to come outside with a tray of hot food.

The narrow terrace runs along two whole sides of their house. The walls are a pale yellow, the floors covered in white tiles, and the outside arches and corners are crowded with dozens of plants in white pots. That's Shamis's touch. She's worked hard—in part to kill the boredom of what sometimes feels like a prison—to create a homely atmosphere. The terrace could almost be a little café, with its plastic chairs and round tables, each with a plastic tablecloth.

Shamis brings out a thick, porridge-like soup called *marak*, which Tarzan loves, a plate of fried liver, some pasta—a nod toward Italy's role in Somalia's colonial past—and then Turkish baklava to finish.

Camel market, Mogadishu, 1960s. OFFICIAL MOGADISHU GUIDEBOOK, 1971

She's wearing a long yellow dress, and she drapes an arm on his shoulder. It's a casual gesture, but here in Mogadishu, where women now feel the need to wear a veil in public, it seems boldly intimate. It's not the first time I've been aware of the electric jolt of affection that seems to flicker between Tarzan and Shamis, even after all these years together. I know their children are quietly proud of it—other Somali parents seem so much more restrained.

Tarzan speaks English quickly and confidently, in a guttural accent—part London, part Somali—pronouncing "months" as "month-es," with an emphasis on the last syllable. Most plurals get the same treatment, and it's only some time later, when I'm talking to an Italian who grew up in Somalia, that I realize where that extra syllable might have come from.

"I was born in the Martino hospital. Room 18," he continues, wafting his hand in the general direction of the sea, then waving at two men who have just walked onto the terrace and quietly taken seats in the corner, as if waiting for a doctor's appointment. Tarzan is in his casual clothes—bare legs and feet, a long sarong-like *macawis*, and a black short-sleeved shirt.

"National health! Free. The Italians controlled the hospital. Nuns. Nuns! They were my midwives. It was 1954." Tarzan is enjoying himself.

The San Martino Hospital—a ruin these days—was once a landmark in the city, right on the seafront, about a mile away from here. Tarzan looks nostalgic as he describes the circumstances of his birth, how his mother dutifully made the long trek from the wilderness of the Ogaden, where the family lived as nomads; and then how she returned with her newborn son, to her husband and firstborn, immediately after Tarzan's birth.

Except that it's not true . . . none of his birth story is. But it will take me a while to discover that, and much longer to work out why he feels the need to reinvent himself.

Shamis has brought more tea to the table now, and some honey to stir into it. I've got my notebook out and I've written "Room 18" and underlined it. It's a resonant detail, I'm thinking. Not something I'd have remembered about my own birth.

At this point, I've been visiting Somalia, on and off, for twelve years, as a journalist for BBC News. I can feel the place burrowing into my skull. There is something uncomfortably bewitching about some conflict zones. I've felt it in Chechnya, Iraq, Afghanistan, Liberia, and in plenty of other countries. But there is a particular intensity to the experience of visiting Somalia, and it's hard to pin down why. The sunbaked ruins are spectacular, and the people are impossibly, jaw-droppingly resilient, but it's more than that. It feels like a place untethered from the outside world. A city that has suffered for so long that war has become the status quo.

It's August 2012—two years before the attack on Villa Somalia's mosque—and two years since I first met Tarzan.

Visiting Mogadishu, particularly as a foreigner, is a risky, expensive, and, above all, logistically complicated process. Who guards you—a particular clan, foreign peacekeepers, the UN, private security contractors? Do you stay with the military, or in a hotel, or with the government? Which rumors to believe? What security advice to trust? Should you avoid all convoys? Is it safer to keep a low profile in a small car, or to hire a dozen guards? Will the budget stretch to bulletproof windows? What does bulletproof even mean, in practice?

The result is usually a string of short, slightly frantic trips.

Tarzan caught my attention from the start. It is, you might say, in his nature to do so. He's impatient, outspoken, and refreshingly different from almost every other politician I've met here. Most are cautious to a fault. And who can blame them? Perhaps Tarzan is a little too media savvy. I always feel slightly suspicious of anyone who actively wants to talk to a journalist. But still, I'm intrigued.

Boom . . . There's a hollow-sounding explosion, a small one, a few blocks away. Shamis has joined us at the table and looks around sharply, as do I. Tarzan continues to sip his tea and quietly announces, "Grenade." Sure enough, tomorrow's Somali news websites will confirm that a grenade was thrown in the market, just a few hundred meters away, in an area known as Shangani.

This is the third evening in a row that I've spent breaking the Ramadan fast with Tarzan and Shamis at their small home, and I'm slowly getting used to the unusual feeling of being outside the regular security bubble that has, in varying forms, dominated every other trip I've made to Mogadishu.

I was dropped off at around 6:00 p.m. Eight local armed guards, from the foreign-run guesthouse I'm staying at near the airport, drove behind our car and waited at the security barrier at the end of Tarzan's rubbish-strewn cul-de-sac, as we went on through. A tall, cheerful, eastern European security advisor—who rather spoiled the mood on the journey by reminding me that the bounty on a foreigner's head is between US$1 million and $1.5 million—then got out of the front passenger seat of our car, briefly assessed the situation, came to open my door, and escorted me into Tarzan's house, past an elderly man sitting beside the bright green gate with a Kalashnikov on his knee.

And now I've been transferred—and it's hard not to feel just a tiny bit like a hostage—into the hands of Tarzan's own security team. On previous nights, his eldest son Ahmed drove me back, on his own, to my fortress-like guesthouse, picking his way through the dark back streets, past several sleepy crowds of goats, and through a handful of army checkpoints.

It's a year now since the militants of Al Shabab abruptly withdrew from Mogadishu, in the middle of a famine, and the city is currently enjoying a period of relative calm.

On the terrace, Tarzan turns in his seat to beckon the two men who've been waiting for a chance to talk. It's been like this every night—a steady stream of uninvited visitors hoping to bend the ear of the mayor of Mogadishu. The men are from his clan. One wants to become an MP, the other is his lobbyist. They've traveled 400 kilometers from the town of Beledweyne, in the hope of securing Tarzan's endorsement.

"I don't know," says Tarzan, when the men finally leave. He thinks the would-be MP "talks too much." He scratches at his elbow and then lashes out at the mosquitoes around his ankles.

Shamis, meanwhile, has had enough of playing the politician's wife for one day.

"When Ramadan is finished I'm not allowing it anymore. I tell the guards, 'Don't let anyone to come here after five o'clock! No more.' Cos I want to be alone with my husband. When you are at work people should go to your office, but this is my place and I want to be alone with you." Her English is less polished than her husband's, but she speaks with warm, almost theatrical intimacy.

Tarzan chuckles. It's evidently not the first time they've had this discussion.

"You've become English woman! You are not Somali anymore," he teases.

More visitors come and go. Fresh tea is poured. Late in the evening, the business calls thin out, and an old school friend drops in, then the lady who lives across the street. And finally I'm back in Ahmed's car, and he's driving too fast as we go down the hill, through another, bigger security barrier beside the old national theater, then right and along the main road toward the airport.

Ahmed repeats his mantra, "Mogadishu is quite safe," in a distinctively London accent. But he's clearly still edgy about the militants of Al Shabab. "You can't trust anyone here. At least with your own clan you can vet people, and trace stuff back if things go wrong."

Ahmed—his father later admits to me—has been brought back to Mogadishu in order to be "straightened out."

"I'm just trying to find my niche here, cos it's—like—a blank canvas, a lot of things missing. So I'm importing security equipment for now . . . from Dubai." Tarzan's critics claim Ahmed has been winning contracts improperly, because of his father's influence.

Ten minutes and a maze of side streets later, I'm knocking on the giant metal gates of my guesthouse, watched by the displaced families still camped out in their ragged tent across the street, and by the armed guards manning the guesthouse's turrets, who peer down and then give a shout to let me in.

⁂

FOUR MONTHS PASS, AND finally, I manage to get hold of Tarzan's younger brother, Yusuf, on the phone. It's not been easy to track down his number. Tarzan will talk all night, face-to-face, but he's notoriously sluggish when it comes to answering phones, emails, and texts.

"He's not a good communicator," Yusuf concedes. It's a bit of a family joke. "We Somalis prefer talking to writing anytime."

Yusuf is at home in the United States, with two teenaged daughters and a crumbling marriage. He's a professor, driving every week into Kokomo, near Indianapolis, where he teaches business studies at the university. In his spare time, he's become a fanatical mountain biker.

"It's a two-hour drive. Let's chat."

We fall into a pattern of arranging phone calls while he's doing the commute and, later, on his travels—to northern Somalia, Dubai, and even Taiwan, where his two daughters end up spending a summer teaching English before taking their father on a cycling holiday.

"Hands free, I assure you," he says on the first call. "I'm heading north on Highway 37. It connects my little town to Indianapolis. Sometimes I spend the night at the university. Like tonight—I have a late class. I wish I lived in the countryside, but the children would not let me do that. I'm the only Somali in Bloomington, believe it or not! Well, I wouldn't know for sure, but there's no community, so the only way I'd know if a Somali was in town is if they come to the mosque. There are no Somalis at my campus, either. Indianapolis started bringing refugees in the late nineties and I went to their section of town. They have a restaurant—no food, but a hubbly-bubbly, a water pipe [hookah]. And people chewed khat [a mildly narcotic leaf chewed with vigorous enthusiasm across Somalia]—illegally I guess. I can't stand smoke, so that was first and last time I went there."

As you may have gleaned, Yusuf is a details man, a natural teacher. He's garrulous and charming, too, with a light American accent and an unquenchable enthusiasm for explaining Somali words and customs.

"He told you that?" Yusuf laughs when I ask him about Tarzan's birth, in room 18 at the San Martino Hospital.

But then he quickly changes tone. His brother is a public figure, and he doesn't want to be disloyal. Eventually he settles on a diplomatic but still revealing truth.

"There are no records. So you can claim whatever you want."

"I was born under a tree. It was the most natural birth imaginable," says Yusuf, and as his neat, precise tones zip down the phone line from Indiana, I start picturing the dry wilderness he's talking about.

⁂

"IF YOU DRIVE NORTH out of Mogadishu . . ." As I write that sentence, I realize it should probably finish with "then you would be a fool." It's not a journey to be attempted these days, with roadside bombs, kidnappings, and unexpected roadblocks targeting civilian buses, trucks, and armored African Union military convoys alike. But let's put those risks to one side for now, and imagine coming out of Tarzan's house, and turning left onto Corso Somalia, the main road that snakes through the city and out, past the old pasta factory, into the sand-blown, low-rise outskirts. You'll quickly find yourself crossing a dusty plain on a straight but almost comically potholed road. Perhaps an hour out of town, the dry countryside suddenly turns green as the road enters a region irrigated by the Shabelle River, where most of Mogadishu's food is grown. The road follows the river's path upstream.

The Shabelle, meaning a place of leopards, is a meandering river prone to flash floods. It wouldn't get much notice in most countries. But Somalia has only two rivers of any size or significance. The Shabelle begins in the green Ethiopian highlands on the eastern edge of the Rift Valley, then crosses a high plateau into Somalia, heading straight for the coast before losing its nerve outside Mogadishu,

swinging south, and dwindling into a few brackish puddles somewhere in the sand dunes outside the port of Kismayo.

After about 450 lonely kilometers, the long road north eventually
forks at the tiny town of Jawiil, otherwise known as Kala Bayr, which
simply means "fork in the road." It's home to some of Tarzan's extended
family, and "the only one town we claim as our own," says Yusuf.

It's rough country—the ragged fringes of the geological bruising
caused by the giant Rift Valley. It's not quite a desert, but rain is often
rare and always precious.

I've not managed to visit Jawiil. But I once flew to Dusamareb, a
much larger Somali town about 200 kilometers to the northeast.

I have two particular memories of the trip. The first is of sitting
in the negligible shade of a thornbush just outside town, beneath a
blazing afternoon sun, talking to an understandably gloomy man who
was scraping a living by gathering scarce firewood from the surrounding plains to sell by the roadside. "I'm waiting for change. But things
are just getting worse," he said, as his wife remained hidden behind
him inside a tiny tent, constructed from thorn branches and a blue
plastic sheet provided by the UN. He'd once had a home and a job
in Mogadishu, but the family had been compelled to flee fighting
there, then to flee more fighting in Dusamareb, and was now stranded
in no-man's-land. I looked around me at the flat, hot earth and the
scorched sky, wondered how it was possible to survive here, and
thought of the well-thumbed book tucked in my rucksack.

Warriors is one of the few foreign accounts of rural life in Somalia.
It was written by a British army officer charged with policing the region during the Second World War, and composed in tones as dry as
the place. Somalia was "a desiccated, bitter, cruel, sun-beaten" wilderness, marked by its "mad stubborn camels, rocks too hot to touch,
and blood feuds whose origins cannot be remembered, only honored
in the stabbing," Gerald Hanley declared.

"But of all the races of Africa there cannot be one better to live
among than the most difficult, the proudest, the bravest, the vainest,
the most merciless, the friendliest; the Somalis."

My second memory from Dusamareb is from later the same afternoon in 2009. It was, we discovered, Somali Independence Day. A moderate Sunni group was in control of the town and had just fought off a ferocious assault by the militants of Al Shabab. Outside the bullet-riddled government headquarters in the town center, a group of children, women, and heavily armed fighters had gathered together in a touchingly neat line to sing the national anthem of the period. A local student generously attempted a translation for me and said it was about "waking up and leaning together." The chorus is, indeed, an unusually and pleasingly bossy list of instructions—a distinct change from the wordless old Italian anthem and the more recent, flowery, and forgettable version. Here's a more formal translation of the chorus we heard:

> *Somalis wake up!*
> *Wake up and support each other.*
> *Support your country.*
> *Support it forever.*
> *Stop fighting each other.*
> *Come back with strength and joy and be friends again.*
> *It's time to look forward and take command,*
> *Defeat your enemies and unite once again.*
> *Become strong, again and again.*

Back on the main road north from Mogadishu, a few miles past Fork in the Road, is the long, impossibly straight, contentious border with Ethiopia; the very definition of one of those careless, arbitrary lines drawn on a map decades ago by colonial officials in distant boardrooms. In this case, Britain, Ethiopia, Italy, and France were the main players in a scramble for territory and influence that stretched back at least as far as the sixteenth century, and was only settled in the aftermath of the Second World War. Or half settled.

If you look on any map, you'll see Somalia hugging the shoreline of the Horn of Africa, along the top edge and down the Indian Ocean, in a fairly clear approximation of the number 7. To the west, Ethiopia appears to jab into Somalia, like a rhinoceros trying to push it, rather aggressively, into the sea. And that's how many Somalis still view it—that Ethiopia's border "bulge" is stolen Somali territory, a high plateau still populated by people with far closer ethnic and historic ties to Somalia than to Ethiopia.

"Any child my age grew up knowing of Ethiopia's enmity to Somalia. Ethiopia is our main enemy. It's a hyena. It doesn't want us to stand on our own two feet," Tarzan says.

On Google Maps today the border is marked by a dotted rather than a solid line "to reflect the ground-based reality that the two countries maintain an ongoing dispute in the region," as Google puts it.

It is on the far side of this dotted border, inside Ethiopia, that Yusuf was born. And Tarzan, too.

"Our grazing land was almost exclusively on the east side of the river Shabelle, north of the border," says Yusuf, sketching out a vast chunk of territory inside Ethiopia, widely known as the Ogaden.

"The furthest we go west is the river town of Mustahil. That means 'Prohibition' in Arabic. I don't know why they called it that."

I've not been to Prohibition, but I have visited a town called Gode, a little further upstream inside Ethiopia, and a nearby settlement called Danan. It was one of the first trips I made after moving to Africa in 2000, and I was unprepared for the experience. The region was in the grip of yet another drought, and on a wind-lashed plain outside Danan, I walked toward a cluster of flimsy shelters made of twigs and rags. "Huts like molehills. Dust swirling," is what I wrote in my notebook at the time. I'd never seen such poverty before. The families inside the molehills were starving, skeletal. They told me they'd traveled 150 kilometers—five days' walk—to get help.

So that is the picture I'm holding in my head, as Yusuf begins describing his own early childhood.

"WE WERE DIRT-POOR," Yusuf says, of the Nur family.

But he's not looking for pity. Quite the opposite. There is a quiet pride in his voice.

"I was born at a place called Mayr-Qurac," he says. "*Mayr* is a special kind of reed, used to make thick mats to cover nomadic huts and camels' backs. *Qurac* is the most common tree in Somalia. In Kenya the bark is light, yellowish green, but in Somalia they're darker brown and shorter. It's an acacia tree, but a special type. The hardiest tree. That would be our national tree."

And so I begin to piece together the family's humble, but for Somalis very typical, nomadic origins. Tarzan's grandfather had been nicknamed Nur-Baadi.

"*Baadi* means a lost flock of goats or camels." Yusuf is driving through a snowstorm in Indiana as he explains this.

"My grandfather's mother was looking for lost goats and when she found them she went into labor. So she named him after that. All Somali names have meaning. We cling to those meanings—like a Toni Morrison novel."

Nur-Baadi's son was called Ahmed, and he inherited his father's nickname along with a prominent gap between his front teeth and a share of the family's camels, goats, and cattle. Yusuf would inherit the teeth, too, and he now signs his name "Yusuf Ahmed Nur 'Baadi,' PhD."

And so they moved, as nomads do, around their grazing lands, following the rains and the fresh grass, keeping their wells clean and clear, sometimes staying in one place for a few months, sometimes moving every night to keep up with the livestock, always on the look-out for lions and for strangers.

It must have been a grueling life. And it continues to this day. Indeed many Somali families, wherever they are, still own camels and still have relatives looking after them in the wilderness.

In many ways that nomadic spirit—something both entirely

literal and wildly romantic—holds a key to understanding Somalia. It is a country of proudly independent families, deeply suspicious of outside authority, linked together horizontally by paternal bloodlines, clan allegiances, and carefully arranged marriages.

"So and so begets, who begat, etcetera," says Yusuf crisply.

On a continent so often shaped by chiefs, and by top-down authority, Somalia presents itself as a radical exception, as a constellation of equals. In some ways, it's a source of great strength and stability. But in the wrong circumstances, it can be quite the opposite. As the old Somali proverb goes:

Me and my clan against the world;
Me and my family against my clan;
Me and my brother against my family;
Me against my brother.

It must have been in about 1950, or shortly after, that Ahmed Nur decided to remarry. His first wife had just died, leaving him with four young children—two sons and two daughters.

Ahmed's second wife was young and unenthusiastic. Her name was Habeba, and she was about twenty-two years old, an orphan whose parents had died during a drought. Her full name, or at least a good chunk of it, was Habeba Abdi Abdille Omar, and then her nickname, "Libaax."

Somalis carry their family trees with them in this fashion—a rattling sack of male ancestors stretching back as far as an individual can be bothered, or made, to recall. Some can count back ten or twenty generations. For nomads, it's a way of defining and shoring up their identity in a world without passports or bureaucracy.

Libaax means "lion" and was a reference to a moderately famous relative, a poet who had fought under the command of a considerably more famous poet in the anti-imperial wars against Britain and Italy in the early 1900s.

Yusuf still remembers a handful of Libaax's verses.

A married man without a herd of goats
Is like an empty vessel.
His wife will always be destitute and thirsty.
His daughter will go unnoticed,
Looked down on.
Oh Lord, multiply my goats for me,
I will be ever so tenacious in safeguarding them.

Every Somali who has been to school knows the works of Libaax's commander, the charismatic, divisive resistance leader Muhammad Abdullah Hassan. The British sought to mock and marginalize him as the "Mad Mullah," but his searing, bloodthirsty poems have endured alongside his legend. Indeed, listening to "The Death of Richard Corfield," where he celebrates the death, in battle, of an impetuous British colonial officer, you can almost trace a link to the swagger of modern-day rappers, dissing each other, head-to-head:

Say: Beasts of prey have eaten my flesh and torn it apart for meat.
Say: The sound of swallowing the flesh
and the fat comes from the hyena.
Say: Crows plucked out my veins and tendons.

(TRANSLATED BY ANDREZEJEWSKI AND LEWIS.)

But none of this meant much for Habeba. Her rich lineage counted for little in a society that, at least in crude terms of reparation and value, seemed to rank camels above women.

"She was forced to marry," says Yusuf. "There were a lot of orphans in those days. People died young—still die young. So she was brought up by an uncle who just said, 'Look, you have to marry the old man or I'll curse you.' In Somalia that's like invoking God's wrath. Somalis believe their parents have that kind of power. She thought she'd avoid the curse by marrying Father—but just for one night, and then escape to town. But she said Father then put a spell on her, and she no longer wanted to leave."

Ahmed was a tall man, even by local standards. Perhaps six foot four inches. It was said he could load a hand-woven, fifteen-gallon water container onto a camel's back without needing to force the animal to the ground first. Habeba, by contrast, was unusually short. "Much shorter than average. Barely five feet," says Yusuf. They made an odd couple. But Habeba soon proved her worth by giving birth to five boys in quick succession.

First came Mohamed, then Mohamud (who would later become known as Tarzan), then Yusuf, Muse, and last, Abdullahi.

Birthdays are not much marked or celebrated in Somalia, but Yusuf, true to form, has since tried to work his out. "My mother told me I was born in Ramadan month. Early on the ninth morning. I used a calculator to convert Islamic calendar to Gregorian calendar. So I was born around May 3, 1955 or '56."

I'm keen to understand what it must have been like to grow up as a nomad, to live in a way that can barely have changed in centuries. Tarzan and Yusuf both steer me toward their younger brother, Muse. "It's the same word as Moses," says Yusuf. Unlike all his surviving brothers, Muse stayed with the family until he was a teenager, and so it is to him the others defer for the detail, the family history.

But Muse is a hard man to reach. It's just as Tarzan suspected. "Most likely he will want nothing to do with a book." He works in Mogadishu these days, for the country's biggest mobile phone company—an industry that has thrived here with staggering resilience and inventiveness. "He's the tower guy," Yusuf says. It's a job that requires Muse to be able to travel freely around the country, navigating his way through potentially hostile areas to access phone masts and so on.

Muse, displaying the caution only Tarzan seems to lack, makes it clear that he's worried that any publicity could jeopardize his security and his ability to travel. At one point I hire a local Somali journalist to see if he can track him down in Mogadishu and convince him, but I'm soon told, by email, that "he refuses to be part of the book, saying 'I am not ready by any means good or bad.'"

So I make other plans.

MY HOME, FOR NOW, is in South Africa, a country with a big Somali community. In a way the Somalis are like any other group of expats. Over the years I've had plenty of opportunity to tap into, say, the Ghanaian community in Johannesburg during their country's giddy journey through the 2010 World Cup. Or to look for advice from Ivoirians and Malians when their countries were collapsing into civil war.

But the Somalis are different. I've never encountered a more closely connected, efficient network. It's like jumping from dial-up to broadband. Perhaps I'm getting carried away, but I start thinking of all those constellations of nomads, linked across the wilderness by tendrils of blood and marriage, and now extending across almost the entire world, as an alternative manifestation of the internet.

Not for the first time, the Somali novelist Nuruddin Farah kindly offers to help me out. I've come to know him first through his books, later at lectures he's given, and finally through a mutual friend—a Kenyan Somali who used to work for the BBC and is now a member of parliament in Nairobi. He was injured in a grenade attack—probably the work of Islamist militants—and Nuruddin and I met up when we were both visiting him in a hospital in Johannesburg.

So I email Nuruddin, who lives in a book-cluttered apartment just below Table Mountain in Cape Town, with what strikes me as an unreasonably tall order. Can he put me in touch with a young Somali who lives in Johannesburg, speaks strong English, and who was, until recently, a nomad, living, ideally, in the Ogaden region of Ethiopia, where Nuruddin's clan is also from, and not too far from the Nur family's pastureland.

"I've asked around," comes the near-instantaneous reply, "and been given the name of a young man. Bashir."

Sure enough, a day or two later, I'm sitting in the sunshine outside a cafeteria at Wits University in Johannesburg, watching Bashir's long, strong fingers mimic the steady actions of milking a camel.

Wits is one of South Africa's top universities and occupies a hilltop and steep, well-manicured hillside just north of the city center. It's lunchtime and tables around us are filling up.

At first Bashir doesn't notice he's even moving his hands, as his thumbs work their way instinctively across the other fingers, in a gesture that seems both rough and oddly tender.

"Psheee, psheee, psheee," he says, imitating the sound of the milk jetting out and hitting a container. "Even now I can remember exactly how to make milking. This is for the camel. You put like this the breast of the camel. She has four." Teats? "Yes. *Pshee, pshee!* But the goats it is like that. *Sheee. Sheee,"* and his fingers move more gently across each other—more of a stroke than a rub.

Bashir was born in 1985, outside a town called Degehabur, which means "boulder." It's just north of Tarzan's family grazing land in Ethiopia. Their clans were neighbors and would often intermarry.

Bashir Omar "Qaman" in Johannesburg, 2016. COURTESY OF THE AUTHOR

"You see, I found it here," says Bashir, peering at the map on my mobile phone. He is a tall, gregarious man, with a high forehead, an angular face, and eye-catchingly hollow cheeks that he keeps turning, like a sunflower, toward the winter sun. His upper teeth jut forward as he grins, and his long arms move extravagantly as he acts out scenes.

"I was born outside the town, in a small area with wells for cattle. Bulalle—a very famous place." So an oasis? I ask. "Yeah. I can't tell exactly which night I was born, but I estimate it was the first of January. Somalis don't give the day much attention. That's not the tradition. I like to but . . ." His voice trails off.

"My mother and father have both passed away now. We were a big family with about five hundred sheep and a hundred goats, and seven children. My nickname is Qaman—it means 'hero.' I inherited it from my grandfather."

A few days later Bashir emails me to explain that his nickname is a bit more complicated than that. Literally it means "the one who does not wait," indicating a child that gulps at his camel milk and implying a greedy, and perhaps brave, temperament.

The day Bashir was born, his father chose a newborn camel for his son, and to mark their bond, Bashir's umbilical cord was tied around the camel's neck. Her name was Duwan.

At the age of seven, Bashir became a *dabadhon*, or camel herder. "There is one or two of you, depending on the number of camels. My father, most of time, he has between seventy and a hundred cattle. The old ones died because of the famine. So I was a dabadhon, and there is an older man who you go with to find fresh grass for the camels."

I imagine the two herders trekking into the bush for a few days but Bashir puts me straight.

"Sometimes several months. Then back to where our father is."

So much for childhood.

Bashir describes one particularly long, grueling trip he says he made as an eight-year-old—just him, a man his father had hired named Shafih, and about 160 camels, the herd swelled by others belonging to an aunt and uncle. Shafih was not good company.

"There is such unkindness toward the young, the dabadhon. They always beat you. He will beat you. He must beat you. If you do a big mistake he'll say 'come' and then he takes a stick from the tree. Not the fist. It is *tchee, tchee, tchee.*" And Bashir mimes a beating, his arm swinging from high behind his head.

For more than a month the group traveled southwest, heading to fresh pastureland. Finally they turned toward home. At this point Bashir stands up in the cafeteria, to imitate the plodding gait of both man and camel.

"You just walk after, like that. So at about eight at night you need to rest. The older man tells me, 'You stay with the camel, I need to go ahead. I leave you and camel. You will see the fire at midnight.'" And Shafih disappeared into the scrubland ahead with his small machete, in order to cut thorn branches.

"He's making a place, a house of the night . . . What is the word in English?" A cattle pen? "Exactly. Because maybe there is hyena. Sometimes lion." And he draws me three circles in my notebook, like a Venn diagram, with a big one for the camels, a smaller one inside for the young camels, and another, linking both, for man and boy.

The sun set, and in the dark, Bashir noticed a few drops of rain. He began talking to the camels stomping around him in the dark.

It started with a few instructions. *"Whoo,"* he half-whistled in a strange, haunting style. It's a warning note, designed to keep the camels together, "to protect them from being eaten." Except tonight it didn't seem to be working. *"Hai, hai, hai,"* said Bashir, ordering one group to move to the right. *"Whee,"* he whistled, trying to make another group speed up.

By now he knew every camel, by sight, by name, and by toe mark. And in the darkness he began to sing to them, and to one camel in particular.

"Duwan!" Bashir beams at the memory of his childhood companion. It's as if he's talking about a favorite sister. "If you put such a famous name in your book I'm sure many in the Ogaden will buy it! *Duwan* means that the camel is 'different'—in color, or taller, than its mother. So everyone loves this one—because it's the one who perseveres during difficult times, who produces more female babies, and more milk." He could follow Duwan's trail in the sand by tracking the large gap between her toes, and her left-curving nails.

There are plenty of traditional camel herders' songs—indeed poetry is something of a Somali obsession. But the song Bashir sings to Duwan is his own composition, delivered with intense, quiet affection.

"It is you. It is you. The one. The camel who is always more powerful than others. A beautiful expensive woman—only you can equal her. Not sheep-es [he shares Tarzan's habit with plurals], not goats."

At first I don't realize he's singing. His talking voice slides into something lilting and tender, a grin spreads up to his eyes, and I find myself smiling too, as if we're sharing some happy secret, while he translates the next verse of the song.

"Sheep and goat-es died for drought and famine. It is you—come, elder one who is still alive. It is you who produce milk and meat. It is you, the most expensive one. It is you who allows me to survive."

"Colokolo . . ." Bashir abruptly changes his voice to make the noise of a wooden bell. "Duwan had a bell, because always she likes to stray, alone."

But late that night, Bashir heard another sound. "Galubkolugh" is what I've written in my notebook, followed by an attempt to describe it as "a guttural sound, like someone swallowing tin pans." It's the sound, Bashir explains, of the same bell now being broken in the jaws of a lion.

"I heard it nearby. I had such fury. I can't control. I heard galubkolugh, for lion destroying bell. Nearby, maybe about where that gate is." He gestures to the university gate, thirty yards away from us. "And I ran toward the place to see what has happened. I can see the face of the lion. I have a small stick and small knife here." He gestures to his belt. "And I can see the lion and Duwan, just like that. Her last seconds of breath." His head flops to the side, as if his neck were caught in the lion's mouth.

"There are five other lions standing there. The female, who killed Duwan, she removed some blood from her mouth toward me. *Phooo.*"

You mean she spits?

"Yes, she spits, so I ran away. There are some rock-es. I collect, then I start attacking them." Bashir remembered that a solitary lion will often attack several camels, but a pack of six will almost always settle on just one, so he left them to eat Duwan, and rushed away to try to gather the rest of his herd.

"I tried! I spent the whole night like that. The sun comes up. Then the guy, about nine in the morning, he came to me. He looks terrible. I said, 'Last night I escaped from being eaten myself by lion. Look—the blood on me. The rest of the camels . . . I don't know.'

"You can imagine how I look. He didn't beat me that time. He shouted at me, blaming me, like I'm weak. Not a clever boy. But the way I look—all my clothes are cut by the trees from walking that night."

⁂

I NOTICE THAT BASHIR is getting quieter as we talk. His last mimicry—a *howaaahoooaa* sound he used to make as an alarm call to the camels—is almost a whisper, followed by an embarrassed glance around the lunchtime crowd now filling the university terrace.

These are not easy times to be a Somali in South Africa. As we're talking, there are xenophobic riots going on at the coast in Durban—provoked by the Zulu king, who told a crowd that foreigners "dirty our streets" and should pack their bags and leave. Before that, there were vigilante attacks and riots in Soweto, near Johannesburg. Bashir shows me a photo of a friend named Abdul in Durban, sent to his mobile phone over the weekend. I count twelve stitches on a gash stretching from the bridge of his nose to the corner of his left eye, and four more wounds on his forehead.

"I have lots of friends in Durban. It's mostly black people who attack. They have this attitude." And Bashir remembers sitting in a crowded minibus taxi here, listening to those around him complaining about immigrants. "We were seven Somali students on the bus—the others were talking in their language, but we understand. They are saying, 'Oh, they are taking our places and the government is paying for them.' But it's not true. Maybe these people don't know how to start a business. The majority of people here are peaceful, good. But there is no proper action by the government to stop such xenophobia by bad elements in the community."

Bashir has been in South Africa for seven years now, but not as an asylum seeker. "I asked first for asylum. They rejected." So he went back north, to Kenya, where he'd once been registered, as a teenager, having strolled across the long unpatrolled border from Somalia. His Kenyan passport shows he was born in Garissa, in the east of the country. Not true, of course, but logical. How else should a nomad behave when his worldview, dictated by rains and wells and horizons and family, clashes with the bureaucracy of borders, nation-states, and visas?

So Bashir took his Kenyan passport, applied to take a business course at Wits, and returned to South Africa on a study permit. He describes what must have been a long and difficult process with the breezy confidence of a man at ease in any country.

"We don't feel like citizens of any government. Not of Ethiopia. Not even Somalia. I can go anywhere. I've experienced a lot of hardships, so I laugh and sleep well. No big stress. And I believe if worse happens to me, I can survive, no problem.

"People are always scared of the small things. Maybe my life [as a nomad] made me a bit harder. I don't tell myself, 'This is difficult, I can't do.' I don't believe that. I have to try. My life is divided in two—half as nomad, half not. I can't laugh at the small things like other people do. Ha! Lah! Sure I can laugh—but not at the small things, because I was between seven and ten when I considered myself as a mature, big man. My father, and the life there, taught me—you are a big man. All things taught me—do what big men do."

And so within three months of arriving in South Africa, Bashir had started his own shop. "Some university students asked me, 'How can you own a shop and you've only been here a few months?' and I say, 'I can get business anywhere. I believe if I got to New York I can start something quickly.' We start in the countryside. Somalis—we're connected. I went to a place called Duduza, outside Johannesburg. I start a shop, for 45,000 rand. After one year I sold it for 270,000 rand. Then I established another one in Pretoria. It's quite risky. Thieves come to my shop more than three times. They put a gun to my head, but luckily I survived."

Bashir and I meet up from time to time in Johannesburg, and I'm surprised to learn that he has a wife and child living in Morocco. He's also got a BA in politics now. Sometimes we're joined by other Somali friends, who tell their own nomad tales.

The city's largest Somali neighborhood is called Mayfair, over the ridge from Wits and down beside the train tracks to the west of the city center. Bashir's eyes light up on rumors that a fresh consignment of camel milk has just arrived. "Haha! I like so much! It never expires—you put in container, wait a month, and you can drink without protection. Maybe more salty when older."

He reminisces about the food of his childhood—honey made not by bees but "more small insect-like. And roots, you scrape and dig into the earth, or you climb tree and find something like berries up there to eat."

He describes the squabbles over muddy watering holes, and women, and the ways in which elders would settle disputes between different families. One fight, which began when young men at a well slapped an older woman, ended in a gunfight and a fine of nine camels.

The most precious watering holes would often be elaborately divided, like a pie, with a slice for each family and their camels. During a drought, a fight began when one of Bashir's camels wandered over to drink from the wrong side of a watering hole.

"My older brother took a gun from that guy and started slapping, beating, hitting him! I started with my stick to beat him! I was so young! Maybe seven."

Bashir's brother, Osman, won the fight, but then had to go into hiding in the bush until the elders could strike a deal to prevent the losers from coming to kill him. "Lots of guns at that time, lots of conflict over water, for bushes, trees. Such things happen. Some people love camels more than people. Ha!"

Bashir's earliest memory is of an Ethiopian jet bombing his family's encampment, looking to target Ogaden rebels who were fighting against the central government. "I was four years old. I was crying—*Ahhhh! Ahhh!* We run in the bushes." He mimes the way his brother was holding his hand as they ran, how his aunt was hit by shrapnel in the head, and then a few years later, how another brother was killed by a government militia, and how he's just heard by phone that his brother Osman has been arrested for, allegedly, giving "one goat to Ogaden rebels. It's like house arrest—he has some goats, some camel with him."

Bashir insists he, himself, is "not a rebel, not political." But the suburb of Mayfair is full of ethnic Somalis from the Ogaden plateau who campaign, plot, and argue over the best way forward for their region and whether it should remain part of Ethiopia, seek greater autonomy, or take its chances with a reemerging Somali state.

Bashir keeps talking, and I'm reminded of Yusuf and, to a lesser extent, of Tarzan, who both have similar skills as raconteurs. Then again, so do most other Somalis I've encountered over the years. It stands to reason. Nomads have little use for paper or the written word. In fact, there wasn't even a Somali script until the 1970s.

In Somalia, you are, in ways both casual and significant, what you say you are. And there's another lesson I take from Bashir's anecdotes—a fundamental truth that helped shape his childhood and shaped the country, too. When trouble comes, you look out for your camels, your family, your clan. And you fight.

⁕

"ALL I REMEMBER, VIVIDLY, is being naked." It was 1960, or maybe 1961, and Yusuf was probably turning five, and Tarzan seven.

A particularly severe drought had forced the family to leave its grazing lands and cross to the west bank of the Shabelle River, and the outskirts of the town of Prohibition. Their father, Ahmed, was sick.

"He was weakened by famine, but people said he had flu," Yusuf says.

He can't be sure what are his own memories of those days, and what his brother Muse has since filled in for him. But one day Ahmed accompanied his sons to bathe in the river near Prohibition, to watch over them, because of the crocodiles. Ahmed was already an old man, and his tall frame was stooped. "He was in his late sixties if not early seventies. In that area, that's old."

"Father died. He died a natural death. It was difficult at that time," is the way Tarzan describes what happened next.

It's a curt epitaph, and I'm left wondering whether it's just because Tarzan remembers so little, or whether it is all wrapped up with what happens soon afterward.

Muse was just three at the time, but he's since told Yusuf that he remembers the scene. Their father's body was taken to a patch of ground, designated as a cemetery, outside Prohibition. There were rough pieces of stone to mark other graves, and no writing. "Most people don't read or write," Yusuf explains. Ahmed's long, wizened body was laid out on a stretch of woven straw and washed for burial, then wrapped up in a length of cloth.

"He's supposed to be covered with a sheet for burial. But they didn't have enough clothes to cover him. Either because he was too tall, or because they didn't have enough . . ." For once, Yusuf's steady voice trails off. He means the family didn't have enough money. Muse's memory has become his—the image of his father's feet sticking out, awkwardly and humiliatingly, from the end of his burial sheet, as he's lowered into a shallow, sandy grave.

Then things got much harder. Without a husband to help look after the animals and five young children, and with the drought tightening its grip, Ahmed's widow Habeba was struggling.

Yusuf remembers his mother as "the kindest, nicest person."

Tarzan, once again, has a more curt assessment. "She could not cope. You have to get water, put water to camel, so a woman cannot do that. So she cannot look after herself and five children."

Reading his words back now, I am immediately reminded of another young woman from approximately the same era, region, and background.

Ebla was an eighteen-year-old orphan who had the same instinct as Habeba, to run away from her nomadic encampment to avoid an arranged marriage. She is a fictional character—the subject of *From a Crooked Rib*, Nuruddin Farah's first novel.

Ebla, he writes, "wanted to fly away from the dependence on the seasons, the seasons which determine the life or death of the nomads. And she wanted to fly away from the squabbles over water, squabbles caused by the lack of water, which meant that the season was bad. She wanted to go away from the duty of women. . . . Even a moron-male cost twice as much as two women in terms of blood-compensation. As many as twenty or thirty camels are allotted to each son. . . . 'Maybe God prefers men to women,' she told herself" (*From a Crooked Rib*, Penguin Classics, 1970, 13).

But escape was no longer an option for Habeba. She had five boys to care for, and she moved the family under a bridge outside Prohibition, camping on the dry riverbed, the herd left to fend for itself.

"We were starving. It was terrible. All I remember is that bridge," says Yusuf.

"We all were sick. All crying. I remember it was near a river. So mosquitoes. All of us had malaria," says Tarzan.

At which point a message was sent to Mogadishu for help. The details have been forgotten, but it cannot have been easy to arrange. Someone—a passer-by perhaps, or a friend—must have agreed to walk to the nearest telegraph office, in the Somali border town of Beledweyne, about 50 miles downriver. It's the same town Ebla first ran away to in Nuruddin's book. From there, someone in the Nur family's network, who was working for the city council, sent a telegram to Mogadishu, and to a woman both Tarzan and Yusuf describe as an aunt, although in fact she was their father's cousin.

Her name was Fatima, but everyone knew her as Guura. It's a nickname given to a child born "on the move," but Yusuf, as usual, elaborates. "It refers to someone traveling at night, usually with stealth and perhaps even during hostilities."

Guura, by all accounts, took some time to respond. Her son, Mohamed, was an ambitious, well-read student who would later become a diplomat and have his photo taken with President John F. Kennedy. Eventually he persuaded her to take a bus to Beledweyne, and then to hitch a ride on a truck crossing the border to Prohibition, and "see what she could do."

It's possible that what happened next was meant as a temporary solution—a brief respite for a family in a desperate state. But it didn't work out like that.

Guura made the long journey from Mogadishu and arrived to find Habeba in the shade on the riverbed, with all five boys, filthy and naked, beside her.

A decision was quickly made that two of the children would return with Guura to Mogadishu. Habeba could perhaps cope with the other three. But which children to take? The oldest two?

As the second child, Tarzan—or Mohamud as he was still known—was immediately selected. But when Guura suggested taking the oldest boy, Mohamed, as well, Habeba objected.

"Not having any daughters, my mother depended on Mohamed for her biggest help. So as fate would have it, she said she wanted to keep him," says Yusuf. As the third born, he found himself chosen instead.

"So that's how I ended up coming along, and getting educated. Otherwise I would have ended up as a camel boy. Now I don't remember anything about my father or mother. Strange."

Tarzan is more blunt. "I was very lucky for my father to die. Believe me. It was a miracle Allah sent to us. Had my father been alive I could end up as a camel herder."

Guura looked at her two new charges. Neither had ever worn clothes in their lives, let alone been in a vehicle. "Let's put a cloth around your waist before we leave," she told them.

If there were farewells, neither boy can recall them. They walked with their aunt to the main road, then clambered down into another dry riverbed to find shade under the bridge, and waited for a passing truck heading south, from central Ethiopia toward Mogadishu.

Over the years I push both of them for more details. Yusuf is adamant. "I have no recollections at all." But Tarzan gives the impression of someone consciously shutting a door.

"I never went back. Believe me. Even when I grew up. Never."

2

A Slate Scrubbed Clean

"They call us bastards. Fatherless bastards."

—ALI MADOBE

Minnaaradda
Cabdi-Casiis

From the long ridge overlooking Mogadishu, the new arrivals watched the fireworks crackle and fizz above the old town.

It must have been a bewildering introduction. For weeks they'd been lying, close to death, on camp beds inside their aunt's house, both boys skeleton-thin and racked with diarrhea. But now they were on the mend, and they stood on the road outside, still scratching at their first clothes, confronting the drama, noise, and bricked-up horizons of their first city.

There were no streetlights in those days, and precious few headlights to graze the darkness and give the boys a sense of the size of Mogadishu. But it was tiny, and the fireworks illuminated much of it. There were just two main tarmacked roads and a population of less than a hundred thousand packed into an ancient, cosmopolitan trading port.

Yusuf couldn't take his eyes off the fireworks. The flashes picked out the walls of Villa Somalia, the two tall towers of the cathedral, and the palace of government beside it. There was another light, too—a beam from the old lighthouse that swept timidly across the blackness of the Indian Ocean.

Tarzan's memories of their arrival are minimal. Or at least he's still choosing not to share them. Perhaps I'm reading too much into it, but I'm guessing he finds it too uncomfortable to talk about being sent

Abdul-Aziz mosque, Mogadishu, nineteenth century. COURTESY OF RASNA WARAH AND SOMALI CULTURAL CENTRE, COLUMBUS, OHIO away by his mother—however compelling her reasons might have been.

There's something else at work, too. The sense of a slate being scrubbed clean, a fresh start, a man choosing not quite to reinvent himself, but to grasp the opportunity to control his own story.

It was July 1, 1960. For two boys whose world had only ever been loosely pegged out by the rains, the phases of the moon, and guesswork, this was their first encounter with a formal calendar, their first date. And the reason we know the day—although Yusuf concedes the possibility that it might have been exactly one year later—is because of those fireworks.

Somalia was celebrating its independence, or rather the second stage of its independence, from colonial rule. Five days earlier, the British Union Jack had come down in Somaliland, the northern region that forms the top part of today's 7-shaped, sort-of nation. Now it was the Italian flag being lowered in Mogadishu, as the rest of the country was freed from a protracted, fractious, postwar trusteeship that had seen the Italians—on the losing side in World War Two—allowed back to chaperone their former colony toward independence.

Neither Tarzan nor Yusuf joined the crowds gathering to watch Somalia's new flag being raised. They were too small and still too frail. Newsreel footage shows a sizeable parade in Mogadishu, the men mostly dressed in neat white short-sleeved shirts, some with white caps, too, while many women wore elegant patterned dresses with scarves draped around their shoulders or heads. Watching those faded, grainy recordings online is a strange experience. The optimism is almost overwhelming. A screen full of proud, earnest, modern faces. A new nation straining at the leash. There's one unidentified young man who claps and grins so hard it feels like Somalia could not possibly fail.

In the middle of the parade came two lines of boy scouts—Italians and Somalis. At the head of the Somali column, a young boy carried the Italian flag. Beside him, twelve-year-old Lino Marano clutched Somalia's blue and white flag and, despite his best efforts to look appropriately serious, kept grinning like everyone else.

Lino's father had come to Somalia from Taranto, in southern Italy, in 1938. The Italians had built a submarine base in Kismayo, further down the coast from Mogadishu, and Sante Marano, a civilian engineer contracted to the navy, was sent there to run the submarine workshop.

When the war came and the British took control, Sante was taken to Mogadishu and, as a civilian, put to work in an Allied engineering unit. After the war, he decided to stay on, and the Italian government, anxious to play a role in its former colony, made it easier for men like him by shipping out wives and families. Sante and Anna quickly opened the "Italia" bar and restaurant, a few blocks back from Lido beach, and before long, Lino was born. He and his older brother attended an Italian government school, run by nuns, while their parents expanded the family business into property and imports.

The prospect of independence had scared away some Italian families. But that night, those who'd decided to stay on gathered at the grand Italian club, the Casa Italia, to watch the fireworks and celebrate with a big party. There was enormous relief that the new president had sounded so conciliatory toward Italians during his speech.

"He confirmed that Italians would be treated like Somalis," Lino remembers now. "Everyone was so happy. I remember the fireworks. All the ladies brought food to the club. There was a band, and music, and it went on until after midnight. What I remember most is the president's speech. He was peaceful and respectful toward Italians."

Lino is speaking on the phone one evening, from Malindi, 800 kilometers south of Mogadishu, on the Kenyan coast. It's taken me some time to track him down. There's a small Italian community living there now—families who couldn't imagine returning to Europe when Somalia eventually collapsed and hunted, instead, for an approximation of the life they'd once known in Mogadishu. I'm not sure why I'm so keen to hear his small part in this story—perhaps because I'm curious about embers of empire. My own grandfather spent two decades studying termites in rural Tanganyika, now Tanzania. I'm intrigued by the fact that it is not just Somalis who cling to memories of what their country once was.

Lino tells me he has a Tusker beer in his hand. I can hear the waves fizzing up the beach behind him and know it must be high tide there.

"It was a great day for Somalia," Lino says. "I use-ed to consider it my country."

At first I just notice the extra syllable. Exactly like Tarzan's. But in the long pause that follows it, I can hear something else. Or rather I imagine I can. It's a sense of loss and of dislocation—a very Somali sound.

In Mogadishu, Tarzan's family had an extra reason to celebrate that night in 1960. The country's first president, the man who had just reassured the Italian community about the future, was named Adan Abdulle Osman. He wore a double-breasted cream suit, narrow tie, spectacles, and white cap, and in the evening, after his speech, he went up the hill to Villa Italia, to receive the keys, and to rename it Villa Somalia. President Osman wasn't a close relative of the Nurs'. But not far off. In Somalia's intricate clan system, he came from the same small group.

"Our only claim to fame," says Yusuf.

The new national flag was promptly raised over Villa Somalia. It was a simple, elegant design, a five-pointed white star on a sky blue background. But those five points were more than decorative. They were a provocative reference to Somalia's own sense of itself as a truncated, unfinished nation, sliced apart by colonial powers.

Two of the points represented, and indeed still represent, Somalia and Somaliland, Italy and Britain's former colonies. Years later, in 1991, peaceful Somaliland would turn its back on the rest of the country in the hope—as yet unfulfilled—of being recognized internationally as an independent state. The split would save Somaliland from being dragged into the abyss of civil war.

The other three points represent something more nebulous and far more awkward, namely, the dream of a "Greater Somalia" that could one day bring together all the territories dominated by ethnic Somali populations. That dream, which has gone in and out of fashion over the years, explicitly involves taking land from all three of Somalia's neighbors. The resulting Somali state would then control the entire triangular ear of Africa.

One of those coveted regions is the tiny port nation of Djibouti, further north up the Red Sea coast. Another refers to a giant strip of Kenya's arid eastern plains, known in the colonial era as the Northern Frontier District. British officials had initially agreed that the area would end up as part of a new Somalia. But the choreography proved to be a mess. By the time Kenya gained its independence three years after its neighbor, the government in Nairobi had shrugged off the opinions of the local inhabitants and decided it would rather keep things as they were. For a time, Somalia severed diplomatic relations with Britain in protest.

The last flag point—and certainly the most contentious—is eastern Ethiopia, the plateau that bulges into Somalia's back, known as the Ogaden, or Region 5, or Western Somalia, or eastern Ethiopia. The Great Powers granted the region to Ethiopia in the carve-up that followed the Second World War, but it remains unfinished business for many Somalis, and their claims to the territory have stirred decades of nationalism and war, alongside a lingering suspicion that Somalia's neighbors have deliberately conspired to keep the country weak in order to prevent it from seizing more territory.

TARZAN STAYED WITH HIS aunt Guura and her family for three more months. They had a big house not far from the cul-de-sac where Tarzan and his wife would one day live. Guura was an only child who had married well. Her husband had brought her from the Ogaden, first to Beledweyne and then to Mogadishu.

One day in October, Tarzan was taken aside and told that new plans had been made for him.

Aunt Guura's son, Mohamed, had made some inquiries at the

Education Ministry where he worked. A place had been found at a
free state institution, at the bottom of the hill, on the southern edge
of the city. Yusuf would stay with his aunt.

It was a brisk announcement, and no discussion followed. Again,
Tarzan is gruffly reluctant to go into detail, and Yusuf was too young
to remember much.

Why was he sent away? There are plenty of theories—some more
generous than others. Guura was already looking after other relatives'
children. And they were paying her for her troubles. Tarzan was the
older of the two newcomers and, self-evidently, better able to take care
of himself. Besides, you could argue, surely this was another lucky
break—first a rescue from starvation, then a trip to the city, and now,
a coveted place at a free state institution.

I was dropped off myself, when I was eight years old, at what
seemed at the time like a coldly forbidding boarding school. No doubt
that is why I initially assume that Tarzan must have been feeling utterly
overwhelmed as he was led down the hill on foot. He admits to feeling scared. But that's only part of it. Over time it becomes clear to
me that he has chosen to remember the entire experience in a very
different way. As a beginning, a liberation of sorts.

I start working this out one afternoon when Tarzan takes me on
a tour of Mogadishu.

Our car stops on a stretch of newly tarmacked road, already half-
clogged with debris after heavy rains overwhelmed the new storm
drains. We heave open the armor-plated doors, and Tarzan immediately points to a high wall made out of local breezeblocks—cement
mixed with ground-up coral and painted white. "I think that was the
original wall. I used to jump out here to go into town."

I can see him smiling at the memory. The place, he says, was
called the "Orfano Masculin," or simply OM. It sounds like a grimly
functional name. But when I check, the correct phrase in Italian
should be the more elegant Orfanotrofio Maschile. It must be a Somali
abbreviation.

Whatever its name, the orphanage had a forbidding reputation as an overcrowded, brutalizing place. It occupied a triangular corner plot at the shabbier end of Via Londra, or London Road, an important access route into the city that ran down from the ridge, then parallel to the shoreline, past the rather grand new British embassy, and all the way to the old lighthouse.

Inland from Via Londra were Via Mali, Via Congo, Via Moscow, and Via Morocco—all signposting a young nation's ambition to place itself on the world map. Not that many locals seemed to know the names, or, for that matter, to agree on the origins of the word "Mogadishu" itself. Was it a reference to an Arab shah who once ruled here, or, more prosaically, did it simply mean "a place where sheep are slaughtered"?

Behind the orphanage was another, smaller dirt track called Peking Road, and across it was a place known to the boys as "Ferrari"—a separate orphanage for the children of police officers.

Standing at the corner with Tarzan, I remember that I drove past the same spot a day earlier and turned off just south of the orphanage to head onto a dirt road, toward the shore. These days it's actually the back route into the heavily guarded international airport, and to the brand new British embassy, a low-rise fortress that crouches behind an elaborate, almost beautiful array of mesh fences and moats, with its back to the sea. We'd stopped some distance before the first security gates in order to see four wooden posts hammered deep into the sand, at the foot of the tallest dune. It's where captured Al Shabab members are sometimes taken to be executed by firing squad.

I notice now that we're surrounded by more armed men than usual. My six guards, in their own pickup, have been joined by Tarzan's team of eight, who've been racing through the city to catch up with us. And so we stroll down the road, like camels in a moving pen of thorns. Only the schoolchildren stare. Most locals have become used to such sights.

Suddenly Tarzan gestures inland, to a distant cluster of ragged homes made from scavenged metal scraps. They're perched on top of a huge sand dune, just visible above a mass of thornbushes.

"That's where the military trained their horses," he says. At first I cannot picture it at all, and then abruptly, but all too briefly, it's as though Mogadishu's past and present are alive around us simultaneously.

The orphanage was built in the decade before independence. It was knocked down some years ago and turned into warehouses for the new port on the far side of Via Londra. But in 1960 the site was filled with military-style concrete barracks around a series of courtyards. The corrugated iron roofs nearly touched each other. Inside, the dormitories had wooden floors with bunk beds for the smaller boys. It was built to house five hundred.

"It was tough. It was survival for the fittest," says Tarzan, nodding to himself intensely.

And yet as he describes the fights and the brutality, I detect no trace of anger and no search for sympathy. Nor is it the blank, defensive voice I'd heard before, brushing aside memories of his mother. Instead it is something more like pride, as if this is where he wants his life story to begin.

"I really surviv-ed," he says.

ON ARRIVAL—AND SEPARATED from all family for the first time in his life—Tarzan was put in a dormitory for the youngest boys. There were about fifty of them. In the morning they would cross the Via Londra to attend a state primary school. But the fights began on the first night.

"There was this gang of five, intimidating the boys. They come at night, then they wake you up and say 'come outside,' then they start punching you," Tarzan says.

The battles seemed to be almost constant, and not just older boys picking on the new arrivals. It was a semi-formalized way of establishing a pecking order in each dormitory, of testing character and resolve.

"I'd fought before of course, but not like this. It was so well organized," one of Tarzan's friends, Ali Madobe, told me. The dormitory monitor was still known by the Italian phrase "Capo Squadrone," and it was his job to preside over the more formal battles and to police the dangerous ones.

At the time, Tarzan was still known as Mohamud—a conventional Arabic name shared by dozens of his peers. But that didn't last for long. Every morning, before dawn, the orphanage instructors would call the boys out of the dormitory and order them to form a queue outside the dining room, sometimes making them stand for up to an hour. The kitchen served bread and tea for breakfast, rice with a bit of oil for lunch, and beans for dinner. Mohamud considered the early line-up a form of punishment and so, exhibiting a cursory disdain for procedures, or as he would put it, an activist's impulse to challenge authority, he regularly sneaked back to his top bunk, took his shirt off, and dozed.

Then came the morning when he was woken in the dark by the creak of a floorboard, and realized that one of the instructors had come back to inspect the dormitory. There was a window by the bunk bed, and outside it a large tree that produced small yellow fruit. Seconds later, the instructor glanced out the window to find a small boy, naked but for a pair of blue shorts, hanging from a branch. How Mohamud became Tarzan, you can probably guess.

There can be very few countries or cultures that cherish, and elevate, nicknames with such teasing, tender, crude, enthusiastic longevity as Somalia. It is, in a sense, an extension of the national obsession with the poetry of the spoken word.

In Somalia, you can inherit a nickname, as Tarzan's father did with "Baadi." You can suggest your own, and even declare that you've changed it, like a signature, when the mood takes you. But usually you have to leave it to friends, fate, and, less imaginatively, to physiognomy. If your own name is unusual to start with, then you may never get a nickname, but if you're a Mohamed, or a Mohamud, or a Mahmoud, you'll need a way to distinguish yourself from the crowd.

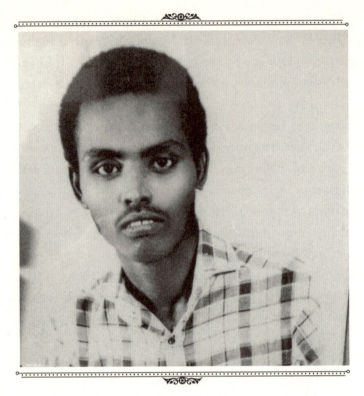

Mohamud "Tarzan" Nur, circa 1974. COURTESY OF THE NUR FAMILY

There are plenty of Somalis called "Dheere," which means "tall," or "Yarisow," which means "small." You can be branded for life as "left-handed," or "chipped-tooth," or "big mouth." There are some flattering nicknames, like "Diamond" or "Sweet" for a woman, but Somalis' sense of humor leans toward the crueler, and sometimes filthier, end of the spectrum.

So "Tarzan" it was. And it's tempting to imagine the eight-year-old grabbing hold of his new name with the zeal of an immigrant clutching a new passport and mentally consigning his old identity to the dustbin. Besides, he was in good company. Around him, a group of friends was forming that would become more like a second family.

There was Ali "Madobe," an orphan from the south of the country who had darker skin and whose nickname simply meant "black," although because someone else had the same title, he was initially known as "Madobe Wayne," or "Big Black." There was Bashir—known as "Goobbe" or "hunchback." Hussein was a talker and quickly became "Gabyow" or "poet." Omar "Ringo" was a keen boxer and earned his name from the ring he fought in, but he was also known by the more colorful phrase "Wasmo Carbeed," or "Arab fucker." It was a schoolboy stereotype about Yemenis and sodomy, and a phrase which, it seems, Ringo may have been in the habit of shouting at enemies in his dormitory.

And then there was "Hayo." Tarzan chuckles, tries to stop, and then splutters through an explanation. Hayo was a reference to the way a boy called Abdullahi used to speak, in a particular regional accent "that people just despised." A few years later, Hayo declared he'd had enough of the nickname, and from now on would be known as "Asbaro." "From the tablet, aspirin, you know, for the headache. The painkiller!"

The orphanage bestowed its own sort of nicknames, too. Every boy had an official number. Tarzan's was 795. Madobe, a tall, thoughtful, un-sporty boy, remembers his was 499. To this day, he still calls another friend "Sei ventisei," rather than 626, using the colonial Italian that clung to some of the orphanage's traditions.

In the early days, it was a given that every child had lost one or both parents, although there was confusion about some who weren't even registered at the orphanage but were street kids who had slipped in like stowaways. Ringo says they were known as the *fuorilegge,* or fugitives, and made up a significant portion of the population.

Over time the orphanage filled up, and indeed overflowed, with far less needy cases.

"It was ministers, wealthy people, they sent their kids there if they couldn't control them. They sent them there to tame them! Ha!" Ali Madobe remembers.

"Or sometimes, because Somali families are very large, ministers or high-ranking officers could not afford to take care of all their relatives." So the orphanage director would be prevailed upon to take in a few extras. And of course, each new director would bring in his own clan's relations.

"You know Somalis," says Tarzan, scathingly. "The Italians left it in good shape. But after they left the numbers increased drastically. Thousands. It became unmanageable."

For now, though, Tarzan was among boys who understood what it was like to be abandoned. And in most cases, the blame seemed to fall on a stepmother.

Ali Madobe's mother had died when he was two years old and an only child. His father, a nomad, remarried, and his new wife "got a problem with me," as Madobe puts it. So he was sent off to live with an uncle, Loyan, a soldier serving at the time in Beledweyne. But then the uncle—who would go on to become the head of Somalia's immigration service—got married, and "so I get the same problem," Madobe says with a generous belly laugh.

Gabyow, the "poet," tells a similar story, and laughs like Madobe. "My mother died when I was four or five, or something like that. We were three boys, and when she died, my father married another woman, and we had a problem with the woman."

The orphanage had high walls, but the boys were not isolated from the rest of Mogadishu. They would cross Via Londra each morning to go to primary school in their distinctive uniforms—blue shorts and a white shirt to match the new national flag. And they would take part in national ceremonies, too. Every year, on Independence Day, they would parade through the city. Yusuf, still living with his aunt, remembers listening to the event on the radio, perhaps three years after they'd arrived in Mogadishu.

"*Salaan Midig!*" It was Tarzan's voice, suddenly crackling to life on the radio, as he told his *horin*, or platoon, to "Salute Right!" Tarzan was now a Capo Squadrone at the orphanage, and had been chosen to salute President Osman at the annual parade.

"He was always kind of a leader," Yusuf says with sincerity.

The orphans may have been given a curt nod of respectability at the annual Independence Day parade. But for the rest of the year, their uniforms—with "OM" stitched on their shirt pockets—marked them out for a very different sort of reception.

"Bastard! *Wahal!*" The taunt followed them around Mogadishu.

"They call us bastards . . . fatherless bastards. Ha!" Madobe gives a small splutter of contempt. The jeers seemed to come from every doorway, every day.

"The people in Mogadishu thought we were illegitimate. That's what they thought," says Tarzan.

The effect of Mogadishu's collective sneer was considerable, and lasting. It brought the boys together into a united, defensive huddle that would, for Tarzan and for many others, linger for a lifetime. And in the process it rendered irrelevant—or at least it suspended—the one issue that could otherwise have caused so much trouble within the orphanage. The one issue that would later rip the entire city apart.

I've glossed over the issue of Somalia's clan system until now—in rather the same way one might cross the road to avoid a crowd of neighbors arguing over the meaning of life, or the position of a garden fence. It's a complicated, fluid, emotive topic, and—depending on when and where you sit—either a defining aspect of Somali society and culture, a source of all the country's troubles and wars, a meaningless anachronism exaggerated by cynical politicians, a distraction from the path of Islam, or a combination of all that and so much more. Outsiders seem almost guaranteed to get it wrong.

The first thing to stress is that Somalis are—however much they sometimes lose sight of the fact—extraordinarily homogenous. Most nationalities in Africa are fairly new constructs, political experiments, colonial carve-ups roping together different religions and ethnic groups. Not so with Somalis. They speak one language. They share one religion and culture. They occupy a single chunk of territory—albeit not all within their own borders. They consider themselves a race apart. And they look, well, Somali. The Hollywood film *Black Hawk Down* may have captured the spectacular mayhem of Mogadishu in 1993, but the apparent casting of non-Somali actors was sometimes ludicrous. To anyone in the know, it was like watching blond Scandinavians starring in a film about Hezbollah.

And yet, within that Somali identity, clans matter profoundly. At times they offer the only credible source of protection and justice. At times they divide and destroy.

Tarzan was born into the Hawiye—one of the "big four" family trees, as he puts it. The others are the Darod, the Dir, and the Digil-Mirifle. The Hawiye are a powerful group in Somalia, tracing their lineage back more than a thousand years, via written references in the thirteenth century, to a patriarch from Yemen who crossed the Gulf of Aden.

The Hawiye are spread around many parts of Somalia, particularly in central regions and along the coast around Mogadishu, and inside Ethiopia and eastern Kenya. But they represent merely the trunk of a long, elaborate, disputed, and sometimes thorny family tree, which branches off into powerful clans, then into sub-clans, and beyond. Each with its own habits and stereotypes. And those smaller branches, or even twigs, have often ended up fighting as bitterly against each other as they have against non-Hawiyes.

Not that it's easy to tell them apart. By accent, perhaps, but certainly not by their appearance.

Tarzan's clan is best known for being tiny. It's usually the first thing people say about it, before going on to mention the fact that Somalia's first president belonged to it, and that its fighters have a fearsome reputation. It's called the Udeejeen, but people often get it wrong.

"Except for the clan itself, hardly anybody pronounces it correctly," says Yusuf with a hint of indignation.

Depending whom you ask or what website you check, the Udeejeen is either a clan in its own right, a sub-clan, or a sub-sub-clan of the Hawiye. Yusuf, as usual, is fastidious and intriguing when it comes to details. "Actually the name of our ancestor was Ciise, which is Jesus in Somali and Arabic. So, it's a clan, not a sub-clan, by Somali reckoning. It is said that the original nickname of the clan ancestor was Sii Jeedeen, which translates as 'back always turned away'—for his legendary obstinacy."

A detailed World Bank analysis of Somalia's clans offers a range of spindly tree-diagrams, which it admits are all "partial" and "by no means exhaustive." The Udeejeen barely make it onto any of them.

At the orphanage, clans did not exist. Or barely existed. Perhaps it's best to say that the boys ended up creating their own clan—"the bastards." And Tarzan seemed to embrace that new identity with particular fervor.

"Usually if you grow up with your family and mother you learn all that. They teach you. They count it out. But a person like me, who grew up in an orphanage, I was lucky if I know my three names. Mohamud. Ahmed. Nur."

It became a matter of pride, and principle. Orphanage first, then country, and then, later, if at all, clan. Indeed, Gabyow is quite indignant when I ask him about his own clan. "You ask me for my tribe now? Believe me no one asked me then. We fight as an orphanage."

"Forget everything else. Everything is prioritized by our brotherhood—by the years we grew up together," says Madobe.

***

BACK AT HIS AUNT'S house halfway up the hillside, an increasingly lonely Yusuf was turning into a studious, daydreaming, and pious teenager.

"I escaped into books. *To Kill a Mockingbird* was on the shelf. And *Gone with the Wind. Anne of Green Gables.* I ended up reading most of the British and American classics. Some French and Russian."

Yusuf was not a fighter. There was a rumor he'd been born prematurely, and as an infant he'd sometimes been called "Dhicis," which means "premature" or "stillborn." "It's not a particularly nice nickname." He left the name behind him in the Ogaden, but he still found himself being picked on and beaten up by some boys in the neighborhood. And so, increasingly, he wandered deeper into the city, to the Via Londra, and to the orphanage. Sometimes he would stay there overnight.

"Tarzan was my protector. I remember one afternoon, when I was being bullied by these two older boys, I walked all the way to the orphanage. Tarzan came back with me to the neighborhood with a friend and he threatens those guys. Then he turns to me and says, 'Look at them! You can beat these guys.'"

Tarzan began trying to toughen up his little brother, who never really picked up a new nickname of his own—Yusuf being rare enough—but became known, for a while, simply as "Little Tarzan."

"One time Tarzan arranged—if that's the word—that I should fight someone. So he got this guy—younger or shorter than me—and he was a fighter, a feisty little guy. They took us to one of the alleys between the dormitories and said, 'Okay, you guys are going to fight,'" says Yusuf.

The smaller boy stood in front of him on the dirty path and said, "Let's fight clean. No dirty tricks. No throwing sand."

"And poor me, I believed him. First thing he did was to grab sand and throw it into my eyes. He started punching me. I was bigger and stronger but I had no idea how to fistfight or punch. So I'd close in, grapple him, and get him to the ground. Then my brother and another guy would stop the fight and we'd start all over again. Tarzan always talks about that time—about when I accepted the no-sand deal. He always gets a kick out of that."

There are no photographs of the boys from that era. Nor, as far as I can tell, of the orphanage. We have to imagine two brothers, arms draped over each other's shoulders. They look almost like twins, but Tarzan is slightly taller and much stockier. Perhaps he's staring a little imperiously at the camera while his scrawny brother offers a gentle smile.

Everyone remembers Yusuf as a "polite" boy, a scholar, and a devout Muslim. Tarzan's strengths lay elsewhere. He was quickly turning into an accomplished fighter. Someone you didn't mess with. And as I gather more anecdotes, I start to wonder whether this was just a survival tactic, or whether it was becoming something else. The bigger boys were still coming around most evenings to pick on the boys in the younger dormitories, and Tarzan remembers the night they came for him.

"They pull my bedsheet, then say, 'Hey, Tarzan.' They knew that they can beat me up. They were bigger than me." But then the largest boy intervened. "Leave this guy, leave him." And as Tarzan explains why, I catch a glimpse of the sort of ferocity, of single-mindedness, for which the adult has become known.

"They know I will not stop," he says. "I will take my revenge. Whether it is an accident, for example, or I will hit him while he is sleeping. Or hot water while the person is sleeping. I will take my revenge."

The image sticks in my mind. I got into the habit of taping our conversations on a small voice recorder and typing them up later. And as I listen back it strikes me that he's not talking about an imaginary incident, but something real. I picture him standing over someone's bed in the dark, with a saucepan of steaming water.

The fights weren't just contained inside the orphanage. As the staff began to lose control, the boys spent more time in the city itself. Tarzan had no clothes of his own besides his uniform, and so would have to borrow trousers, shirt, and shoes from wealthier friends if he wanted to go out in civvies. The taunts of "Bastard!" continued, and sometimes that was enough to trigger a confrontation. But it's probably fairer to say that the Orfano Masculin boys had become little more than another street gang, one of many that roamed the old town.

"I was with him when he was losing one of his ears! Ha!" Ali Madobe is sitting on the porch outside his home in Mogadishu, sipping tea and reminiscing, with undisguised delight, about Tarzan's fights. These days General Madobe is a grand figure. His white, two-story house is on the crest of the hill right beside the walls of Villa Somalia. Armed police guards patrol the courtyard. It's ten in the morning and there's a Mediterranean feel to the city, with a fresh wind blowing off the sea and a cloudless blue sky. A silent assistant brings out tea. Madobe, the lanky orphan boy, has turned into a suave, commanding presence with a thick gray beard and mustache.

"We came from the sea, we were swimming together near the San Martino Hospital. And we found another guy near the military camp. So they fight together," he says, as if it was the most common thing, and I can hear his military bearing in his choice of words. "Normally if one of us fights another, we all fight. We will be allies. But Tarzan is stronger, so we leave him alone. Tarzan hits him heavily. *Boom. Boom. Boom.* But then the guy catches him one time and *Drrrrr!*" Madobe makes a sound like a dog with its teeth clamped on a rope. "He bites his ear. He removes it!"

Tarzan remembers the incident a little differently. It was 1963. He'd have been about ten years old, and the big gang battles were still a year or two ahead. He says they were crossing the road from primary school, not coming back from a swim. And he intervened to defend a girl who was being beaten by another boy.

"It was here. Just here," Tarzan says, pointing at the mud on Via Londra, and then touching the cartilage above his missing earlobe.

"I just came to defend the girl, so I fought against that boy. I was punching and he grabbed me. And he bite me and cut it off and throw it out!" You mean he spat your ear out? I ask. "Yes! They took me to the emergency room. I was holding the piece. They could put it back, but they didn't. They didn't want to, so they throw it out."

The missing earlobe caused new problems for Tarzan. Inevitably, some people wanted to give him an extra nickname—Dhagey, or "earless" Tarzan. "But this I cannot accept." And so he fought every person who tried to pin the new name on him. "I fought so many people, not to be called this. Because I was very sensitive."

IT MUST BE NEARLY six in the evening by the time Tarzan and I finish walking around the walls of the old orphanage. My guards are anxious to leave—partly because it's never safe to linger too long in one place, and partly, I presume, because they're hungry.

It's dusk now, and we drive back through the city toward Tarzan's home, first along Via Londra and then veering off to the left onto the smaller and bumpier Via Roma, which cuts through the old town of Hamar Weyne, the name locals use instead of Mogadishu. *Hamar* means "red," a reference to the reddish sand to be found on the outskirts of town.

Beside me in the backseat, Tarzan is sitting forward, squinting into the gloom ahead, looking for something. Perhaps it's the sunset that has jogged his memory. He's trying to find the telltale silhouette of a particular building, or type of building, that was once the focal point of life for many in Mogadishu at this time of day. "I know the road. But it's difficult to see it."

Our small convoy is speeding up, the guards perched on the backs of their pickups shouting and waving at the dwindling crowds of pedestrians ahead, ordering them to get out of the way. We're near the old bus station and a market, racing through the neighborhood where, in 1993, the first American Black Hawk helicopter was brought down, by a rocket-propelled grenade, during what came to be known as the Battle of Mogadishu.

Suddenly, Tarzan barks, "Stop!" and up ahead, I can see an oddly shaped yellow wall, more than two stories high, which drops down incrementally, like a set of giant steps.

It's the El Gab cinema—the name means shallow well, or watering hole—and it's part of Mogadishu's heritage, one of more than a dozen cinemas dotted around the city center. Most are now in ruins or have vanished. Not a single one of them has functioned for over twenty years.

It's too late to do more than peer out of the window at El Gab this evening—the security guards make that immediately clear—but I go back another day for a better look. Or at least I think I do.

It's only much later, going through some photos, that I realize the driver took me to a different derelict cinema, the Africa, a few blocks closer to the orphanage.

"That was in a rougher neighborhood. There were whorehouses across the street from the Africa and the area flooded whenever it rained. They used to have turf wars between the orphans and the town boys. No guns. They used knives. Educated people would not go there," Yusuf explains.

The Africa's walls are a rustier yellow than El Gab's. I wander down a side street, imagining what it might have looked like if Mogadishu had managed to preserve its architectural heritage.

A hole has been punched through the wall to create a crude new entrance, plugged by a gray metal gate. There's a minaret just behind

Africa Cinema, Mogadishu, 2012. COURTESY OF THE AUTHOR

the building, and a tall wooden telegraph pole beside the gate appears to be carrying an entire city's worth of sagging wires, which brush the roofs of the adjoining buildings. I knock and walk inside to find an open-air courtyard packed with old tires, engines, and exhaust pipes. A couple of workmen look up, then ignore me. Most of the cinema's terraced stalls—wide concrete steps—have been knocked out, and the interior has been subdivided with a breezeblock wall across the middle. But at one end, half-hidden behind a small tree, a mobile phone mast, and some crude corrugated iron sheets, is a smooth, white, plastered wall rising high above the surrounding rooftops and spoiled only by a small door and a hole for a new air-conditioning unit.

I feel like I've stumbled on hidden treasure. It's the screen.

As a boy, Yusuf preferred the Hamar cinema, a block from the cathedral.

"It was a smart place. Sophisticated viewers and functionaries went there. It had a café. My oldest memory is a billboard for *West Side Story*, of a man and woman walking away from the viewer, with a jacket on his shoulder. The three fashionable cinemas were the Hamar, the Missione, and the Centro. They showed Hollywood movies dubbed in Italian."

When Tarzan and Yusuf first mention the cinemas I imagine the boys packed inside dark, and presumably sweltering, theaters. But, of course, they were almost all open-air structures. And the moment I realize that, I can picture them, the terraces filling up after sunset, boisterous children perched high above the city—now forgotten in the darkness around them—as the outside world flickers into life on a white wall.

"I remember watching *It's a Wild, Wild World*. There was an English duke character in it. Very hilarious." It's Yusuf, of course, who remembers sitting near the back of the Centro cinema, trying to follow the Italian translation. The film he's describing is, I suspect, 1963's *It's a Mad, Mad, Mad, Mad World*, with Terry-Thomas playing a bumbling aristocrat.

In those days, the colonial language was receding fast in Mogadishu, but Yusuf knew enough to catch the jokes, and just behind him an Italian family—there were still several thousand Italians in the city—was laughing at his laughs, pleased to see someone still following their language.

The cinemas were a defining feature of Mogadishu's nightlife. People would surface from their siestas at about 5:00 p.m., stroll along the seafront, eat some stew with flatbread made from maize flour at a local restaurant, and then stand at the counter at a café for a macchiato. After that, it was time to catch a film. The cinemas would be open from around six each evening, and for one Somali shilling you could stay until midnight.

The smarter venues would sometimes show Fellini films, just two months behind the cinemas in Rome. El Gab was always crowded and boisterous. It specialized in American cowboy films dubbed into Italian, and before long it was showing spaghetti Westerns, too. One famous American actor became a particular favorite. His name was Levan Khalif. Or at least that was how the crowds in Mogadishu claimed him as their own. He's better known abroad as the mustachioed villain of Sergio Leone's films, Lee Van Cleef.

The orphanage boys tended to go to the Benadir or to the nearest cinema, the Africa. Both played mostly Bollywood movies in the original Hindi. The dances and the songs didn't seem to need translating, but money was always an issue. The boys often clubbed together and shared a ticket, taking it in turns to go inside and then relay the plot to the others. Another trick was to pick up discarded tickets and repair them with glue. Occasionally they would climb a tree in the grounds of a hospital beside the El Gab, which gave them a half-decent view of the screen, but that often ended with the police coming around to order them down and scold them.

Then there was Tarzan's method.

"So we wait outside and sometimes intimidate those buying tickets, so they let us in at the end." Really? I ask. Intimidate? It seems like a revealing choice of words.

"I was not a thug. I was a survivor. We would ask them . . . so they let us," is his explanation. He's insistent, almost indignant. "Always I was on the side of justice. Not stealing, but fighting injustice," he says, and he then launches into a long story that he clearly feels captures the essence of his orphanage years.

⁂

IT WOULD HAVE BEEN about 1965. Late afternoon. Tarzan was standing on the street outside the Africa, looking for a particular face in a crowd of boys. He was planning to make a scene, to beat someone up in front of an audience.

His target was a boy known as Congo. He was an orphan, perhaps sixteen years old, who had struggled academically and was now working, unpaid, in the kitchens. There was a bunch of boys doing the same job, and it's easy to imagine how a rivalry might develop within the orphanage.

"These guys become bigger because they lifted heavy containers of meat, so every day they're lifting, and eating too much, so they get muscles. They get strong." Congo had polio as an infant and still walked with a limp, but he was "a little bigger than me, and huge. He's the head of this gang."

Ali Madobe remembers Congo, too. "Ha! He was a very famous limping guy. His legs were not perfectly controllable to him. He was so huge."

Tarzan was still a Capo Squadrone and at mealtimes would accompany the boys from his dormitory into the dining room. In past years, the food had been set out on each table and left to the Capos to divide as they saw fit. But the orphanage was getting overcrowded, and the boys were now required to line up by the kitchen door to be served, one by one.

Tarzan believed the kitchen boys were stealing food supplies and selling them at the market, sharing the proceeds with the cooks. As a result, the boys at the back of the queue would sometimes go without. To stop this, Tarzan says, he stood at the front and watched to make sure each boy in his dormitory got his "50 grams of rice."

"So all of them—they hate me," he says of the kitchen boys, the cooks, and the storekeeper, all of whom were in on the scam, and even the director of the orphanage, who didn't want trouble. "Because all of them were stealing." Twice he'd even chased after a kitchen boy who'd clambered over the wall heading to the market. "So I'll go jump and catch them and take them to the director. And he hates even that."

Things deteriorated to the point where Tarzan started to come to the dining room each day dressed for a fight. He'd leave his expensive school shirt in the dormitory and "put oil on me so when we fight they cannot hold me.

"So today one boy will fight with me; the next day another. Congo taunts and insults me. But then I say to him, 'Come on then, let's fight.' And I know he doesn't want to fight me in public. He's afraid if he fights with me in the compound and then loses, he will lose face. Usually he has a knife. I know he fights with a knife, so he came to me once with a garment covering the knife, and I said, 'OK, but I have to go to my room,' and I've got a big stick there and I bring it out with me. And now he doesn't want to fight, he just says, 'You will die one day.'"

A few days later, two of Congo's gang caught Tarzan off guard in the dining room, punching him in the face.

Tarzan acts out the scene for me now, pushing his chair back on the patio, teeth bared, face livid, showing me how both his eyes swelled up and he flailed around, unable to see. The orphanage staff grabbed him, and then let the fight resume. "I was completely mad. I cried with anger. Then they took me to the director and he suspended me for a month."

Suspension meant leaving the orphanage. But in the years since he'd arrived, Tarzan had almost never slept anywhere else. His aunt's house was not an option, even in the holidays.

And what hits me now, as I search through all the interviews I've transcribed, looking for a mention of other relatives, is that I've never once asked him what happened to his mother. And more tellingly, he's never once offered any information. It's as if we've both quietly agreed to close the door. Did she ever come to visit her boys in Mogadishu? Was Tarzan in touch with her? I make a note to ask him. All I have, for now, is a comment from Yusuf.

"Once a year, if we were lucky, my mother would come to Mogadishu and spend a few days with us. Not with Tarzan. She might see him once."

So Tarzan's solution was to hide in his dormitory. He couldn't show his face in the compound, but over the years he'd discovered he had other relatives in Mogadishu. Hassan was his older half-brother, his father's son from his first marriage. He'd ended up in Mogadishu after his mother had died and had since found a menial job in the same neighborhood as the orphanage.

"I had a big brother. He's dead now. He would go and get me food," Tarzan says.

For a month, he brooded in the dormitory. "I'm tired of fighting. The only way I can get out of this is to beat this guy. I have to beat Congo."

And so, late one afternoon, Tarzan stood scanning the crowds outside the Africa. He couldn't find Congo, so he walked over to El Gab cinema, and there he was, with the other kitchen boys surrounding him. Tarzan could see that "he'd sold our bread and our rice, so his pocket is full of money."

Tarzan walked up to Congo and pushed him.

"Hey, listen, do you think I'm going to quit the orphanage because of you?"

Before Congo had time to answer, Tarzan punched him and threw him to the ground. There was, however, an established etiquette to such fights, and as they grappled, Congo quickly argued that he needed to take his shirt off, to protect it. Having bought a little time, he then suggested that they take the fight elsewhere.

"Let's go back to the orphanage."

"No. I'll be suspended again if we fight there. But anywhere else is fine."

"Okay, but it's just me and you. The others can't follow."

"Fine, but if one of your group does follow us, then all the other children can come, too."

So the two of them set off, alone, toward the city center. At the foot of the hill that leads up to Villa Somalia, there was a tiny abandoned quarry with a pool of stagnant water in the middle of it. It was known to the local kids as Kala Reeb, or "the place where fights are settled."

Tarzan does not dwell on details of the fight itself.

"So it was me and him only. And I beat him up."

But he lingers on the aftermath and a troublesome conundrum. He'd won the fight, but he lacked an audience.

"So who will be able to tell if I beat him or not? So there's—what do you call it? Gravel?"

At which point, we must now picture Tarzan, straddling Congo's writhing back and, like an artist signing his own work, rubbing his defeated opponent's face into the quarry floor until it was a collage of cuts and bruises.

The next day the director called both boys into his office, noted the contrasting conditions of their faces, and ordered two older boys to mediate an end to the feud.

"And from that day, great peace. No more fighting, no more trouble. And I would even sit with him in the kitchen and eat with him," Tarzan concludes.

***

YUSUF KNOWS THE CONGO story well. But he's worried I'm getting the wrong impression of his brother. It's December 2012, and I'm on the phone with Yusuf, who is now in Hargeisa, the capital of Somaliland. He's traveled there alone from the United States for a holiday, with a bit of consulting work added on, and I can't help but think he sounds more relaxed, more at home, than he does in Indiana.

Hargeisa, bombed to dust near the beginning of Somalia's modern wars, sits on the northern edge of the same high plateau where

Bashir used to graze his camels. It's a fine, even booming, city in its own right these days. But for many Somalis who've spent their best years abroad in the diaspora it has also become something more than that. It's a foothold, a safe place to come and reminisce about the good old days elsewhere in the country, to wallow in a familiar culture, and to ponder why Mogadishu still can't manage to be half as stable or secure.

Yusuf tells me he's sitting on the patio outside his hotel, enjoying the breeze and the altitude, and ready to chat at length. He's always quick to laugh at Tarzan's stories, his temper, and his wilder claims.

Still, Yusuf is anxious to show that he's not trying to undermine his famous brother; rather he wants to make me understand a side of Tarzan that he rarely shows to outsiders.

"We Somalis are not good at expressing feelings. We're unsentimental, and Tarzan shows a tough front. But he appears to be tougher than he actually is. One time I ran away from my aunt's house to the orphanage, and was telling him why, and suddenly I caught him crying, tears in his eyes. I was so surprised."

Then there was the time that Yusuf "drowned."

Via Londra runs parallel to the shoreline in Mogadishu, and for the last stretch, before it swings sharply left into town to become Corso Somalia or Port Road, it emerges from behind a cluster of houses to overlook the sea itself. And ahead is the broad promenade, perched above a slightly forbidding collection of dark, jagged rocks. At high tide the waves are deep enough to dive into. Deep enough, as Yusuf puts it, to drown a camel.

Yusuf had taught himself to swim. It was another way to escape from his home. In his early teens he'd begun to venture beyond the rocks and out toward the bigger boats that would moor offshore on their way south down the coast toward Kismayo or Mombasa. On some days there would be more than a hundred wooden dhows, sails down, rolling in the swell.

At about noon, Yusuf and two friends left their clothes in neat piles on the rocks and swam out to the boats. "We were way out in the ocean." They clung to the sides of several boats and chatted to the sailors. An hour passed, perhaps longer. And then one of the boys ashore, sitting on the rocks in the sun, noticed the untouched clothes and decided to raise the alarm. Everyone knew Yusuf's brother. The boy rushed off to find Tarzan at the orphanage.

Mogadishu seafront, 2012. COURTESY OF BECKY LIPSCOMBE

When he heard, Tarzan sprinted from the orphanage all the way down Via Londra and stood on the rocks, panting and shading his eyes with both hands to scan the sea for his brother. Three hours passed. Tarzan was not a swimmer. Finally, he assumed the worst and picked up his brother's clothes and walked with them back up the hill to his aunt's house.

Half a century later, at his daughter's wedding, Tarzan chokes up as he recounts the incident to a crowd of relatives. How he ran so fast down Via Londra. How he paced along the rocks. And the relief he felt when Yusuf arrived, as if back from the dead, at his aunt's house.

"All I remember," Yusuf says now, with the smallest hint of a chuckle, "is his sad face. Inside he's a very kind guy. Much kinder than I am. He's really soft. A soft heart."

⁂

I THINK AGAIN ABOUT Tarzan's soft heart a few months after our tour of the old orphanage in Mogadishu. We're in London, and I'm trying to fill in some holes about his time at the orphanage.

I start with his mother. Why doesn't he ever mention her visits to the orphanage? Embarrassment is not in Tarzan's repertoire of reactions these days. But as a child, a "sensitive" child, he found his mother's visits deeply embarrassing.

"I love my mother. I feel sympathy for her because she wanted to raise her children by her own hand, but she couldn't do it. She used to visit me in the orphanage once a year. But I don't want her to come. You know why?" I shake my head. "Because she doesn't have good clothes. She didn't even have shoes. She's barefooted. She has nothing. She can't even buy me a drink."

Tarzan couldn't cope with the other boys' teasing. "I don't want people to ridicule me. There's nothing she could offer me."

That last phrase seems particularly harsh, and I can't help saying: "Apart from love."

"Yes," he replies without a hint of emotion.

The exchange confirms my sense of the way Tarzan has been shaped by the orphanage. There's a hardness, a self-reliance, that I'm sure many who've experienced boarding school will recognize. It's a picture he recognizes, too.

"I don't feel lonely. You can take me to Siberia and I don't feel lonely. I love my family but sometimes . . . When I was at the orphanage, on Fridays people go to houses, to families. They get their hair oiled, take shower, get something sweet. I never get that. I never go anywhere. I stay year in, year out. Nobody buys anything for me."

He takes a breath, and the moment passes. "I don't regret the way I grew up. I'm proud of it. I really love it."

But a few seconds later, Tarzan pauses. I look up and notice with shock that he's sobbing quietly. Tears are flowing. His arms remain outstretched, and he makes no attempt to wipe them away.

We talk a bit more about Yusuf. In all my phone calls with Tarzan's brother, he's been very careful about what he's said about his aunt. He doesn't want to upset her relatives with any criticism. But it's become obvious to me that his childhood in her household was a miserable one, and that his aunt was the cause.

I ask Tarzan about it, and he starts describing the first time Yusuf ran away from home and sat on his big brother's bed at the orphanage. He told Tarzan how he was treated—given different food, forced to sleep in a sort of outhouse reserved for nomadic visitors, shouted at, criticized, sent to do errands. Nonstop.

"I think the pressure became too much for Yusuf. He didn't know where to go. He told me the stories and I cried. Because I'm growing up in freedom. Yes, it's difficult, there are fights and struggles, but I'm a free man. He's made inferior to the other boys. He's treated like a maid."

Tarzan found an extra mattress and hid Yusuf under his bed for four nights. Eventually his aunt sent a relative, who found the boy and took him home.

But then Tarzan launches into a very different story. He suddenly remembers that he fell sick as a child. "I think I get smallpox. I was shaking. Fever." And it was his aunt who came to the orphanage and carried him home on her back, brushing away the objections of her relatives who feared he would infect the others.

"So whatever happens, I think she was good," he says, and begins to sob again.

"It was not her heart. Whatever she did to Yusuf, it was not because of hate. She just loved her grandchildren more than him.

Yusuf was still angry, but last Ramadan I convinced him to forgive her."

Yusuf confirms the story. After all, his aunt had brought him to Mogadishu. And then her cruelty pushed him out into the city and eventually into books, and beyond.

"The ultimate escape. And I'm still a restless person. I've moved twenty times since I came to the USA."

3

Us against the World

"His mouth speaks faster than his mind."

—HUSSEIN MAO KHERE "GABYOW"

Nostalgia doesn't quite capture it. It's more like a yearning—the keenest of sensations, part grief, part joy, and more often than not, part shame, too.

I've seen it spread, like a trance, across so many Somali faces and sometimes even hands. How else can one account for Bashir's fingers mime-milking Duwan? Then the words start to flow, and I wonder, once again, if this is the real reason why Somalis talk so much. It's not just the oral culture. It's as if the generations that fled are trying to reminisce their old country back to life, as if an act of collective memory could reset the clock, wipe out the intervening years, and restore Mogadishu to the best of times.

I'm sitting on the corner of a cluttered sofa in a council flat in Brixton, south London, looking at a pile of black-and-white photos, and feeling like I've just slotted another small jigsaw piece into place. In the armchair beside me sits a tall, portly man with rimless glasses, a day or two's gray stubble, and a thin mustache. It's Gabyow, the "poet" from Tarzan's orphanage.

There's a faint medicinal smell in the flat, and the gloom of a March afternoon seeping through the windows. Gabyow, now a retired accountant and a widower, met me earlier outside Brixton Underground station, sporting a rather dashing duck egg blue flat cap, having called me four times to make sure I'd be standing in the right place. Then he drove me back here, joking about how dangerous the

Orphanage basketball team, Mogadishu, 1970.

neighborhood used to be and letting me know that he's "checked up" on me on the internet.

To put him at ease, I try to call Tarzan on the phone in Mogadishu, and, unusually for him, he picks up immediately. The two men chat fast in Somali, and, as usual, my first reaction is to think there's an argument building up. Somali is that kind of language—gulping, guttural, percussive, like a gunfight in a sandstorm. But then Gabyow grins with something like relief, hangs up, and proceeds to explain to me, three times, about a falling-out the two men had six years ago over some possibly imaginary snub, now successfully overcome.

The photographs in front of us show uniformed teenagers playing basketball, at night, in what looks like a smart, open-air, floodlit stadium. Gabyow asks me if I can recognize him, and, after a couple of false starts, he points to a team photo and a young man squatting on his toes in the front row. "Ah. Same nose and same teeth," I say, and his answering smile is warm and wide.

I have no trouble spotting Tarzan. He's standing in the row behind, staring impassively at the camera, legs crossed, teeth exposed as usual, an arm draped over the coach's shoulder. He looks to be one of the smallest players.

Gabyow slides his fingers across the photo to conjure up the rest of "Team Orphanage."

"That one is the coach. Mohamed died two years ago. Musa is in Sweden somewhere; this man is in Canada; this man died. Mohamed Abdi is in Sweden. Sei Cento, six hundred, that was his nickname—he lives in Minneapolis."

Mogadishu was so small in those days that the orphanage team quickly found itself playing in Somalia's brand new national league. Basketball didn't have quite the popularity of football, but it was not far off. There were about sixteen teams, all from the capital, and mostly sponsored by government departments, unions, or businesses.

"It was a very, very happy time, believe me," says Gabyow, putting the photos back in a box. "The country never had any sports before. We became celebrities overnight. We were all friends. All friends. Anyone would die for you." The cadences of Gabyow's delivery and the yearning tone make it sound almost like one of Bashir's poems to a camel.

Hussein Mao Khere "Gabyow" with the author, London, 2014. COURTESY OF THE AUTHOR

"Things were good. Free food, free school. Always, I adore it. I prayed for it. We were always a team. All the time."

Tarzan was turning sixteen and had secured a place on the orphanage team, despite his size. He was number seven.

"I was very fast. Not tall, but fast and a good scorer. Even now I'm a very good shooter. If I throw ten balls, I'll score eight," says Tarzan. And somehow, when he says it so earnestly, it doesn't come across like a boast.

But the desire to win did not seem to translate into the classroom. Tarzan had recently moved from his primary school near the orphanage to a new secondary school further up the hill, where his brother

Yusuf was also a pupil and was beginning to shine academically. Before long he'd leapfrogged into the grade above Tarzan. These days Tarzan admits, "I was the dumbest of all my brothers." But at the time, he tried to explain it by claiming Yusuf was older than him.

"I let him get away with it. It was the best way for him to explain why I was ahead—a way to reconcile for him. From that time on, he always said I was older. Jokingly, of course," Yusuf adds diplomatically.

The orphanage had no court. So the team arranged to play on one belonging to the nearby police academy, where they often sat and studied their better-trained opponents. Tarzan played center.

"He was very aggressive all the time. That was the one thing he was good at, believe me. And very competitive, *all* the time. When he loses, he couldn't speak!" Gabyow is grinning, enjoying the tease.

Orphanage team playing in Mogadishu, 1970.

Women playing at the same stadium, later named
after Wiish, in 2015. COURTESY OF THE AUTHOR

"The only problem he had—was with his mouth. He could not keep it shut!" says Gabyow. "If someone is doing something bad, he'll shout, 'Look, the referee is blind!' He won't say it behind your back. He never punched first. But he insults!"

There is a mixture of admiration and exasperation in his voice. It's a blend I've come to recognize.

"All the time he had big rebellion on his mind. In the school, if there's any demonstration, he's first to go. Any problem with the teacher, he calls the others and says, 'Let's go.' The only reason is because his mouth speaks faster than his mind."

⚜

NONE OF WHICH WOULD have mattered much, if Mogadishu had stayed as it was.

But as the first decade of Somalia's independence was drawing to a close, the political atmosphere was clouding over. The optimism and openness were fading. Corruption was growing. The clans were becoming more prominent, and more divisive, in parliament and government. And then, during the course of a little more than a week in October 1969, everything changed.

Lino, the Italian boy scout who'd brandished Somalia's flag on Independence Day, was twenty years old now and in the middle of his business administration exams at Mogadishu University.

Early on Tuesday morning, October 21, he woke at around 5:00 a.m., intending to finish some last-minute revision. He had an exam at nine.

By now, Lino's parents had sold their restaurant and moved into the property business. They were doing rather well. Lino was staying at their new venture—a big three-story apartment block some four kilometers from the city center, beside the aptly named K4 roundabout.

Lino looked outside and noticed that it was drizzling. Then he looked toward the main road, and in the gloom he saw an armored car. He woke up his brother and switched on Radio Mogadishu to find out what was happening.

It was a military coup—and by no means an unexpected one. The country's new president (its second—Tarzan's clansman had distinguished himself by setting the precedent of stepping down) had been shot dead by his bodyguard a few days earlier in what appeared to be a clan dispute. Now the radio was playing music, interrupted occasionally by a male announcer who declared that the army had seized power "to save the country." A strict curfew would be put in place.

Lino and his brother briefly weighed the risks, then decided to leave the apartment to get some money from their parents' office, just in case. They drove carefully, on side streets, but they could see the city filling up with soldiers.

At about 8:00 a.m. they were nearly back at the apartment block when a small army truck pulled them over. Lino noticed immediately that it was a Soviet vehicle, known as a UAZ, and sitting inside, behind the two Somali soldiers in the front seat, were, he was sure, two Russian officers.

"I saw them! Yes, yes! The Russians were behind the coup! I saw them around the city in the next few days, in cars with the Somalis." Lino is insistent on this point.

The soldiers escorted Lino and his brother safely back to the apartment and told them not to leave until the curfew was relaxed. They did as they were told. The armored vehicle they'd seen earlier on the main road was still there, parked outside a government minister's house. They heard he'd been arrested.

Three days later, it was all over. Across the country, the coup had been a spectacular success—well organized and virtually unopposed. The constitution was suspended, and a Supreme Revolutionary Council was established, led by the army commander General Siad Barre and twenty-four officers.

The extent of Soviet involvement in the coup itself has since been disputed, but there's no doubt that Somalia and the wider region were becoming the focus of a new Cold War power struggle. Somalia was now firmly in Moscow's camp.

TWELVE-YEAR-OLD SAMIYA STOOD ON the roadside, watching the crowds flood past.

"It looks like a river. Like a river of people," she thought.

She'd never seen anything like it. The daytime curfew had just ended, and people were emerging from their homes and, overwhelmingly it seemed, showing their support for the coup. They were singing and holding up branches or bits of cloth in celebration.

Samiya rushed back to her house, which was just off the main road, the Makkah Al-Mukarramah, which leads from the K4 roundabout into the city, slipping over the ridge from the west and down toward the coast.

Her mother, Fatima, was a glamorous figure, one of Somalia's most popular musicians. Samiya was slightly in awe of "our first female superstar." Her stage name was Fatima Kenya. She'd divorced Samiya's father long ago, had spent time in Moscow on a scholarship, and was now married to her third husband, a news presenter and linguist, also Soviet trained. The couple both worked at the state radio station in Mogadishu, where Fatima co-hosted a slightly flirty, romantic, and hugely popular call-in show.

The family had spent the curfew cooped up, comfortably, in their house. That day, Samiya ate some dates, *canjeero* pancakes, and later some pasta for lunch. She stood at her window and heard the crowds still passing nearby, and she listened to her parents discuss the coup.

Mogadishu had always been—and indeed thought of itself as—a cosmopolitan city. Samiya's family was part of an increasingly assertive new urban, middle-class elite, one that worked alongside the Italian colonizers, attending their schools and adopting many of their tastes—for siestas, cappuccinos, and Fellini. Now they were appalled by the new, crude, clan-dominated politics that seemed to have taken over since independence. It struck them as an alien aberration, a virus imported into the city by unsophisticated nomads.

They even had a name for themselves—the "Beizani." The word comes from the Italian *paesano*, or rustics, and was meant to reinforce the idea that the cosmopolitan elites were somehow the "real" Somalis and a cut above the feuding newcomers.

Samiya's mother and stepfather grumbled about the clans—the

way they rewarded blood and loyalty over brains and integrity. It didn't help that Fatima came from a small, "low-ranking" sub-clan, and her husband was from Eritrea and considered himself clan-less. They saw power and arrogance being concentrated in a few unaccountable hands, jobs being handed out, and withdrawn, on clan lines.

"You could be a retard and you'd become a minister, because you're from clan so-and-so," is how Samiya later described her parents' scathing perspective.

And so, in their household, and in many others, the military coup was seen as something necessary, something corrective, a resetting of the clock. Besides, many people had simply grown tired and suspicious of the conspicuous wealth flaunted by Somalia's new political class.

AT THE ORPHANAGE DOWN the hill, Tarzan heard the tanks rumbling out of the military barracks and along Via Londra, and he cheered with everyone else.

For Tarzan, as for Lino and Samiya, the coup initially changed very little. Within a few weeks even the nighttime curfew was lifted, the soldiers withdrew from the streets, the schools and cinemas re-opened, and the basketball league resumed its regular matches.

Soon after that, Tarzan and Gabyow both quarreled with their coach and quit the orphanage team in protest over something neither can remember. They switched to a team sponsored by a local trade union, and Gabyow became the new captain.

A few months later, they played a league match against the orphanage team and won. The next day, a minister in the new government came to the orphanage to find the two defectors and ordered them to return to their original team. "So, what choice did we have?" Tarzan remarks.

It was trivial. But it was also the smallest hint of things to come.

The laissez-faire atmosphere of pre-coup Mogadishu was turning into something more controlled and repressive. The Soviet influence was becoming clear. The main basketball stadium in Mogadishu, the Centro Sportivo, otherwise known by its Italian name, Lucello, was promptly renamed "21st October." Every district in the city was given an "orientation" center, or as Tarzan saw it, "an indoctrination center."

One day, the military officials running the Hodan district interrupted a basketball game between their local team and the orphanage. With ten minutes still to play, they declared that Hodan had won.

"So I grabbed the microphone and said whatever I want," says Tarzan. By which he means that he screamed and swore at them. The next day he was ordered to pay a visit to a building in town now occupied by the national security services—a place known as "the hole."

"They thought I was politically motivated—that I was against the revolution, and had insulted the idea of these indoctrination centers."

They detained Tarzan for four days, until someone senior intervened and convinced them this was about sport, not politics. Back at the orphanage, one of his friends tried to persuade him that the new revolutionary government "will look after you, give you an apartment, health care, education, this and that."

"Maybe I'm from a poor family but I want to buy my own home, and maybe a big farm," Tarzan replied. The idea of the state providing everything for him made him think of the way a dog owner would look after a pet.

The smaller things started to irritate him. District officials ordered women to come onto the streets and bang drums to encourage people to help sweep their neighborhoods clean. But they did it just after lunch, at siesta time—one Italian tradition that Mogadishu's residents were reluctant to forfeit.

In a small city, Tarzan's antics slowly began to gain him a reputation. He wasn't the best basketball player by any means, nor the most famous, but he was wild and, it seemed to some, principled. He was a "character," someone with "gumption."

Samiya and her friends started talking about this Tarzan as a "lion."

⁂

A YEAR AFTER THE coup, the orphanage team reached the finals of the national basketball league. The police and army teams had already been merged in what was either a practical step to control their increasingly fierce rivalry or a transparent attempt by the Supreme Revolutionary Council to ensure that the security forces would field the strongest possible team and win.

It didn't work out that way.

"It was night, it was open air, it was downtown," Gabyow sighs contentedly. "It was very close."

The stadium was down by the seafront, in one of Mogadishu's older neighborhoods just north of the lighthouse. There were palm trees in the corner, and on each side of the court, the stands, made up of five big concrete steps, were overflowing with supporters.

Perhaps one shouldn't read too much into one match. But the players all felt it that night. Something more was at stake than just a trophy. In the year since the coup, the public mood had changed. There were too many rules now and too many arrests. There was a whiff of protest in the air.

Gabyow can't quite explain it. "It was a good time. But it's a bit confusing. People liked the coup, but they didn't like the army. So instead of insulting it, they cheered for us."

What he means, I suspect, is that fear had arrived in Mogadishu. Quietly at first, perhaps. But it was already starting to change the way people behaved in public and interacted with authority.

The match was close. But the orphanage team scraped to a narrow victory. Gabyow remembers walking off the court, out of the glare of the floodlights, and into a roaring crowd. He and his teammates were trying not to smile. Looking casual, contemptuous even, seemed like a far better way to put the army players in their place. But Gabyow couldn't help himself.

ON THE DESK IN front of me, I have a copy of an old tourist guide to Mogadishu. I'd heard of its existence some years back, but so much was destroyed in Somalia's wars, and so few souvenirs remain, that it took me until a few weeks ago to get my hands on it.

The front cover is missing, and on the inside page, someone has scribbled illegibly around the title, which reads "Mogadishu—Pearl of the Indian Ocean." Beneath it is Somalia's coat of arms—two leopards standing upright, tails pointed, tongues out, holding a shield with a single white star on a sky blue background. It was published in northern Italy, on behalf of Mogadishu's local government, in 1971.

I turn the page and find myself staring into the small, dark eyes of General Siad Barre. Somalia's coup leader and the president of its Supreme Revolutionary Council is seated before a red curtain, welcoming readers and offering the official guidebook his wordless endorsement. He's a jowly man with a closely cropped mustache and blank, unreadable expression. He's wielding a cane and wearing a pale khaki uniform and cap. Unmentioned in the brief caption below his photograph is his nickname, given to him as a child by fellow herd boys in the Ogaden. It is Afweyne, or "Big Mouth."

It would be easy to read the guidebook through a fog of historical irony. Who would be mad enough to spend a holiday in Mogadishu? And yet the city that comes to life in these pages is an earnest, attractive, sympathetic one. There are neat lists—of all fourteen cinemas, twenty embassies, five libraries, six nightclubs, seven hotels, four newspapers, and twelve restaurants. There are color photographs of the city, of an Italian tourist grinning as she perches on the back of a camel, a fisherman clutching a giant shell, the national bank and theater, and the imposing twin-towered cathedral.

In an introduction, an army major who calls himself Mogadishu's

President Siad Barre, circa 1970. OFFICIAL MOGADISHU GUIDEBOOK, 1971

"Extraordinary Commissioner" promises visitors unspoiled beaches, year-round "sun-baths," elephants, monuments, and the hospitality of a city that dates back to 700 B.C. And in an overt nod to Somalia's political upheavals, guests will also be witnesses to a "gigantic effort of revival" in a new "revolutionary era."

But what catches the eye, on almost every page, are the advertisements, which seem to reveal so much more about the city and its changing affiliations than all those lists and captions.

Here's a three-quarter-page advertisement for the Somali Commercial Bank, which has five branches nationwide and now incorporates three big Italian banks that have been nationalized. The National Bottling Company is now on the newly named Via V.I. Lenin. Somali Airlines is the general agent for the Soviet carrier,

Aeroflot. The Agenzia Marittima has changed its name to Somalia Shipping Agency Ltd.

On page after page, you can sense a state trying to shed its colonial past and reaching out, not least toward Moscow, for new patrons and allies.

And yet, squeezed between those bigger advertisements are plenty of defiant little reminders of Mogadishu's enduring relationship with Italy.

Foreign tourist on camel near Mogadishu, circa 1970.
OFFICIAL MOGADISHU GUIDEBOOK, 1971

There's Lugli and Zini's watch shop on the Duke of Genoa street, the gnocchi and cannelloni specials at Ristorante El Trocadero, Alfa Romeo's exclusive agents Francesco Boero and Sons, the fresh pizzas at Cappuccetto Nero, and what looks like Gino

Capone's thriving business importing Innocenti motor scooters direct from Milan.

⁂

CURIOUSLY, AMONG THE FIRST people to take the brochure's promise of an old-fashioned, "open-armed" welcome at face value were two tall, prodigiously talented Americans.

Oscar Robertson and Kareem Abdul-Jabbar were, and remain, basketball royalty. The pair had just won America's NBA championship title for their team, the Milwaukee Bucks.

They could have chosen to visit almost any city, in any country in Africa. They were clearly looking to inspire young black players on a continent engulfed by the upheavals and opportunities presented by the end of colonial rule. Guided by a prominent black American athlete turned diplomat named Mal Whitfield, they settled on Mogadishu, flying in to the beachfront airstrip in 1972.

It's easy to picture them walking down the steps from the plane and into the waiting crowd. Oscar Robertson was 6 feet 5 inches, and a muscular, powerful presence. Kareem Abdul-Jabbar—who'd recently embraced Islam and changed his name from Lew Alcindor—was 7 feet 2 inches and a giant even by Somalia's lanky standards.

In the decades ahead, Somalis would become among the most globalized people on earth, with communities spread across every continent. But at that moment they were acutely aware of their relative isolation and appropriately grateful to the two Americans for their endorsement.

Gabyow and Tarzan both grin and cackle like excited teenagers when they talk about the week that followed—how Kareem Abdul-Jabbar needed two beds pushed together at the Shabelle Hotel ("five star—the best, believe me," Gabyow gushes) in order to stretch out his giant frame.

Tarzan remembers how the front seat of a car, perhaps a Fiat, was removed to enable the American to fold himself inside. "We were like chickens beside them!" Kareem gave out some of his shirts. "They went all the way to my knees!"

There were banquets and picnics and a national tournament with coaching sessions provided by the visitors—a few minutes for each team. And finally, toward the end of the visit, Somalia's two top league teams put on an exhibition match with their foreign guests invited to play.

Kareem Abdul-Jabbar coaching, Mogadishu, 1972.

It should have been the crowning moment of the trip. Several thousand people—the great and good of Mogadishu—had squeezed inside the 21st October stadium for the evening match. The flood-lights flickered on, and the rest of the city vanished into the surrounding darkness. Kareem Abdul-Jabbar was to play with Tarzan and Gabyow's team. Oscar Robertson was with the combined police and army team, called Horseed.

It started well enough. Nuruddin Farah, who had just begun his career as a novelist and was teaching English at Tarzan and Yusuf's high school at the time, was in the crowd.

"The Americans made fools of the Somalis, who couldn't get to the ball," he remembers dryly.

But then the Somali referee started to intervene. His nickname was "Wiish," which sounds, appropriately, like a whistle but actually means "crane," in reference to his height.

Tarzan had had plenty of experience with Wiish's refereeing. He considered him pedantic. A "show-off." Today, Gabyow and Tarzan both wince when they think back on what happened next.

According to Gabyow, Kareem Abdul-Jabbar took more steps than he was allowed while carrying the ball. There was a dispute. Wiish sent Abdul-Jabbar off. Tarzan has a more elaborate story. He insists that Oscar Robertson was dribbling the ball in a manner that Wiish had never seen before. His hand would come under, then over the top of the ball, almost as if stroking it. It was normal practice among the professionals of the NBA, but not in Mogadishu. Wiish believed the American was "carrying" the ball. He blew his whistle and declared, "Technical foul." A few minutes later, he blew it again.

"Oscar came to him and shouted at him," but Wiish would not be swayed. The American was sent off. The crowd began to boo, and then to walk out. It felt like someone had ruined a wedding.

"So Wiish spoiled it. The game did not finish. He didn't realize that all these guys came to watch them, not us." For years afterward, Tarzan would berate Wiish for his "stupid" behavior. He clung on to that anger until 2012, when a suicide bomber killed Wiish inside Mogadishu's national theater.

I've tried repeatedly to get both American players to talk about their trip. Kareem Abdul-Jabbar told me by email that he remembers having "a good time," but nothing more. "My memory is not that great on these types of things." Through a spokesman, Oscar Robertson, or the "Big O," seemed to doubt whether the trip took place at all but also suggested that Tarzan's memories were "quite far-fetched."

And yet, that week stands out for me, as it does for Tarzan, Gabyow, and many others, as something greater than the sum of its parts. I'm not suggesting it marked a high point for the city, let alone a turning point. But listening to them reminiscing about it all these years later, I can sense two teenaged boys closing a chapter. They'd met their heroes. The outside world, in the shape of two famous black Americans, had loudly endorsed their city. And then came the adult realization that life—on court and off—had become more complicated and more disappointing.

⁂

THE ORPHANAGE BASKETBALL TEAM broke up, with the best players poached by other teams. The orphanage itself suffered a similar fate. It was divided up among the army, the police, and the prison service. For the older boys, it was like being conscripted. They were expected to join one of the services and to drop out of high school. Tarzan and a few others insisted that they wished to complete their education. They were promptly told there was no longer any place for them in the orphanage and were thrown out almost immediately.

It was a difficult moment. Tarzan's aunt refused to let him stay with her. But an elderly neighbor, a relative known as "Cross-eyed Osman," eventually offered him a bed. And then Tarzan had an idea. He approached the head of the Somalita, the state-run National Banana Enterprise, who had always sponsored the orphanage team and was angry that it had been broken up.

"Pay us pocket money to survive and we will come and play for you," was Tarzan's offer. And after some haggling, it was agreed. He, Gabyow, Asbaro, and several others all signed up with Somalita and continued to attend high school.

The boys were coming to the end of their teens. That meant more scrutiny from the increasingly Soviet-orientated military government, which was honing its skills in tracking "anti-revolutionary" behavior, real or imagined. It wasn't just political parties that had been banned after the coup. Student groups and unions were outlawed, too. In 1973 Gabyow helped one of his best friends, another basketball player, to escape arrest and flee abroad.

Tarzan's confrontational nature was getting him in trouble, too.

These days he says he can't remember the exact words to the "revolutionary" song they had to sing every morning in his final year at secondary school. "Something about Siad Barre 'keeping power forever . . . keeping us on the right path.' Something like that," he says, with an edge of contempt. The song's title was "O Triumphant Siad."

One morning in January 1975, Tarzan decided to arrange a small classroom protest. A day earlier, the military government had caused outrage in the city by executing ten prominent religious leaders. President Siad Barre was trying to implement something called "Scientific Socialism," which involved balancing an impulse to follow communist ideology with the need to respect Somalia's deeply held Muslim traditions. He had changed the law on inheritance to give women equal rights. There were immediate protests in the mosques, where the new law was seen as proof that the government was undermining Islam.

"Look, this guy is an atheist," Tarzan told his classmates. "So when they ask us to sing the song, we read verses of the Koran."

The headmaster at the 15th May Secondary School, on the hill right next to Villa Somalia, was a gentle man. When the pupils began reciting the Koran, rather than singing, he did the same. Then he urged them to sing, as required, the next verse of the revolutionary song. They ignored him. After the third time, a member of the Supreme Revolutionary Council, who was attending school assembly that day, ordered the students to return to their classrooms, and then came to each one in turn, asking them to sing. There were four classes in the year. The boys in 4D had been together since primary school. They agreed to keep reciting the Koran, regardless. As a result their class was promptly abolished, and its members split up among the other three, while Tarzan was identified, once again, as a troublemaker and ringleader.

By now, his brother Yusuf had already finished school. He'd come in top in his year. "He was the best, very intelligent. The military targeted him. Medical exams, then three days later—*phweeee!*—he's off to Russia. A SAM missile guidance engineer," Tarzan recalls.

Tarzan's own future seemed much less certain. Like most kids out of school, he was required to do military service: six months of training followed by six months of community work, which usually meant being a teaching assistant. And so he left the orphanage for new barracks in an army camp on the edge of town, beside the airport.

The army did not suit Tarzan. There were more songs, a lot more propaganda, daily drills on how to handle an 82-millimeter mortar, and constant surveillance.

"They're like the Nazi SS, or the Russian Secret Service," Tarzan ended up complaining to a group of colleagues one afternoon after training. He was exaggerating wildly, but he seemed to mean it.

"They tell us they're cleaning the hearts and minds of the people, but this is where they plant the seeds of corruption and tribalism." He saw the richer, better-connected students being able to get out of the camp whenever they wanted, or their relatives would bring them food inside.

As if to confirm his suspicions, someone reported him, and the next day a soldier escorted Tarzan to the commander's office at the camp.

"You're a reactionary. You're pro-American," the major shouted at him. "We know what you've said. We know what you are." Tarzan was put in solitary confinement for two days, then brought out for another withering lecture.

"You're from a poor family. You can't afford to be kicked out of here. You'll never get a job. You'll never get to university. You have no chance in this country. You will be blacklisted."

Tarzan claims he knuckled under. But he's not very convincing.

As a member of the Somalita basketball team, Tarzan was still going out of camp three times a week for matches and practices. With Gabyow, Tarzan, and Asbaro on board, Somalita had reached the last eight teams battling for the league championship. They were the favorites to win the trophy. The quarterfinals were held, as usual, at the 21st October stadium, and for the evening game, the vice president of the military council was sitting courtside.

Earlier in the afternoon, Somalita had played another team in a game that would count toward the championship. No one can remember the exact details. "I'm getting old!" Gabyow shouts down the phone to me when I call him to check. But Somalita felt they'd been cheated of victory—that the referee had deliberately steered the game toward the weaker team. As Somalita's captain, Gabyow had demanded a rematch and insisted that a decision should be made before they played the next match, against the military's team, Horseed, that evening. Otherwise they would boycott the tournament.

It was the old orphanage mentality at work again. Us against the world. The conviction that Mogadishu's new elites—now the military—were trying to put them, the city's bastards, in their place.

Somalita came out onto the court for the evening match. And there was Wiish, "very powerful, very show-off," ready to referee once again. Wiish muttered something about the possibility of a rematch for the disputed game in a few months. But no guarantees. "Now you must play," he said.

Gabyow would have handled it a little differently. But he knew that Tarzan was not to be controlled, that his friend spoke and acted from the heart.

"I became wild," is how Tarzan puts it.

"Fuck you! Fuck you! You're stupid. You're not honest. We're never coming back again!" Tarzan screamed into Wiish's face. Then he charged over to the scorer's table, at the edge of the court, and hurled it across the ground. The director of sports tried to grab hold of him. Tarzan spat in his face and wheeled around to have another go at throwing the table. The crowd began a slow handclap. The game was suspended. The vice president walked slowly and pointedly out of the stadium.

Tarzan's teammates dragged him back to the army camp that evening. Phone calls were made. The minister of sports and the head of the Olympic Committee, anticipating the military government's instincts, procured a warrant of arrest. The police were sent with it to the army camp, and left soon afterward, with Tarzan.

"Why don't you fight Wiish with me? Why don't you come and fight when I make a move?" Tarzan asked his teammates that evening, before his arrest. He was still raging and crying.

"Because you're crazy," Gabyow remembers one of the others saying. "And we're not crazy."

A Girl Called "Mosquito"

"Blow us a kiss! Look at us! Hey—Comrade Siad."

—SAMIYA LEREW

I T FELT A BIT LIKE they were going to war. But in a fun sort of way, if that makes any sense.

Samiya sat in the back of a small, open truck, in a long, orderly convoy that trundled through the outskirts of Mogadishu. It was 1974, five years since she'd watched the crowds surge down the main road to welcome the military coup. She was seventeen now and sat with her feet on her luggage, her school friends squeezed in beside her. They were off to the countryside as part of a grand, unprecedented mission to drag their young nation out of ignorance.

The girls would normally raise their eyebrows sarcastically when it came to singing revolutionary songs. But today they all joined in, loudly and without irony, their grins bouncing around the truck.

"A revolution dawned in Somalia today."

"Forward forever, backward never!"

"March on, our beloved leader!"

The convoy reached the southwestern edge of Mogadishu, the city ended abruptly, and their truck picked up speed as it slipped behind the dunes. Before long the singing eased off, and Samiya wrapped a shawl around her face and turned to face back toward home.

Beside her was a much taller girl, her head framed by a fashionably bouffant Afro hairstyle. At sixteen, Shamis was a year younger than Samiya and "pretty. A lot prettier than me."

Shamis kept looking down to inspect her brand new sneakers.

Mass literacy convoy leaving Mogadishu, circa 1974. POSTCARD COURTESY OF

SAMIYA LEREW

Like the others, she'd never been allowed to leave Mogadishu on her own before. The shopping and other preparations had been going on for weeks. Her aunt had bought her the sneakers to protect her against the snakes and other "biting things" that she'd been warned about in the countryside.

Shamis felt she knew a little more about rural life than the other girls. She wasn't really a Beizani like them. Her father was a veterinarian who drove around rural Somalia in his own truck, with a big mosquito painted on the side. He was, inevitably, nicknamed "Dr. Mosquito," or "Kaneeco" in Somali. He used to tell Shamis about the dangers of nomadic life—the crocodiles, hyenas, and malaria—and perhaps to show she wasn't scared, and more likely to keep him close after the divorce and her mother's death, she adopted his nickname, as one might put on a favorite sweater. Shamis Kaneeco.

A few days before they set off, the girls had gathered at a big parade ground in town, beside a brand new Soviet-built hospital, to listen to President Siad Barre tell them about their mission.

"The battle . . . has more value than anything you have known," he declared in the tone of someone who did not expect to be doubted.

Five years after seizing power, the president could not be accused of idleness or a lack of ambition. There were regular "crash programs" designed to eradicate the very notion of clans and to reform the economy, all under the banner of "Scientific Socialism." And with the president's lofty goals came a growing need for tighter controls and louder propaganda. Visiting dignitaries—Uganda's dictator, Idi Amin, for example—would be treated to a stadium filled with thousands of dancers performing tightly choreographed spectacles and wielding giant cards to spell out revolutionary slogans.

In hindsight, it's easy to mock such Soviet-style extravaganzas. But Somalia was developing rapidly, and the president's latest campaign had caught the public mood like no other.

Every school in the country was closed. Every Somali student aged fourteen years and above had been summoned to take part. More than thirty thousand people—teachers, volunteers, and officials—

were poised to join. Somalia had never seen anything quite like it; nor, in terms of size and ambition, had the African continent. There was an overwhelming public thirst for education.

But there was a problem. For years Somalia had been wrestling with the fact that it had no written script. It was an oral culture, after all. People would write in Italian, or in Arabic. Or they would use one of those alphabets to come up with something that approximately resembled Somali words.

It wasn't just awkward and unwieldy. It was humiliating.

Somali academics had been tinkering with new or hybrid alphabets; others insisted that anything less than a formal Arabic script would be "un-Islamic." The arguments had been stewing for years. But the military government wanted a decision, and Samiya's stepfather had been part of an official commission charged with analyzing all the options, picking a Somali script, and then drawing up plans for standardized spelling.

For such an acutely proud nation, the final decision was surprisingly pragmatic. New printing presses were expensive. Most existing presses used the Roman script. Therefore . . .

It's easy to imagine Siad Barre's large, impatient hand coming down on a desk somewhere, and brooking no further argument.

It may well have been among the best things he ever did for Somalia. And having taken the decision in favor of the Roman script, the next step was to spread the word.

ON THE DAY OF their departure, Samiya and Shamis found their designated truck in a huge column of vehicles on the roadside and clambered on board. Just before they were about to set off, they saw an open car drive by. The president was standing inside it, saluting his "troops" and exhorting them to take the "Somali Rural Literacy Campaign" to the farthest corners and the most isolated nomadic communities of the country. This was, he said, a cultural revolution that would break the old divisions of tribe, clan, and sect and unite Somalia. It was, in essence, a war against ignorance.

For a moment, teenaged instincts trumped revolutionary fervor.

"Blow us a kiss! Look at us! Hey—Comrade Siad," the girls shouted out from the back of their truck. If the comrade heard them, he didn't show it.

On time, and in unison, the convoy moved out of the city, heading southwest, on the main road toward Kenya. After a hundred kilometers, just outside another ancient port city, Merca, the girls' truck turned right off the main road, heading inland. Half an hour later, it came to a stop in the middle of a small town.

It was called Qoryooley, the "place of firewood." Although, of course, no one had ever written its name like that before. Now it was official—no more Arabic approximations, no clumsy Italian. Somalia had its own official script and spelling—no letters *v*, *z*, or *p*—and the girls were in Qoryooley to teach it to the uneducated masses.

They stayed one night at the local school and then headed out, deeper into the countryside, to their designated village, where they were to be billeted with local families. They had their luggage with them, a blanket each, and special teaching kits, which consisted of some chalk, pens, and books inside a wooden box that was crudely designed to fold out into a blackboard.

An old black-and-white photograph of their group has survived. Samiya dug it out and emailed it to me a few days earlier, and at first glance it seemed unremarkable. Seven figures in white shirts stare aimlessly at the camera, as if interrupted during the dullest of picnics. Behind them is a sun-bleached field, with some small trees in the distance.

But kneeling in the front row is a girl who seems to have wandered in from another era altogether. Her black curly hair cascades— yes, that's the right word—down past her right shoulder. She's wearing a tunic over an elegant long-sleeved shirt and the most enormous, glamorous sunglasses that reflect the sun, the horizon, and a smudge that must be the photographer.

Shamis (standing, second from right), Samiya (sitting on right), and friends,
Qoryooley, 1974. COURTESY OF SAMIYA LEREW

The girl with the curls is Samiya, and as she breaks into a half pout,
half smile, the figures around her suddenly seem to catch a glint of
that same city swagger. It's as though everyone in the picture has just
woken up, and my eye flits from languidly folded arms, to another
fashionable pair of sunglasses, to a hint of flared trousers, to something in Shamis's casual poise.

They're Beizani, of course. The offspring of Mogadishu's cosmopolitan elite might have been roughing it on their very first adventure, but they could still flaunt their Italian clothes and urban
sophistication.

I'm intrigued and call up Samiya to ask her what else defined the
teenaged Beizani, besides clothes and attitude. The answer, she explains, lies in the relationship between Mogadishu's elites and the former colonial power, Italy.

"Unlike the British and the French, the Italians integrated with the natives. You talked like them; you dressed like them; you thought like them; you were one of them!" Samiya remembers.

But surely the colonial Italians still considered themselves superior to the "natives . . ."

"Yes. But those who adopted their way of living were superiors, too. So to be inferior is to be one of the 'bush' people."

And of course it was that sharp social division, between urban and rural, rich and poor, that the language campaign was supposed to help break down.

The teaching began. For the next seven months, the girls held daily classes in the open air, with their blackboards suspended from the trees. In Mogadishu, they'd learned the basics of their new script. Now they taught not only the children but their parents, too. The adults, who'd cheered their arrival in the village, were earnest and appreciative from the very start and would gather around the Beizani in the afternoons, seated on small stools in the shade.

"I was snooty," Samiya admits with a small grin. But Shamis did not feel so out of place and seemed to have the knack for teaching. With her, the new script "flowed like water. She would laugh and chat with them in a way I couldn't."

At night, the girls slept, like everyone else, in small mud houses. Sometimes a calf would be brought in to share the floor.

"Not a tent. Not a proper house. They make their own . . ." Shamis hunts for the right word. "I don't know how you call it in English. Igloo? Igloo! That's it!"

The rains had been failing for some time. There was nothing particularly unusual about that in Somalia. But toward the end of 1974, the girls noticed that the nearby Shabelle River had dried out completely. Samiya's mother, visiting them from Mogadishu, shared some worrying news she'd picked up from the radio station where she still worked. It was the worst drought in living memory, a national crisis that would come to be known as "the long-tailed drought."

The villagers knew what to do. The girls watched them as they dug deep holes in the riverbed to find water. They built underground grain stores for their corn to see them through the hardest times. They were short of cash, but no one was starving.

For the nomads, this drought was harder to fight. Their camels, goats, and cattle died. Without them, they were broke and desperate.

The government, supported by the Soviet Union, reacted swiftly. The literacy campaign was not entirely abandoned, but a new and even bigger nationwide mobilization took place. Many students found themselves reassigned to huge government relief camps, which were quickly set up for the nomads in more fertile areas. Before long, a quarter of a million people were being looked after in the camps.

In the years ahead, that huge displacement of people would create new clan and ethnic tensions, with the haughty nomads bristling at the idea that they should till the land like mere farmers. But for now the government's reaction to the drought was rightly deemed a success. Some eighteen thousand people died, but that was a small figure compared with neighboring Ethiopia, where famine was pushing the country toward open rebellion.

History has not been kind to President Siad Barre. He was a coup plotter, a dictator, and a warmonger. But 1974 marked a genuine high point. He'd steered Somalia away from famine, and by the time his literacy campaign had finally come to an end, the number of Somalis who could read and write had risen from under 10 percent to around 50 percent. It was an achievement that other postcolonial leaders around the continent could only watch with envy.

In their village, Shamis and Samiya continued to teach. They made a few friends, learned a great deal about ploughing, weaving, poverty—"an alien world to us"—and sometimes they got bored. A few months before they were due to return to Mogadishu, Shamis tried to sneak away for a night in Merca. She hitched a ride and went to see a cousin in the town. But this was still a country where everyone seemed to know everyone. Shamis was almost immediately spotted, detained, and, as punishment, promptly reallocated by the authorities to a new village, along with her blanket, blackboard, and snake-proof sneakers.

⁂

IT WAS A MONDAY morning, a week or so after the girls had come back to Mogadishu, having spent about eight months in the countryside. Shamis and Samiya sat near the back of the classroom in their yellow uniforms, waiting to see which awkward, gangly conscript—finished with his military training and now forced to do six months as a teacher's assistant—would be assigned to their history class that term.

A muscular man of unremarkable height, in a white shirt and dark trousers, walked into the room and moved toward the blackboard. The class fell silent, chairs scraping back on the stone floor, as everyone stood up.

Shamis peered at the stranger as he picked up a piece of chalk and turned to face them. He was not handsome, that was for sure, she said to herself. But then she heard some of the boys nearby whisper in recognition. Some pronounced it "Tarsan." After all, there was no *z* in their new script. Others said "Tarzan."

Shamis was tall and reasonably athletic, but she had never been to a basketball match and had never seen this famous character before. She preferred the cinema. Still, she knew of Tarzan by reputation.

"A tough man. Very popular. Everybody knew him," she says.

"If someone was getting bullied, he'd stand up and say, 'No! This is wrong!'" That's Samiya, who still talks about Tarzan with a mixture of awe, fear, and the giggly tones of a schoolgirl crush.

"He was a lion of a man," Samiya gushes. "Not outstandingly good-looking, but firm. Always clean and smart. Shirt ironed. We were all skinny little shrimps, and he had this chunky sort of build. He walked past you and you were scared. Maybe because he has burningly beautiful eyes—that makes you not want to mess with him!"

Following his arrest for disrupting the quarterfinals of the basketball league championship, Tarzan went to jail, but only briefly. Once again, a senior figure—this time the head of the Somalita team—intervened and persuaded the authorities to drop the charges.

They reluctantly agreed, and instead, Tarzan was banned for a year from playing or training with the team.

Instead, he taught the history of the Austro-Hungarian Empire and the origins of the First World War to Shamis's class. And after lessons, with more time on his hands because of the ban, he started coaching boys and girls in the school basketball club.

Shamis felt moved to sign up and found him approachable and straightforward—not overly flirty like some of the other conscripts. The school was perhaps 50 meters away from the home they would share nearly forty years later.

They began chatting and soon worked out that Shamis had almost certainly insulted Tarzan, a decade earlier, on the street outside her aunt's house.

Every Thursday, before the coup, the police band marched around Mogadishu playing trumpets, drums, and trombones. It seemed to have the same impact on the city as an ice cream van's jingle, and children would rush outside to watch the bandleader, left hand perched on hip, throwing his baton impossibly high into the air. And most weeks, trailing behind the band like extras from an *Oliver Twist* musical, came the orphan boys, doing their own swaggering imitations of the police.

"We used to run when we heard the orphans were coming," says Shamis with a pretend shiver, remembering how everyone would taunt and fear the boys in equal measure. "We shouted 'Orphan!' at them." And, no doubt, "Bastard!" too.

"That was me," Tarzan confirms.

IT WAS NOT UNTIL well over a year after Tarzan and Shamis had met, properly, that Samiya found out that the two of them were now in a relationship. She'd left school by then and was taking typing classes at a small academy down the hill from Villa Somalia. Late one afternoon, she popped out to get a drink at the café across the road and stumbled upon her best friend sitting inside and holding Tarzan's hand across the table.

Tarzan seemed mortified. "This lion of a man, suddenly holding hands with one of my girlfriends . . . a bit of a come-down? So he was shocked," Samiya recalls.

"Now she'll tell everyone," Tarzan muttered.

"No. I know Samiya well. She won't tell," said Shamis, leaning across the table.

Shamis, Mogadishu, circa 1976.
COURTESY OF SHAMIS NUR

But Samiya's explanation for Tarzan's awkwardness at being discovered—that his stature was somehow lessened by the relationship—doesn't ring entirely true for me. If he was a lion, he was a penniless one, a troublemaker from a poor family and a tiny clan. Shamis, on the other hand, was a real catch.

SHAMIS WAS BORN IN a small rural town called El Buur in 1958, but her parents split when she was three years old. Divorce seems particularly common, and uncomplicated, in Somalia.

"If wives have a problem, they just say, 'Divorce me,' and you have to divorce," says Shamis with a shrug.

Soon afterward, Shamis's mother died in childbirth, and her father, "Mosquito" the vet, remarried. Then, like so many of the boys at the orphanage, Shamis found herself in an awkward position.

I can't go into the details. Like her brother-in-law Yusuf, Shamis is uncomfortable talking about such delicate matters. Or rather, she talks at considerable length but then asks me not to repeat it because it will cause problems within the family.

"Did Yusuf talk to you about that?" she asks with an inquiring smile.

At the time, Shamis was her father's only daughter. He approached his sister, who was living in Mogadishu, and asked if she would be willing to look after the girl. Shamis's aunt appears to have been an even more formidable woman than Samiya's mother—the radio and singing star. She immediately agreed to the arrangement, and it proved to be a happy one.

"My aunty said, 'Don't worry, I'll look after her.' And she looked after me like her own daughter. Like more than that. She loved me and I loved her."

The aunt's name was Hawa Awale Abtidoon. Everyone knew her as "Little Hawa." She wore high heels, smoked in the street, refused to wear a head covering of any sort, and possessed a deep, booming voice. She was the first Somali woman ever to campaign for a seat in parliament.

"People say, 'She's like a man,'" Shamis recalls, proudly. "She was a very tough lady."

Hawa's first husband was a wealthy businessman from Yemen. Her second was a bank manager. The family lived in a large villa near

Samiya's house, by the K4 roundabout, on the main road heading south-west out of the city. Shamis shared a room with one of her aunt's five daughters and took a taxi to school each morning. On Fridays the whole family would head to the cinema, followed by dinner at an Italian restaurant and perhaps a stroll along the beachfront.

Tarzan, in other words, was a little out of his depth.

Nonetheless, it didn't take too long for news of the relationship to spread. "We used to date normally," says Shamis, by which she meant they began going to restaurants together, and to the cinema. She wore miniskirts. They both wore flares. They argued over which films to see. She loved the Hindi films. He refused to go and would take her instead to see the latest Italian releases at the Equatore. Before sunset, they would often *fare una passeggiata*, the Italian ritual of the leisurely evening stroll, which had long ago become a Mogadishu tradition, as enthusiastically practiced as the siesta.

Shamis would dress up for the occasion. High heels, billowing dresses made by local tailors copying Italian fashion, big earrings, and elaborate hairdos.

"She was slender. So pretty," says Samiya with her usual enthu-siasm.

When I ask Shamis if Tarzan was her first boyfriend, she starts to answer, blushes furiously, and tells me I'll get her in trouble. "Tarzan was my first," she finally declares.

"The boys were after me. A lot of boys were after me," she recalls with a grin. The braver ones would call out to her during *la passeg-giata*, telling her she could do a lot better than Tarzan. Or warning her that she was dating a thug, that he would beat her black-and-blue.

It seems clear to me that the relationship was changing Tarzan more than Shamis. Once they begin dating, there are no more men-tions of fights or tantrums.

Shamis was studying to be a teacher; Tarzan began attending the university and working on his geology degree. Shamis still wasn't a true member of the Beizani—for that she should have been born in Mogadishu and attended a private Italian school. But her sophisticated ways were rubbing off on Tarzan. And he had another reason to feel more settled, too. The allowance he'd been receiving from Somalita for playing on their basketball team had given him the means to reach out to his mother, still living as a nomad, and bring her and her two youngest sons to live in Mogadishu.

"Two hundred and fifty shillings!" Tarzan remembers. He kept a hundred, rented a new room in town for twenty-five shillings, and ate at a cheap restaurant for fifty shillings a month. The rest of the money was enough to rent a house for his mother and a growing crowd of relatives. Before long, he was looking after the six children of a jailed half-brother, too.

The half-brother's story is a curious one. He was a policeman who'd been part of a firing squad called to execute a woman convicted of murder. The woman had killed another in a jealous rage. Three times in a row, every policeman on the squad deliberately aimed to miss, and all were sentenced to a year in jail. When his half-brother came out of jail, Tarzan used one of his orphanage contacts, now working as an exam supervisor, to help him cheat his way to a job at the national printing press.

Tarzan was now twenty-three, and with Yusuf training in Russia, he was shouldering a growing number of responsibilities. Money was tight, and his prospects seemed limited.

Perhaps he would have found a job, and stuck it out. Perhaps he could have won over Shamis's family, who were opposed to their relationship, and settled down in Mogadishu. But Somalia was changing tack once again, and the Cold War was about to intervene.

PART 2

The Sky Has Turned
to Smoke

1977–2009

". . . and now my home is the mouth of a shark,
now my home is the barrel of a gun.
I'll see you on the other side."

—FROM *CONVERSATIONS ABOUT HOME*,
BY WARSAN SHIRE

5

A Lonely Impulse

"This is not my country anymore."

—MOHAMUD "TARZAN" NUR

IT WAS THE STEADY, CLICKING rhythm of Ali Madobe's typing that got him noticed. Fifty words a minute, for hours on end, as he sat in the open-air passageway just outside the commander's office.

Madobe was a quiet, grounded young man. Nothing like Tarzan. At times he liked to imagine he was playing a piano rather than typing up another army report.

It was a couple of years since Madobe had left the orphanage. With no money, no basketball skills to cash in, no close family, and no obvious career options, he had gone to live in town with an aunt who worked as a cleaner at a nearby girls' school. It had been a struggle, but she'd helped him enroll at a typing school—the same one that Samiya attended—and his uncle had chipped in twenty dollars a month.

When he'd completed the course, Madobe joined the army as a typist, working as a sergeant at the military base on the southern edge of Mogadishu. He enjoyed the order and the camaraderie.

His uncle Loyan, the one whose marriage had prompted his move to the orphanage a decade earlier, had recently been drafted into the new National Security Service—a combined police and army department—as an investigator. One day in March, hoping to advance his quiet nephew's career, he asked permission for Madobe to be transferred for a few weeks to his unit, to type up a large, apparently urgent, report.

At first, the eighteen-year-old wasn't aware of the tall figure

Mogadishu, circa 1970s.

standing beside him. His fingers continued tapping away at the type-
writer in a competent, steady rhythm. When he finally looked up, he
sprang to his feet to salute the head of National Intelligence, a member of Siad Barre's Supreme Revolutionary Council.

A few minutes later, the general summoned him to his office,
praised his typing, and asked him who'd brought him to this department. His uncle rushed into the room and explained it all.

"Do you trust him?" the uncle was asked.

"He's my brother's son. I raised him. I trust him."

Ali Madobe, Mogadishu, 2014. COURTESY OF THE AUTHOR

And with that, Ali Madobe was transferred, on the spot, to Somalia's intelligence services. His financial problems were over. He was
made an officer, sent to Moscow for six months' training, and would
go on to rise to the highest positions inside President Siad Barre's in-

creasingly repressive security forces. He had a ringside seat for Somalia's impending collapse.

But first came a short and initially very popular war.

ᴬᵗᵒᵍᵉᶻᴬ

IT WAS THE SUMMER of 1977 and a long-simmering conflict over the fate of the Ogaden was boiling over.

Neighboring Ethiopia had been in turmoil following its own coup d'état against the emperor. Somalia sensed it had a historic opportunity to seize back a huge chunk of stolen territory. But that window of opportunity was closing fast. Ethiopia's new military leader had broken off ties to the United States and was realigning his country as a Marxist-Leninist state. For Somalia's Siad Barre, it was now or never.

At first, the Somali army was triumphant, sweeping across the Ogaden in a matter of weeks with the support of local rebel groups and crushing Ethiopian resistance. There were wild celebrations in Mogadishu. Somalia was being made whole again. People sold their jewelry to help fund the invasion.

But before long, the offensive stuttered to a halt. Ali Madobe found himself touring the frontlines as clerk to a group of more senior intelligence officers who were trying to understand what was going wrong. The answer turned out to be very straightforward.

The Soviet Union suddenly found itself in the awkward position of backing both sides in the conflict. The relatively tiny Somalia against giant Ethiopia. The Kremlin weighed up the advantages of Siad Barre's Scientific Socialism against the far more radical ambitions of Ethiopia's dictator, Mengistu Haile Mariam. There was, it seemed, no contest. Somalia was promptly abandoned—all those, like Yusuf, who were still training in the Soviet Union were sent home—and Ethiopia was aggressively reinforced by thousands of Soviet and Cuban soldiers.

ᴬᵗᵒᵍᵉᶻᴬ

LIKE EVERYONE ELSE IN the city, Tarzan had noticed the change of atmosphere. The military had begun going through the markets looking for idle young men to send to the front. The government's already limited tolerance for criticism was vanishing altogether.

It was a few weeks later, during classes one morning in Mogadishu, that all the science and technical students at the university—those doing engineering, geology, and so on—were summoned to the dining room, the only space big enough on their campus to fit all 1,500 of them. In the dining hall, the minister of higher education told the students they would begin military training immediately. The university's classes were still being taught in Italian, and for the first six months of their course, the students had intensive Italian language lessons each afternoon. Those lessons would be canceled to make time for the military exercises.

"Excuse me?" Tarzan had his hand in the air before the minister had finished talking.

"Minister, the country needs soldiers to fight and defend. But it also needs people with an education. It needs university students. We need those language lessons because Italian is still a struggle for us."

The minister turned away from Tarzan and didn't look back. And when he spoke his tone had changed. He held out his finger, jabbing it around the room.

"One soldier—one soldier in a bunker in the Kara Mardha mountains [the current frontline]—is worth more than all of you here today!"

Until that moment—for all the fights and the headstrong impulsiveness—the larger contours of Tarzan's life had been shaped by the decisions of others. But listening to the minister's indignant, scathing reply, he remembers feeling something within him snap.

"This is not my country anymore," he told his friends after the minister had left. "I cannot survive here. I have to leave."

It sounds like the sort of self-dramatizing thing a young student might say in the heat of the moment. And then quietly forget about. Instead, Tarzan walked into town and bought himself a bus ticket.

Shamis was mortified when he outlined his nomadic plan. She was nineteen and in love. It all seemed so sudden and so serious. So adult. Tarzan had always been the pursuer in their relationship, spurred on, perhaps, by the mockery of her other suitors with their taunts that she could do so much better than a poor thug. Now she would be the one sitting at home, teaching at a primary school, waiting for him to earn enough money. And then he'd send for her, tearing her away from her family, her job, to live abroad, to raise a family somewhere overseas. They had spoken of marriage and she assumed he would honor his promise. But when?

FOR YEARS TARZAN HAD kept a small map of America taped to the underside of the bunk bed above him in the orphanage dormitory. It was the land of basketball, of Kareem Abdul-Jabbar, and of opportunity. Something to aim for. But now he had neither the money, nor the contacts, nor the paperwork to pull it off.

Instead, he said goodbye to Shamis and took a bus to Hargeisa, in the far north of the country. Halfway there, the bus driver stopped for lunch in a small town, then scrambled to get his passengers back on board and on the road as a group of soldiers began sweeping the streets, searching for potential conscripts for the Ogaden war.

From Hargeisa, Tarzan crossed the border into neighboring Djibouti. Then, following a trail set by many other impoverished Somalis looking for work abroad, he went to Yemen and secured a three-day transit visa for Saudi Arabia.

The first time Tarzan tells me about his decision to leave Somalia, he blames the "political situation" rather than the war. It's only when I check the dates that I realize there's an obvious link to the Ogaden conflict. When I ask him again, Tarzan appears to be perfectly open about it all—partly because that's his nature, I think, but also because that's the political profile he's adopted, as "the man without secrets."

"You can ask me anything. Anything at all," he says. "On live television. In a debate. I have nothing to hide."

It's a challenge I've heard him make to others. And he follows it with another phrase that seems familiar. When I do a word search on my laptop I realize that it's become something of a catchphrase of his—a motto that acts like an exclamation mark, and one that still carries with it the echo of a tough orphan on a dusty street daring his enemies to contradict him.

"Believe me."

I mention this now because there's something about Tarzan's abrupt decision to leave Somalia that makes me pause. It seems reasonable to ask whether a young man of military age, who was born in the Ogaden, might not feel a compulsion to fight for it. And by extension, whether a young man who chose to leave the country during wartime might be accused of something close to desertion. I put it to him, in more or less that fashion, and watch him closely as he answers.

"No, no, no. If they send me to fight, I will fight. I was not afraid of the fight. But am I fighting for Somalia, or am I fighting for a regime that I'm not happy with?" He speaks in a measured way, holding my gaze, and then answers his own question.

"Of course it was a regime I opposed. I knew if I stayed I would end up in prison. National Security had already imprisoned me two times."

Later, Tarzan emails me to expand on his reasoning. He talks about the lack of investment in the Ogaden region, the fact that its inhabitants were not yet "ready" for self-determination, and that Somalia's government was wrong to impose its will.

It sounds like an older man trying to prune and polish the impetuous actions of his younger self. His brother Yusuf believes his decision had almost nothing to do with the war, and that his real motivation was simply the need for a poor young man to make money.

THE DESERT TOWN OF Arar, once nothing more than an oil pumping station, lies in the far north of Saudi Arabia, close to the border with Iraq. It is a bleak place, not least in winter, when the wind whips a blur of snow across the plains.

Tarzan was stooped in front of a large tractor, picking out the larger rocks from the dirt and throwing them to the side of the new road that an Italian company was building northward toward Iraq. The intense cold was an unfamiliar sensation for him, and so was the monotony of manual labor.

He'd flown from Djibouti to Jeddah in Saudi Arabia a few weeks earlier, and, after his transit visa expired, had slipped into the twilight world of the undocumented migrant. He'd heard word through other Somalis in his clan that they were hiring in Arar, and had rushed north to see if it was true.

Once hired, his first priority was to get out of the cold. When the Italian manager grudgingly agreed that the workers could set up and staff their own canteen, Tarzan put himself forward as a qualified chef.

He woke in the dark at 5 a.m. to cook porridge for the road-grading team, then went back to bed for a few hours before starting to make lunch at 10 a.m. The first couple of days went smoothly enough. Tarzan knew how to cook spaghetti. But when the men demanded something else—rice, perhaps—his limited culinary repertoire was exposed. The other Somalis promptly demanded a new cook, and when they discovered that the job included overtime benefits, each put forward someone from their own clan.

Tarzan's response was uncompromising, to put it mildly.

"So I don't know how to cook. Fine, but I'm learning. None of us are doing jobs we know. We're all on three-day transit permits. No one has a work permit. The guy in personnel is registered on a Yemeni passport, and he's not Yemeni. If you don't leave me alone I will go to the labor office and tell everything. In the case of the personnel officer, it's a case of forgery. They'll deport the rest of us, but they'll cut his hand off.

"So, do what you want to me, and I'll do the same."

It worked. But not for long.

Two months later, the Italian company asked the Somalis to produce their work permits. Of course nobody had one. The entire team left overnight to hunt for new work. Tarzan had not yet learned to drive, but he talked his way into a new job as a truck driver at another huge construction site. He was found out soon enough, but he just shrugged and moved on. He was cocky and entrepreneurial. And he was lucky. A few months later, the Saudi authorities issued a rare amnesty for Muslims living illegally in the country. As a result, Tarzan got a residency permit and a work permit, and he soon found himself a job in the capital, Riyadh, working for a big American company providing heavy equipment for the oil industry.

"Very good job. A nice job." Tarzan was hired as a purchaser, getting general supplies for the office, and driving an American car around the city. A year slid by. Then one of Saudi Arabia's many princes, who had ties to the company, recommended a new salesman to join the team. The man had been to America and "thought he was above everybody else." One morning, while Tarzan was busy washing his company car in the parking lot, the man asked him to clean his car, too.

"Fuck you!"

Tarzan's hair-trigger indignation took the other man by surprise. He reached for the black band of rope that held his traditional red and white Saudi headdress in place and tried to whip Tarzan with it. Tarzan immediately punched him in the face, at least three times, and then the two men began grappling with each other.

Tarzan relives the fight for me, pulling down the neck of his T-shirt to show his right shoulder.

"He holds me, and bites me . . . here. Can you see?" And sure enough there are two dark marks, like lip-shaped blushes, on his skin.

The incident would almost certainly have brought his brief career at the company to an end. But before the awkward aftermath of the fight had a chance to play itself out, Tarzan received a phone call from Shamis, back in Mogadishu.

"It's my aunt. She is forcing me to marry a cousin. You have to come."

SHAMIS'S FORMIDABLE AUNT HAD been against the relationship with Tarzan from the moment she finally found out about it. He was too poor. Too much of a ruffian. And his clan was too small. He was not fit for her niece. She would make other plans for Shamis.

Tarzan left for Somalia the same day that he received the phone call. He had saved some money and flew straight back to Mogadishu.

Shamis's household was in uproar. Her aunt had selected a young relative who had been studying engineering in Czechoslovakia and had just returned. It was a good match.

Shamis's memories of the period seem fragmented and almost contradictory. At times she told her aunt, point blank, that she would marry no one but Tarzan, that she was in love and would do as she pleased. But then she remembers thinking that she should listen to her family, that it would be wrong to abandon them and live abroad.

"I was not desperate like he was desperate at that time," she says of Tarzan.

Shamis's father, Dr. Mosquito, was summoned from central Somalia to mediate. He was from the same Hawiye tree as Tarzan, but from a different clan. And within his sub-sub-sub-clan, he, and therefore Shamis, were considered to have royal blood. Mosquito sided with his daughter.

"She can marry as she wants," he told his sister.

"No. She is my daughter now."

"But she is still my daughter, too, and she is the one who must live with whatever man she marries. Not you or me."

Somali arguments—not unlike the language itself—tend toward the more ferocious end of the spectrum. I've sometimes been left feeling bruised from an encounter that, I'm later assured, was nothing but a friendly exchange of views. A Somali friend living in the U.K. once laughingly told me how bystanders had called the police to intervene in a mild diaspora dispute between friends that had been mistaken for the beginning of a full-fledged street battle.

And so I picture Shamis's aunt and father locked in a finger-jabbing storm of accusations and indignation, in which the aunt seemed to hold the upper hand. Tarzan was now back in Somalia and heard about the dispute. And the more he learned, the more he struggled to contain his feelings.

"I think he became more in love when my family refused—when he was told he couldn't get me," Shamis observes.

And so, in haste and in secrecy, Tarzan made a plan.

———

TOWARD THE END OF one afternoon, not long after Tarzan's return, Shamis slipped out of her aunt's house and into a waiting taxi. Tarzan had persuaded a cousin, named Yusuf, to lend them his house. It was a rushed, low-key, modest wedding. Just Tarzan, Shamis, Yusuf, and three close friends. Everyone was sworn to secrecy. Shamis remembers they drank Pepsi and ate sweets immediately after the formalities were over. Then they spent the evening celebrating with their friends, first at a restaurant in the city's brand new stadium, and then at Lido beach. Mogadishu was still the sort of place where you could walk around all night without running into trouble. Sometime after midnight, Tarzan gallantly returned Shamis to her aunt's in a taxi.

Late that night, she stood alone in her bedroom, staring at her face in the mirror, wondering if anyone would be able to tell just by looking at her. She felt exhilarated and very young.

The following morning, Shamis could feel her secret burning a small hole inside her.

"You know what I did last night?" she whispered to her cousin, who shared a room with her. "I married Tarzan! But you mustn't tell."

Shamis's aunt only found out a month later. By then, Tarzan had already gone back to Saudi Arabia, promising to send for Shamis as soon as he had the necessary funds and a visa for her.

"Why won't you listen to my advice? He's an engineer—a good choice." Her aunt had just returned from a business trip and was in a bad mood, urging her stubborn niece to bow to her good sense and marry her cousin.

"I'm already married. I married the man I want," said Shamis, blurting out the truth. It would be months before her aunt would even speak to her again. Decades later, Shamis seems to blush at the intensity of the memory.

"You know how you dream sometimes when you are that age? I said, 'I want to marry a man like that. A strong man. No one can mess with him. Not talkative. A simple person. But very kind.'

"So he became my dream."

6

From a Trickle to a Flood

"The country is going down into the drainage."

—MOHAMED NUR ADDE

WHEN DID IT BECOME INEVITABLE? Was there a moment when Somalia stopped merely losing its way and began accelerating toward the cliff's edge? It's easy enough to wind back the clock and find traces of a nation's path toward disintegration. But when you're in the thick of it, how do you decide it is time to give up on your own country?

Somalia's exodus began as an unobtrusive trickle. It's tempting to wonder whether a nomadic culture helped to disguise the early signs of the disaster to come—whether the old habits of traveling light and following the rains somehow masked, and only later encouraged, the great uprooting, the spasms of migration that shuddered through an imploding country.

Or maybe the truth is simpler—that only the wealthy and the intrepid run before the alarm bells become deafening, before there is no other choice left.

In a way, you could argue that Tarzan and Shamis were among the first to abandon Mogadishu. A year after he left, he secured all the necessary permits for her to join him in Saudi Arabia, and they settled down to what sounds like a rather dull life. They rented an apartment in the city of Taif, on a high and relatively cool plateau east of Mecca. Tarzan's Arabic was distinctly ropey, and his English was rough, but he managed to bluff his way into an interpreter's job at the outpatient wing of a local military hospital, and then switched to the physiotherapy department, working as a recreation officer and arranging wheelchair sports for injured soldiers. Sports and organizing. The job seemed to suit him. Soon the first of six children was born. Ahmed was quickly followed by Mohamed, then Muna, Ayan, Mimi, and Abdullahi. Three boys and three girls in the space of nine years.

"Yes, she was very fertile. And I was very fertile," Tarzan chuckles.

But if the impulse to leave Somalia had been, at least in part, political, the decision to stay abroad was entirely about money. For the first time in his life, Tarzan was earning a good salary. He was becoming the self-made man he'd always imagined being. He built two houses for his relatives back in Mogadishu. While he was still working at the hospital, he became the Saudi agent for a British company that built hand-control car units for disabled drivers.

Shamis, on the other hand, found Saudi Arabia's conservative traditions restrictive and boring. It was a grim contrast with her carefree life in Mogadishu. "I like to be free, not stuck inside!" She began wearing a headscarf—out of necessity, although later, in London and Mogadishu, it would become the norm. She was unable to leave the apartment without her husband, and she had few friends. "You don't mix. You say 'hi' to the neighbors and that is all."

Still, they were making a family, she'd finally patched things up with her aunt, and on balance life was good.

But in Mogadishu, President Siad Barre's dictatorship was becoming more intolerant and unstable. For those who cared to listen, the sounds of impending trouble were obvious.

Poets and activists were being locked up. Nuruddin Farah was already in exile. His first novels—scathing about some aspects of Somali society—had riled the president, and while Nuruddin was traveling abroad he learned that he would be arrested and perhaps sentenced to death on his return to Somalia.

Shamis's friend Samiya left early in 1982. Her stepfather, disillusioned by the wasteful, foolish, unsuccessful Ogaden war, told her a bigger storm was coming. "He told me, 'Get out of here. Save yourself, the country is going down into the drainage.'" Samiya had already fallen for a British aid worker and soon followed him back to London.

Gabyow, Tarzan's friend from the orphanage basketball team, joined the civil service in Mogadishu, then left to study accountancy. In 1980 he got a scholarship to continue his studies in Britain, and when he returned to Somalia two years later he discovered the place had changed. It was as if people were slowly giving up.

"When I go back, I find people don't want to be accounted! Ha! They all want creative accountants! They say, 'Take your car, take your wages, go back to your house,' and let us continue to steal." He went back to Britain for good, returning to Somalia only once, for the briefest of visits.

So what was going wrong?

LATE MOST AFTERNOONS, AN earnest young man called Ali Jimale Ahmed used to walk across the well-swept courtyard at Villa Somalia toward a large tree that spread its cool shade like a giant carpet outside the president's office. For an hour or two, he would sit in the shade surrounded by a group of perhaps nine men from the president's personal security detail and would teach them a "smattering" of English—enough, he'd been instructed, for them to get by when they accompanied Siad Barre abroad.

Ali Jimale had studied at the nearby 15th May Secondary School with Tarzan and Yusuf. He and Yusuf had been friends since childhood—two bright, academic, serious boys. He used to tease the devout Yusuf about his wild older brother, saying that he'd have to account for Tarzan's sins, one day. But Ali could see how the orphanage had shaped Tarzan—he was "feisty, I don't think he had anyone to turn to for help. He had to fend for himself. His physical prowess helped. You couldn't sort of mess with him, but as I remember he was not a bully. He was not. He was always interested in politics."

Ali was part of a small group of scholars preparing an official biography of President Barre. They worked at a government office across town, but as the leader of the group, Ali would often come over to Villa Somalia to talk to the president.

Siad Barre was an austere, often gloomy, complex man, who had only recently moved his offices from the military barracks near the orphanage to the hilltop Villa Somalia. The giraffes that had roamed the compound in the years after independence were long gone. Barre proceeded to throw out most of the more lavish furniture that had survived, preferring to sit under the tree, where Ali would sometimes join him, scribbling furiously to catch his words.

"You see the difference between the Argentinians and the Somalis?"

It was the summer of 1982, and Britain's naval task force had just regained control over the Falkland Islands after a ten-week war. Argentina's President Galtieri—like Siad Barre, a general who'd come to power at the head of a military junta—had been forced to resign following mass street protests.

"Somalis are noble, honorable," said President Barre, thinking about his own treatment after the disaster of the Ogaden war. "When we were defeated, they did not ask for my head."

Ali sat quietly, his pen paused on his notepad, thinking—but not saying—that no Somali would, or could, dare to demand Barre's resignation. This was not Argentina.

In fact, there had been an attempted coup in Mogadishu after the Ogaden fiasco, and if you're looking to pluck out the threads of history that lead toward Somalia's unraveling, the failed 1978 uprising by a group of army officers is worth holding on to as an early sign of trouble. Specifically, of clan trouble.

Successive Somali governments had tried, since independence, to shake off the influence of clans, to deny them any public role or space. It was a modernizing project for a new nation, a form of social engineering that no one, surely, could argue against. In the 1960s civil servants were told they could no longer mention their clans when introducing themselves. They were all Somalis now. Nothing less.

Rwanda's authoritarian government tried something similar in the aftermath of the 1994 genocide, insisting that there was no such thing as "Hutus" and "Tutsis"; that experiment has yet to run its course.

In Somalia, plenty of people embraced their new, post-clan identity. But others started referring to their "ex-clans" and using other euphemisms that made a game out of the whole process, and inadvertently strengthened the sense of clan as something secretive, something forced underground, a truth that would not die.

Siad Barre took the anti-clan purges even further, burning effigies and insisting that Scientific Socialism had no place for old hierarchies. But what seemed at first like a revolutionizing instinct soon changed into something more destructive. What the president came to mean was that there should be no rival system that could threaten his own grip on power.

Sitting under the tree in Villa Somalia late one afternoon, as the sun dipped toward the inland horizon, Ali could not help but notice the uncomfortable reality in front of him. The president's guards sat in their green uniforms, some clutching their red berets and repeating a few basic English phrases. All nine men were, Ali knew beyond doubt, members of Siad Barre's sub-clan, the Marehan. Many were even close relatives, nephews and so on.

It was the clearest proof that, for all the president's public speeches against clannism, only blood counted when it came to his security. Besides, as opposition to his dictatorship grew, it became increasingly convenient to dismiss his critics as mere clannists. Which is what happened with the military coup plotters of 1978. Tarzan's brother Yusuf—still in the army—knew some of them well and was convinced their motives were patriotic, but the president chose to frame it differently.

Over the next few years, Ali was summoned to Villa Somalia

more often, and not just for the presidential biography or to teach English. Siad Barre's intelligence services had been checking up on him and found that he knew how to keep his mouth shut.

"I have nothing on you," the president told Ali one evening in a manner that seemed to suggest both flattery and threat. He had started calling his young visitor *"compagno,"* the Italian word for "companion," and would often let off steam, furiously denouncing his ministers for an hour or more.

"Thank you. You can go now," he would tell Ali at the end of an evening. It was kind of crazy, Ali remembers. "I was kind of his therapist."

THE CLAN DIVISIONS WOULD not heal. As opposition parties began to form and face persecution, they would retreat into the corners of the country and, by default if not design, into their clans' safety nets. And as President Barre lashed out more aggressively, so the clans became more relevant and more powerful.

Still, Somalia's collapse did not yet feel inevitable, or at least not imminent. Tarzan's old university was churning out graduates. Foreigners were still pleasantly surprised to find the streets far gentler and safer than Nairobi's. There was even a grass-less golf course. There weren't many tourists around—visas had always been a problem—but Princess Ann managed a visit; and Somali Airlines served goat stew, rice, banana, and a "quite decent claret," according to Jeremy Varcoe, British ambassador at the time. Some weekends the ambassador would drive south along the coast beyond Merca, past the newly nationalized banana plantations, to a villa shared by several Western embassies.

"The Italian ambassador—very charming—was still the most powerful diplomat. One Christmas we ate spaghetti and drank a very fine champagne. My wife had given me a pair of Union Jack swimming trunks, rather mischievously, and I wore them on the beach. The other ambassadors were deeply shocked that I would wear a national flag in such a way—that it was disrespectful."

In Mogadishu, the clubs and restaurants were still thriving along Lido beach. But a slaughterhouse had opened north of the city, and the current brought goat blood and other waste straight past the city's beaches. Shark attacks became almost commonplace, even in the shallows just offshore. The German ambassador's daughter lost an arm. Soon, almost no one swam at Lido anymore.

Mogadishu's Italian community was still more or less intact. Lino, the boy scout who witnessed the 1969 coup, had since gone into business with his brother. They would drive around Somalia overseeing engineering projects, particularly the construction of new roads—mostly paid for by foreign aid.

In 1986 Siad Barre was badly injured in a car crash and became even more aggressive and suspicious toward his critics. Summary executions became commonplace. The army leadership was packed with members of the president's clan.

Then, in 1988, Siad Barre lashed out with a brutality that seemed to hurl Somalia toward the cliff, ordering warplanes to bomb the northern opposition stronghold of Hargeisa. The city was almost completely destroyed, and some half a million people fled across the border into Ethiopia. After that, it became hard to imagine a way back from civil war.

Lino stopped driving far outside Mogadishu and hired an armed guard to travel in his car. And then, on a Sunday in July 1989, he heard that the Italian bishop of Mogadishu had just been shot dead by an unknown gunman inside the city's cathedral.

Bishop Salvatore Colombo had lived in Somalia for more than forty years. His death prompted a frenzy of finger-pointing that seemed to highlight all the forces now pulling the country apart. Was he killed by Islamists who claimed he'd been trying to convert Somalis to Catholicism? Was the president simply getting rid of another vocal critic? Had the bishop somehow made an enemy of the wrong clan? Or was the opposition trying to stir up more trouble?

Lino didn't know and didn't care.

"He was my teacher, my religious guide. From that moment I understood there was no chance for Somalia," he says, and as he pauses to consider that, he remembers another moment, a few months later, after his wife and children had moved to Kenya. He was at dinner with a wealthy Somali businessman and found himself sitting next to one of the president's nephews, an army colonel.

"We are a royal family," said the colonel. He meant his Marehan clan. "We're like the royals in Saudi Arabia. And if we lose this fight, all of Somalia will be destroyed."

The Italian embassy tried to reassure those of its citizens who hadn't already made plans to leave. There was "no emergency."

⁂

THROUGHOUT THE 1980s, ALI Madobe had risen fast through the ranks of Somalia's intelligence services. It would be easy to believe that was entirely on merit. He's an imposing character with a sharp mind. But as he himself admits, the fact that he belongs to the same "sub-sub-clan" as the president can only have helped his career.

Since the split with the Soviet Union over the Ogaden war, Madobe had been to the United States, Italy, Britain, and Egypt for training. He became a full colonel and eventually the head of Somali counterintelligence. From within the system, he could see more clearly than most the extent to which the president's Supreme Revolutionary Council was losing power.

At the end of 1989 he tendered his resignation to President Barre, who rejected it with the same indignation that he showed toward the many attempts to mediate an end to Somalia's deepening political crisis. Six months later, Madobe finally persuaded the president to let him travel to the United States to complete a master's degree. The Americans refused to let him bring his family, so Madobe, increasingly convinced that trouble was coming, sent them to Dubai. But toward the end of 1990, without Madobe's knowledge, his uncle persuaded his wife and three children to return to Mogadishu.

When he found out, Madobe rushed back from Colorado, arriving home in mid-November 1990. Just in time.

Fifteen days later, he says, "the civil war erupted."

Madobe could see the situation was desperate. He was still an officer in the intelligence services and was immediately summoned to the National Intelligence headquarters in the center of the city. Opposition groups and clan militias now controlled much of the country and had come up with a mocking new title for the president. He was, they insisted, nothing more than the "mayor of Mogadishu."

Since the murder of the Catholic bishop, the number of killings had risen sharply and, in a chilling glimpse of what was to come, the city was starting to reorganize itself along clan and sub-clan lines, like a pack of cards being un-shuffled, as families moved into relatives' homes in areas they considered safer. In a land where grudges had always held a special value, they were accumulating with dangerous speed. Red berets began appearing on the streets beside the bodies of the dead—an attempt by the government's enemies, Madobe was convinced, to make it seem like the president's personal guards were to blame.

He still felt an intense, complicated loyalty to Siad Barre. Not, perhaps, purely because of the clan system—Madobe still considered himself an orphanage boy at heart—but because he respected the president's character and achievements.

I can hear the admiration in his voice as he talks about him now. His modest, austere lifestyle. Even his ruthlessness.

"I believe he was a kind and good man. He put his personal interests behind those of the country and people. A lot of people say, 'Oh, that dictator created a lot of problems, blah, blah, blah . . .' But he changed this town. He built it. He was very wrong to concentrate all the development in Mogadishu, and leave out the rest of the country. But if I consider the whole history of the world, starting from Napoleon, Mussolini, Hitler . . . these people create history. So Siad Barre created the history of Somalia, or a part of Somalia."

Was he really a Napoleon? Hardly. His ambitions were local and, ultimately, selfish. He destroyed his country by obstinately refusing to negotiate. Perhaps Syria's President Assad would be a better comparison.

Over the next few days Madobe watched the police, the military, and even his own intelligence services begin to disintegrate along clan lines. Moving around town became difficult, especially at night. He decided to stay at home. His house was in Medina, on the southern edge of the city, just up the slope behind the airport and near the American embassy and two big hospitals. It was becoming a stronghold of the Darod tree, from which the Marehan branched. Injured relatives began arriving at his house.

On Sunday, December 3, the sound of gunfire clattered across the city. Opposition forces—mostly drawn from the Hawiye tree, including some who had gathered, with Ethiopian backing, near Tarzan's family pastureland—had begun to fight their way into Mogadishu. The city's cosmopolitan days were coming to an end.

Madobe called his uncle Loyan, who was still living on the far side of the city. He'd been in charge of Somalia's immigration service, but more recently—and presumably for reasons of clan—he'd also become a member of the intelligence services. Madobe begged him to come across to Medina. It would be safer. Loyan insisted that the two men, now the senior figures in their family, should remain apart.

"It should be only me. Or only you," Loyan said, meaning that if one of them were to be killed, the other could take responsibility for the family.

On the night of January 25, 1991, President Siad Barre's family was taken in an armed convoy up to Villa Somalia. The show was nearly over. Twenty-four hours later the president and his entourage would drive out of Mogadishu, never to return. But for now, the first family needed a loyal escort, and Loyan volunteered to accompany them through the streets of Mogadishu.

An armored car led the convoy. Loyan came next in his Nissan, followed by the president's family. Halfway along the still-elegant, tree-lined Somalia Avenue, near the Juba Hotel and the main post office, the Nissan stalled. Loyan jumped out, abandoning his car, and leapt onto the running board of the vehicle behind. The convoy raced off again, but with a gun in one hand, Loyan struggled to keep his footing. By now the convoy had nearly reached the foot of the hill below Villa Somalia.

Madobe has struggled to piece together exactly what happened next, but it seems ambushers were hiding in trees on either side of the road and opened fire on the convoy. One bullet hit the driver of the vehicle carrying the president's family and a swaying Loyan. For a few seconds the driver lost control and, as the car swerved violently, Loyan was hurled onto the road.

The convoy raced on, up the hill toward Villa Somalia. Loyan's body was found the next day. The country was now in free fall.

7

Leave to Remain

"Whatever you can do to save your family, you do it."

—SHAMIS ELMI

THE DOUR WHITE MAN AT the immigration desk was not convinced.

"I can tell you understand me. I think you speak better English than you're letting on," he said.

Shamis stood at the counter in front of him, feeling far less intimidated than she'd expected. Her youngest child, eleven-month-old Abdullahi, was in a stroller beside her. The other five children stood to one side, watched over, in a halfhearted sort of way, by Shamis's seventeen-year-old half-sister Sahra.

"I don't speak English," Shamis repeated to the man, in English. What she really meant is that she couldn't understand his accent or his questions. "I'm a refugee," she said, and again listed the names of everyone in the group.

It was an unusually cold Thursday afternoon at London's Heathrow airport. December 4, 1990. Margaret Thatcher had stepped down as prime minister a fortnight earlier. Britain's economy was sinking into another recession, and a thick blanket of snow was about to cover the country.

When Shamis remembers that day, she veers between two extremes.

Sometimes she talks about "the hardest" time of her life, the exhaustion, the stress, and the desperation to save her family from the horrors unfolding in Somalia. At other times it feels like she's describing an adventure—hectic, unpredictable, but hardly worth

Tarzan with children, London, 1993. COURTESY OF SHAMIS NUR

complaining about. And it's that second impulse that strikes me as a better clue to Shamis's real character, and perhaps to her relationship with Tarzan. They are matter-of-fact people, and neither of them seems inclined toward regret.

Tarzan had waved the family off a few hours earlier at the international departures hall in Sofia, Bulgaria.

"Goodbye. I love you," Shamis remembers him saying. "You know, the normal thing that a husband says to his wife and kids."

They'd flown to Sofia from Damascus. At the time, Somalis could travel to Syria without visas. In the crowded markets of Damascus's old town, Tarzan was put in touch with "people who can arrange to get others into Europe." People smugglers. But he decided the risks were too great, and besides, he'd learned of another option. "Stickers—forged visas. They were easy to get hold of."

"Sweden or England?" The word from other Somalis was that those countries were the best bets for asylum. The choice came down to the language, and Tarzan chose English. The fake visas weren't supposed to fool immigration officials in the U.K. But he was assured they'd be good enough to get the family on the plane in Damascus, through an overnight transit stop in Sofia, and then a couple of hours in Brussels.

It's striking how quickly and resolutely Tarzan seems to have made the decision. There were other options available. London was a gamble, and one that would affect them all for decades to come. But I can imagine him snapping his fingers, as he often does when he's explaining things.

And again I can't help reaching back to Somalia's nomadic culture for an explanation. Home is where you need to be, not where you were born.

A year earlier, he'd decided the family had no future in Saudi Arabia. The work was still good, but they were treated as foreigners there and always would be. Arranging schooling was becoming a struggle, and Shamis was increasingly frustrated. Besides, the country had always been a temporary home in Tarzan's mind. The map above his bed in the orphanage was of America, not the Middle East.

So in 1988, Tarzan uprooted the family and moved them back to Mogadishu. He had plans to use his Saudi contacts to help set up an import business, bringing construction materials across to Somalia. Shamis was already doing some wholesale business of her own, shipping clothes back from the Gulf. They both knew that the political situation was unsteady and worrying, but it wasn't until the plane touched down at the familiar beachside airport, and they drove up and over the hill to their new house, that they realized quite how far things had deteriorated.

All their friends were talking about the curfew, about the night-time killings of prominent people. Suddenly, war seemed almost inevitable. Shamis was worried her aunt might be a target. For the first time in her life she felt the weight of her Hawiye ancestry and her own prominent lineage pressing down on her, marking her out in the wrong sort of way.

Tarzan seems reluctant to talk about their brief return to Mogadishu.

"There's nothing I can tell," he says, curtly. Later he adds, in the voice of someone tired of explaining the depressingly obvious, "It's always the clans. It always splits along clan lines. And that way, the conflict always spreads."

And so they left Mogadishu, returned to Saudi Arabia, and began making plans to fly to Damascus. Shamis asked her father if she could take her half-sister with her to help with the young children, and he agreed.

At the immigration desk at Heathrow, the man asked for their passports. Shamis shrugged and shook her head. Someone in Damascus had told her it was better to arrive with no documents, and so she'd gotten rid of them on the last flight from Brussels. To compound the growing sense of dislocation, their luggage had disappeared en route, never to be found.

For a week, the entire family shuttled back and forth between

Heathrow and what seemed like a very luxurious airport hotel. Shamis was embarrassed to discover that British Airways was footing the bill as a form of punishment for allowing them on the plane in the first place. After that, they were moved to a place called the Thorncliffe Hotel, with other asylum seekers, in a nearby suburb called Hayes. The children watched a new television series called *Mr. Bean*.

By 1990, plenty of families had already arrived in London from Somaliland—the northern region that government airplanes had bombed so viciously two years earlier. Now, with Somalia collapsing into anarchy, the numbers were rising fast.

Before long, bloated corpses littered Mogadishu's streets, a frenzy of looting erupted, and tens of thousands of civilians—above all, the Darod, who bore the brunt of the invading militias' fury—began to flee. It became known as "clan cleansing," as legitimate opposition to President Siad Barre curdled into a battle for supremacy between the Hawiye and Darod. Some of the displaced fled on foot, and some clambered onto trucks, heading first inland to the market town of Afgoye and then on to their clan strongholds and beyond to neighboring Kenya and Ethiopia.

⚜

In London, Shamis came to feel she was being punished, or at least marked out, for being a member of the Hawiye, whose militias were leading the attacks in Mogadishu.

"People who came after me, or before me, got refugee status. But not us. At that time my clan is the one who was fighting with the government. But I don't care. My clan, they are not me. Whatever you can do to save your family—you do it."

It seemed odd to me, at first, that Tarzan did not accompany Shamis to the U.K.—that he would let his young family struggle through the lengthy asylum process in an unfamiliar country without him. Money was one obvious factor. He could return to Saudi Arabia and keep working, for a year or two, while his family tested the waters in the U.K. Then there was Shamis herself—a resourceful, confident woman who could certainly cope with any challenges ahead.

But it's my sense that Tarzan was wrestling with other issues. The years in Saudi Arabia faded into the background. He was now profoundly reluctant to let go of Somalia, to acknowledge that his country had gone past the point of no return, and, perhaps most of all as a proudly self-made man, to submit to what he felt was the indignity of becoming a refugee.

After a couple of months at the Thorncliffe, the family was moved to a council house near Victoria Park, in Hackney, east London, while their asylum application was processed. The older children were enrolled into two local schools, and Shamis—who had grown up with cooks and housekeepers and taxi rides to school—found herself plunging into an unfamiliar, exhausting routine. She'd rise at six, drop the four older children off at their schools, take the younger two with her to a local college where she took English language classes, come home at noon to clean the house and cook, head out to collect the kids from school at 3:30, feed them all, supervise homework, bath time, bedtime for all six children, then ironing, and finally bed for herself.

Her half-sister Sahra was not much help. She was a teenager and quickly found her own life in London, going to college and returning home after the children were asleep.

"How can I be depressed? I don't have the time," Shamis told herself, clinging on to some of that old Mogadishu panache.

She wondered what British people made of her—a dark, skinny, attractive, young-looking woman in Western clothes, her frizzy hair sometimes uncovered, walking through Hackney with Abdullahi in the pushchair, Mimi balancing on the back of it, and Ahmed, Mohamed, Muna, and Ayan all following behind.

"Are those really all your kids?" people would ask, usually more curious than hostile. Even admiring. She looked too young to have so many.

A few weeks after they'd settled into their house in Hackney,

Shamis managed to track down the telephone number of an old friend. Samiya had finally settled in London, marrying a "humble" man who worked on the London Underground.

When Samiya rang the bell, she assumed a weary, worn-down woman would open the door. That's how she felt, and she had only three young children to handle.

"Look at you! You've lost weight, you're even slimmer, and prettier," said Samiya admiringly, as they embraced. "I was expecting a lady with no teeth!" She was referring to Tarzan, still half-convinced the Mogadishu street fighter would prove to be the sort to beat his wife.

"No! I beat him!" Shamis answered with a grin. She explained that Tarzan was still in Saudi Arabia, that he'd gone back to Mogadishu after leaving the family in Sofia, but it was just impossible in Somalia. And now look what was happening to the place. They both shook their heads despairingly and exchanged news about other Mogadishu families who were still trying to flee.

"Fauzia Nur lost seven children. She came by ship from Mogadishu. All the people died. Only she survived."

The news seemed unremittingly grim. And their friends were, by and large, the ones with money, not the masses herded into camps or forced to walk through the wilderness. They'd heard recently of a ship packed with refugees that had been barred from docking at a port in Yemen. The word was that 150 people had died of thirst.

Ali Madobe was safe. He'd finally managed to drive out of Mogadishu with his family, heading to the southern port of Kismayo. But the journey was treacherous, and there was fighting in Somalia's second city, too. They headed inland and eventually managed to cross into Kenya and then, with some sleight of hand, to Dubai. Madobe's brother already had permanent residence there and pretended that Madobe's heavily pregnant wife and children were his own. You do what you need to do. From there, through other Somali friends, they made their way to Tehran, Czechoslovakia, and finally to Holland.

Abukar Dahir, the young banker who would later be caught up in the 2014 attack on Villa Somalia's mosque, was only two years old at the time. His mother, Sadia, a deputy assistant minister of health in the old government, was on a work trip to India—a surreal indication of business-as-usual even in the midst of impending civil war—when her family decided to escape from Mogadishu. They drove south, like Madobe, to Kismayo, and Sadia rushed back, just as the first Gulf War was beginning. She chartered a plane from Nairobi to try to rescue them, but there was too much gunfire at Kismayo's airstrip for the plane to land. Instead the family drove on to the Kenyan border where huge crowds were gathering, desperate to escape the violence. There were stories of starvation and of lions attacking the stragglers.

Eventually, refugee camps were established across the border on a rocky, thorn-infested plain inside Kenya. Over the years the Dadaab camps—a chaotic assortment of homemade huts, donated tents, markets, schools, and white prefabricated cabins—grew until they'd become a seemingly permanent home to nearly four hundred thousand people. In all, perhaps one in seven Somalis, well over a million people, would flee abroad.

But those with money and contacts did not linger in Dadaab. Sadia had brought cash, in case she needed to bribe the Kenyan border guards, and a diplomatic passport. She managed to get most of her relatives to Nairobi, and then the family moved on to Damascus, Moscow, Sweden, and finally to London.

⁂

FOR THREE YEARS, SHAMIS and her children waited for a decision from the British immigration authorities. Finally, in 1993, a letter arrived by post at their home in Hackney. One year's "leave to remain" on humanitarian grounds. Hardly generous. But as grudging as the letter seemed to Shamis, in truth this was the bureaucratic equivalent of a confetti parade. The doors began to open.

One week later, the family was informed it could move from the "temporary" house in Hackney to a roomy top-floor council flat just off the busy market street of Queen's Crescent, in north London, with a glorious view over the city. It would be their home for the next two decades. One week after that, with the help of a lawyer and advice from Ahmed's schoolteacher, Shamis finally secured a visa for Tarzan. He'd been in Saudi Arabia, working and waiting. Now, with the help of a Saudi friend at the Italian embassy, he got a visa to travel to Rome, where Shamis sent his official invitation by courier.

Seven-year-old Ayan was woken by the doorbell ringing late one night in 1993. She wandered out onto the landing from her bedroom and immediately rushed back to check the photograph she kept under her pillow. Shamis had decided not to tell the children anything in case it didn't work out. But it was definitely him.

Tarzan had flown into Gatwick airport, south of London, earlier that evening. It was his second time in Britain. He'd come in 1986 for a short trip to meet the company that was exporting hand-operated car controls to his hospital in Saudi Arabia. By then his old basketball friend, Gabyow, was already living in London, and he remembers Tarzan indignantly rejecting the idea of becoming a refugee, saying, "Never in my life. It's an insult."

This time Shamis had told him to take a train to London and then the tube to Kentish Town Underground station. It was ten o'clock by the time he walked out onto a dark high street and waved down a taxi for the short ride to Gilden Crescent.

Tarzan does not find it easy to admit to weakness. Or to being wrong, for that matter. But from the various descriptions he's given me of the next few months, it's clear that he sank into a profound gloom; refugee blues. The first morning he woke late. The children had already left for school. He stood on the balcony, staring at the gray, distant panorama of London, from the spiky towers of the City, past St. Paul's Cathedral, the Post Office Tower, and all the way west over Primrose Hill toward Heathrow. "So," he thought, "this is what they call London." Then he slunk back inside and didn't leave the house for five days.

Shamis was trying to find work. She'd been attending a teacher training college and soon she'd begin volunteering at the local primary school, helping immigrant children—particularly Somalis—to fit in. But for now, money was tighter than ever, and Tarzan was proving stubborn.

For a long time, he just walked the streets, all the way down into central London and back, along Camden High Street, turning right on Malden Road, up the hill, three flights of stairs, and into the flat. This was not the life he wanted. It was not his to control anymore. He felt emasculated.

One day, an exasperated Shamis finally convinced him to walk with her across to Fortess Road to catch the 134 bus north, up to Archway and a sixteen-story tower that housed the local social security offices.

They took a numbered slip from the machine and sat waiting for Tarzan's turn to sign up for welfare payments. He looked about him. Alcoholic people, he thought. Old people. Rough people. He started shaking his head and turned to Shamis.

"We cannot stay here. Let's go back."

"We need this. I need this. Sometimes we don't have food," Shamis replied.

"I cannot queue with these people. Even if I'm dying. No way."

They left the building, and Shamis gave her husband a few days to calm down. But it was hard. They were really struggling to pay the bills. If Tarzan applied for welfare they could get another £25 a month. Eventually, they came up with a compromise. Tarzan went back alone to Archway Tower and applied, but when the checks started arriving in the post, he signed the backs of them, and Shamis took them to the post office to cash in.

A few weeks later, Tarzan was on one of his regular walks down Camden High Street when he saw a small advice center on the left-hand side of the road, and a decision he'd been wrestling with for some time finally snapped into place.

He was thirty-seven years old. There were plenty of odd jobs around. Cash in hand. Enough to get by on, and who knows, maybe it would lead to something better. Or he could stay on the dole and, as he saw it, end up like the wretches in the queue at Archway Tower. Or he could admit that an unfinished university degree from Mogadishu and all his work experience in Saudi Arabia were worth precious little in Britain, and that he needed to swallow another mouthful of pride and resume his education.

He was told he needed to complete a one-year access course before he'd be eligible for higher education, and he chose business studies at a college in Tower Hamlets, east London. There were plenty of closer, easier options, but he worried that he'd end up finding excuses not to go and would drift toward casual work. It was better if he had to leave early each morning and take the train. It would almost feel like having a proper job.

Each year, the local council gave out a handful of discretionary grants for students who wanted to study at a university. One evening, after a day at college in Tower Hamlets, Tarzan filled in the application form and took it to one of his teachers to polish up his English. He wanted, he wrote, to be "a role model" for the growing Somali community in London.

It sounded like the old Tarzan was back—pushy, ambitious, always the first with his hand in the air.

Twice, when I ask Tarzan what he did to relax in London in those early days, he mentions the television. I assume he means the news. After all, Somalia was constantly in the headlines. But Tarzan was concentrating on something else—O. J. Simpson's murder trial in California.

"I was obsessed," he admits. "I woke up every night at 2 a.m., even when I was studying. At the time I thought he was innocent—that it was about racism. But now I think he must have been guilty."

It's easy to see why a Somali might choose to forget about events in

Mogadishu at that time. The news was unimaginably, shamefully, unspeakably grim.

Any hope that rival opposition groups might reach a power-sharing deal to replace Siad Barre's dictatorship with something—anything—resembling a government quickly vanished. And in the absence of legitimate authority, the vacuum was filled by the only structure still functioning in Somalia, the one system that now seemed bound to make matters even worse. The clan.

This was the time when Mogadishu first became internationally synonymous, justifiably, with anarchy and despair. All the news clichés were true. It was now a bullet-riddled patchwork of clans, sub-clans, and sub-sub-clans whose loyalties and feuds seemed to change by the day and made sense to almost nobody.

It was no better in the countryside. In 1992 clashes between rival warlords triggered a famine in southern and central parts of Somalia. Before long, the United Nations was sending peacekeepers to Mogadishu in order to get humanitarian supplies to those who needed them most, and away from the militia groups and ragged entrepreneurs who could, and would, only see foreign aid as a source of power and profit.

And then at the end of that year, with the world's media already on the beach to film it all, American troops landed at night in Mogadishu, squinting into the camera lights, at the start of a mission to reinforce the UN and "save" Somalia.

I was not in the country to see the iconic calamities that followed—the sight of American Black Hawk helicopters being brought down by nimble clansmen with rocket-propelled grenades, the bodies of American soldiers being dragged through the streets by indignant crowds, the U.S. military's humiliating withdrawal from Somalia, and the UN's startling decision to abandon the country, too.

It was only in 2001 that I made my first trip to Mogadishu. But it was like visiting a crime scene, years later, and finding the evidence undisturbed. The rusting hulk of a U.S. helicopter still lying where it crashed. The archeology of Somalia's implosion eerily intact.

I thought I knew something of war. I'd spent all of the 1990s living in the former Soviet Union and had covered many of the conflicts prompted by its collapse, including Russia's two astonishingly brutal campaigns in the breakaway republic of Chechnya. The ferocity of the fighting there and the sheer firepower available were staggering. Helicopter gunships, fields of artillery, vast tank columns, and fighter jets. Villages, towns, and indeed the entire city of Grozny were flattened like Stalingrad. But that was war at full speed: short, intense battles with astonishingly heavy casualties and specific goals.

Mogadishu was something entirely different.

EIGHT SCRAWNY YOUNG MEN in flip-flops, T-shirts, and combat trousers were waiting for me at a rutted dirt airstrip 50 kilometers outside the city. A hot wind tore across a flat, hazy landscape. This was where the daily khat flights rushed in from Kenya, with their consignments of precious fresh green leaves for the fighters to chew each afternoon. We'd flown in from Nairobi, a few hours after the morning khat scramble, on a tiny charter plane. There were no formalities, no immigration control, just a crowd of cars and armed men.

It's jarring to think that twenty-seven years earlier, Shamis and Samiya had driven past the same spot as their truck took them from a bustling, ambitious city into the countryside to begin teaching Somalia's new alphabet.

Our guards, each clutching a battered AK-47, were responsible for security at a hotel in town, just off the K4 roundabout. The hotel manager, a relaxed young Somali called Ajoos, had driven out in a second pickup with heavily tinted windows. We squeezed into the rear seat, and three members of the security team clambered onto the back, while the rest followed behind in what I can only describe as a sawn-off truck—its roof, windows, anything higher than the steering wheel, all sliced back to the bone.

Between the airstrip and the city, we passed through perhaps half a dozen makeshift roadblocks. Sometimes just a piece of rope dragged across the road, sometimes a metal pole or chunks of concrete. And always more of the same wiry, wary gunmen in flip-flops, peering at our tinted windows.

It was, Ajoos explained, partly a question of math. Eight guards would probably be enough to guarantee a shit storm all around if anyone decided to make trouble. So we'd mostly likely be left alone. But it was also about clans. The checkpoints belonged to a variety of different groups. Murusade, Habr Gedir, Abgal. And Ajoos had carefully selected his guards, as if from a pack of cards, from a range of sub-clans—partly so they wouldn't conspire together and sell us off to the highest bidder and partly so that someone would, hopefully, be able to spot someone they recognized at each checkpoint; maybe even a relative who could wave us through.

On the outskirts of Mogadishu, sweating heavily into my flak jacket now, I saw the first civilians, and it seemed to me that they scuttled, backs to the wall, between doorways. Then again, adrenaline can give even the most ordinary scene a veneer of danger.

Approaching the K4 roundabout, our driver leaned on the horn and pushed the car forward through a herd of goats. Speed clearly meant safety, and as our pickup slowed almost to a halt, the guards in the car behind leapt off and fanned out on the road around us, guns raised, scowling faces hunting for trouble.

The city looked as though it had been bleached. From the dirt road to the buildings, the ruins, the people, and even the air, everything seemed to be variations of the same sand-gray color. Then, as we accelerated toward the hotel's huge metal gates, an impossible burst of scarlet leapt out like an ambush. A giant bougainvillea plant. The city's trees had almost all vanished, chopped down for firewood, but somehow the bougainvillea—planted in more hopeful times—had clung on around the city, providing the occasional, delirious splash of pink, red, purple, or orange blossoms.

An hour later, we left the high walls of the Shamo hotel. Our guards were driving ahead of us now—gun barrels jutting out of the car like a giant porcupine—as we headed down Medina Road, toward the seafront, and past the tip of the airport runway, unused now except toward sunset when a few hundred boys would emerge from the tents and ruins nearby to play football on it.

As the road flattened out near the dunes, it swung to the left, past the old army headquarters where President Siad Barre had once slept during the first years of his dictatorship. If I had known to look at the building opposite, I'd have seen the walls of Tarzan's old orphanage as we swung into Via Londra. Soon afterward we passed the abandoned British embassy, and then, on the right-hand side, the San Martino Hospital where Tarzan claimed to have been born. We were now speeding along the same road he had sprinted down when he thought Yusuf had drowned.

A few hundred yards later, with a bright flash of light, the sea leapt into view on our right, and our little convoy came to a sudden halt.

The scene around us was mesmerizing.

Waves crashed on the dark rocks. Offshore, like a shark's mouth, the tip of a shipwreck seemed to leap from the ocean, gleaming in the afternoon sun. Behind us, a distant rattle of automatic gunfire skipped across the ruins.

It felt like a war zone, for sure. I caught a glimpse of a "technical"—one of the improvised fighting vehicles and warlord status symbols, with a giant machine gun mounted on a tripod—rolling quietly down a side street. But there was something else, something I'd never encountered in Chechnya, something strangely still and unnerving.

I could see it in the seams of ancient garbage that coated the dirt roads and even the rocks along the shoreline, like geological formations, cracking to reveal layers of compressed, grimy sediment. I could see it in the bullet holes that didn't just crowd around a few windows to target a sniper but seemed to decorate every inch of every surface that still stood upright. And I could see it in the ruins, always so fresh and livid in Chechnya, but here transformed, as if by some mad architect, into dusty warrens, festooned with plastic sheeting and scraps of corrugated iron, and repopulated by families—a thousand wary eyes peering out at us—who'd gambled on the hope that an apocalyptic city could be safer than the countryside. And I could see it in what was missing—in the apparent absence of anything of value—every window frame, every street lamp, every wire, every tree, every hint of modernity stripped down, hacked apart, and carted off.

Battlefields are the most terrible places. But the horrors are usually temporary. Mogadishu had mutated into something far more disorientating and rare—a permanent battlefield, staffed by a cast of brutalized thousands who had come to see war not as a temporary aberration to be endured but as a way of life.

There were, for sure, some parts of the city that seemed less damaged, where shops and even universities were operating, and where the electricity poles groaned under the weight of a thousand cables that spoke to the ingenuity and entrepreneurship of Somalis who could thrive in any situation. But not this neighborhood.

We got out of Ajoos's car and I walked toward the old lighthouse at the corner, where the road turns sharply inland toward the city center. A cannibalized gray minibus crawled past us with nothing covering its engine, a set of cow horns tied to the front, and the windshield of a far smaller car ingeniously welded in place in front of the driver.

"Stop!" It was the first time I'd heard Ajoos sounding nervous, and I swung around sharply. A barrier lay across the road just in front of me.

I hadn't noticed the barrier because it was invisible. A metaphorical line in the sand. But Ajoos, and everyone else in the city, could see it. It was as clear as the afternoon rain shower now drifting in from the ocean, or the holes punched into the walls of the lighthouse, or the giant gray ruins of the old Al-Uruba hotel beyond.

We had reached the border of one clan's territory and the start of another's.

⁂

BACK IN LONDON, IN 1995, Tarzan slammed the telephone down in a fury.

In addition to resuming his education—he was now studying business at the University of Westminster—he'd begun trying to get funding for a small community organization he'd set up for Somali kids in the neighborhood around Queen's Crescent.

The local authorities were ready to help, but only if Tarzan's group could merge with three other tiny Somali organizations that also wanted funding. A local church had already offered him space, but he'd rejected that with something close to alarm.

"At the time we were afraid of everything! To go inside a church? We thought you'd change your religion straightaway if you did that!"

So Tarzan had rung up one of the other Somali groups, and an old man had immediately asked him, "Which clan are you?"

"I'm Somali," Tarzan replied indignantly.

"There is no Somali here. I'm Marehan. Are you Hawiye?"

"You destroyed our country, and still you are proud to call your-self that? Still, even here, you are dividing people by clan?" Tarzan was shouting now.

It was inevitable, of course, that some of the battles, the grievances, and the rivalries festering in Somalia would survive the journey to London and elsewhere. How could they not? Throughout the 1990s thousands of Somalis were arriving in Britain each year, and, at the very least, it was logical that they would try to move into neighbor-hoods where they knew they'd find relatives.

The phenomenon is almost certainly exaggerated, but for some, a map of London, even today, is divided into clan territories. The Isaq in the east of the city—Mile End, White Chapel, Stamford Hill, Green-wich, Woolwich, Stratford. Head north to Kentish Town, King's Cross, and that's the Majerteyn. And so on. The theory extends beyond the capital, to cities like Birmingham where the Darod are considered strong. And it has deeper roots in history, from the first Somali seamen who came to ports like Cardiff and Liverpool in the late nineteenth century.

Something similar was happening in America, where more than a hundred thousand Somalis would be granted refugee status and were soon building substantial communities in cities like Minneapolis, St. Paul, Seattle, and San Diego.

⚜

THE 105 BUS ZIGZAGS through the edge of west London, from just beyond Wembley stadium all the way to Heathrow airport. Late one evening a group of young Somali men watched Adam Mattan climb up to the top deck and walk past them.

"Oi! You. You're not from this postcode."

"Certainly I'm not. I'm just taking the bus. I'm leaving your postcode," Adam half-stammered. He was a tall, thoughtful student with an unruly and—for a Somali—unusually long mop of black hair.

"OK, cool. Not a problem. Which clan you belong to then?"

Adam's mind was racing. He could recognize some clans from their accents, but he couldn't be entirely sure. All he knew was that they seemed well educated, and probably went to college like him. He was scared. If he said the wrong clan, or sub-clan, he was reasonably sure he'd get beaten up or perhaps even stabbed.

"I don't know my clan."

"You bastard! You're talking crap."

"Sure. If that makes me a bastard, then that's fine. But I don't know my clan."

Adam grins, his long arms flapping, as he acts out the incident, years later. We're sitting in the office of the organization he now runs, just behind the railway line and the covered market in Shepherds Bush, west London. The organization is called the Anti-Tribalism Movement.

"So what clan are you from?" I ask, a little provocatively. Adam giggles politely and declines to answer. No, he really won't tell me. There's a principle at stake, one that is shored up almost every day, whenever his telephone rings and a member of his clan asks for money to settle some dispute or other back in Somaliland.

"It happens to me every day. EVERY SINGLE DAY. They say, 'Our sub-clan and XYZ clan are fighting over grassland near our village.'

"And I say, 'Is there any way it can be resolved without firing a bullet?'

"And they say, 'What?! How can you ask that? How can we split it?'

"So I say, 'I will not be a murderer with my money,' because if I send a hundred quid, that money pays for an AK-47 and someone is killed. 'Screw all of you!'"

Adam is a natural actor, and I can feel his indignation growing, his hands waving in fury. He talks of a recent clan battle over land that he says led to about three hundred deaths in the northern region of Somaliland—the vehicles, the food for the fighters, the petrol, the ammunition, all paid for by families living in the U.K. And some of them were on benefits here, Adam says with contempt.

"Do anything you want with your own freakin' money. But not the money we all work for and that has been given to you to feed your child!"

And then, of course, the dead overseas must be avenged or paid for with "blood money." We're back to the logic and habits of nomadic life—where, in the absence of any other judicial system, the clan elders would settle disputes. But now the blood money is being gathered in foreign sitting rooms and transferred around the globe by remittance companies. And the value of one life depends on many factors—the status and power of his sub-clan, the size of his family, and the nature of his career.

"Our blood is more expensive than theirs," Adam says in a light, supercilious tone. He's acting again, explaining how four men from a small, "marginalized" clan might be killed to avenge the death of one man from a bigger clan, and how blood debts can be put on hold, banked, sometimes for years, until an appropriately respected figure comes of age to be murdered.

"I remember like daylight—like it was yesterday—someone famous from my clan was killed by another clan." But rather than targeting the murderer, Adam's clan waited for more than fifteen years and then killed "one of the best of the best" from the other clan in a town in Somaliland.

"I couldn't believe what was going on here in London. Boys my age were celebrating," says Adam, slowly shaking his head.

THE CLANS COULDN'T BE ignored. But it turned out that with a little patience and maneuvering, they could be brought together. Up the hill in Queen's Crescent, Tarzan was making progress as a community activist, and in Camden, rival groups finally united to build the Somali Youth Development Resource Centre.

Some people bristled—as they still do—at Tarzan's style. He was a forceful, blunt character, maybe a little intimidating at times. And he was a charismatic public speaker. "He wanted it all for himself. He had puppets everywhere," one colleague grumbled to me recently.

But Tarzan was not the type to be held back by criticism. He began working for the local council as a refugee employment and education advisor and soon set up his own organization—the Somali Speakers Association—offering support and guidance to new arrivals across the borough of Islington.

"A lot of people were carrying all that trauma from the war. It was just really hard coming here. Too many Somali men were just sitting around chewing khat," says Sarah Lee, who hired and worked with Tarzan as he tried not just to find jobs for Somalis but to convince them it was a good idea to work in the first place.

"He was a good guy. Funny. You could tell he was a leader, and the community loved him."

"How could you know that?" I ask.

"Mainly because so many people came to see him. He had masses and masses of clients. And he could convince them."

At home, Tarzan's children were turning, effortlessly, into Londoners, with strong local accents and only a hazy idea of the country they'd left behind. It was strange to hear their father talking so earnestly about Somalia, about the orphanage, and basketball, and how he would like to be buried there one day. From their British perspective, they imagined it as somewhere backward and grim, and asked ignorant questions, and laughed when their parents talked nostalgically about going out to the cinema together in Mogadishu.

"We'd be cracking up!" says Abdullahi.

Shamis with the kids, 1991. COURTESY OF THE NUR FAMILY

For years, Abdullahi was a difficult, hyperactive child. At home, after school, he would crouch behind the television set mixing flour and oil together on the floor, then pelting his older brothers and sisters.

"I swear, if I had this child I would either kill him, or kill myself," said the lady next door. Tarzan sometimes felt almost the same way—"Believe me, he was crazy." Shamis was more patient, but still, she admits, "Abdullahi was DIFFICULT! I could not sit when he was awake."

The oldest boy, Ahmed, had the occasional run-in with the police. "He could be a little bit rude," Shamis concedes. But Mohamed was quiet and earnest, and all three girls were thriving academically.

All six children went to the state primary school in a stern Victorian building just down the street. Shamis had become a support teacher there, helping other Somali children who had arrived more recently to master English. She organized coffee mornings for the new parents, explained the local bus routes and the welfare system, and still struggled with the rent on their council flat. London was growing on her, and she was good at making friends. Even the local drug gangs—Somali or otherwise—would leave her in peace now that they started to recognize her from school.

Years later, I'm sitting outside a café in north London with Abdullahi and his big sister Ayan. He's now a gangly, charming, scatterbrained, information technology graduate looking for a job. She's taking a lunch break from the private clinic nearby where all three of Tarzan's daughters—all university graduates—now work. Ayan has her father's almond eyes, a neat black hijab covering her hair, and a quick, warm laugh.

"I've always been a daddy's girl!"

"He spoiled you," Abdullahi teases, and then adds, "Mum used to spoil me."

They talk about the camping trips that Tarzan would organize through the Somali Speakers Association for families that couldn't afford holidays. A different place outside London every summer. As a teenager, Ayan used to help out. Abdullah, too, but he says he didn't have any Somali friends when he was growing up. Only in sixth form.

"Somalis always used to call me 'white boy' cos I only had, like, white friends!" he says, and with that, perhaps inevitably, the conversation veers toward the subject of clans.

Both insist they grew up neither knowing nor caring about their own famously small clan. Abdullahi says he found out about the Udeejeen when he was a teenager but didn't know where the branch fit in relation to the bigger clan tree. And it wasn't until Ayan was about seventeen that some Somali girls started "acting weird and raising eyebrows," and then one friend said, "Why don't you ask Ayan—she's from that tribe."

"And I remember going home that night and asking my dad, 'Am I this tribe?'

"And I remember my dad laughing, and saying, 'Don't buy into this filth.'"

By now, Tarzan seemed settled in London. Not as much as his children or Shamis, perhaps. But he was certainly busy. He still preferred to walk everywhere, and I can picture him weaving briskly through the regular Thursday market in Queen's Crescent, a well-known figure heading off to a management meeting or to check up on the internet café he'd set up on the nearby Seven Sisters road. The lumpy scar on his forehead came from a fight at the café with some Albanian "thugs" who, Tarzan insists, came off worse from the encounter.

Before long, his ambition started nudging him toward politics. He joined the Labour Party—"I believe in social justice, and I don't like the Conservatives' policy toward immigrants and non-British"—and he applied to run for a seat on the local council. Things might have worked out very differently if he'd won. But he signed up late and was selected to contest an unwinnable seat. The consensus among Labour activists at the time was that his heart wasn't really in it anyway; his real focus had begun to drift elsewhere.

They were right.

Back in Somalia, the years of pure anarchy were ending. A window of political opportunity was opening, and Tarzan could not resist. He felt the tug of home, of patriotism, and perhaps, the nomadic impulse to keep chasing the rains. But the changes in Somalia were uncertain, and with them came the acute danger that chaos might be replaced by something even more menacing.

8

Filling the Vacuum

"No more clan rubbish."

—MOHAMUD "TARZAN" NUR

TARZAN WAS GRINNING. HE COULDN'T stop himself. It was the most extraordinary news he'd heard in years. Peace had arrived, without warning, in Mogadishu.

The phone in the hallway at Queen's Crescent was ringing again. It hadn't stopped since word had got out. But Tarzan was already racing down the stairwell and out onto the street, heading to the travel agency to book a flight straight back to the place he still thought of when he heard the word "home."

"Are you sure? It is still dangerous. The warlords still have their guns," Shamis called out after him.

It was June 2006, and, for the first time in fifteen years, the fighting had stopped throughout Mogadishu.

A few days later, Tarzan arrived back in the sun and heat of Mogadishu and was overcome, almost immediately, by a bewildering sense of dislocation. He wasn't a foreigner, but he almost felt like one. The destruction was disorientating. He found himself struggling to recognize the ruins of familiar neighborhoods. And why were all these children roaming the streets? Were there really no schools anywhere anymore?

But for all that, it felt safe. It was safe. The gunfire really had stopped.

Tarzan went straight to see the men who had seized control. He knew many of them from the old days. There was his orphanage friend and basketball teammate Asbaro—or Aspirin—and Ibrahim

Ugandan soldier on the frontline, Mogadishu, 2010. COURTESY OF THE AUTHOR

Adow from high school. They were part of an organization called the Islamic Courts Union that had just achieved the seemingly impossible.

The ICU had begun life as a loose alliance of local clerics and Sharia courts, mostly from the Hawiye, who were trying to offer Islamic justice to individual districts. Nothing more. But after so many years of clan-based, arbitrary mayhem, there was a vacuum to be filled. People were desperate for an alternative to the warlords, and the ICU soon found itself transformed into a broader political and military movement.

The fighting in Mogadishu had been building up for weeks. But in early June, the ICU's forces launched a final assault. The warlords had formed their own alliance by then. They had years of experience and plenty of weapons. But they were routed.

"These are the right people to make peace in Somalia," Tarzan thought as he looked around the room. "No more clan rubbish." He was on board, ready to help in whatever way he could. Some people would later accuse him of throwing his lot in with religious fanatics—with Al Qaeda. But it didn't feel like that. These were his friends—pragmatists—people who could make a difference. He was sure of it, and he quickly became an advisor to the ICU and later to its successor organization, the Alliance for the Re-liberation of Somalia.

Tarzan describes all this to me in a flood of enthusiasm. Several times. I have dozens of pages of notes detailing his role, in the years that followed, as an influencer, a cajoler, and a mediator—a breathless stream of political intrigue, backroom deals, and brinkmanship. It is clear, as he explains it, that he is in his element in this world, and I feel like I'm seeing a new, unexpectedly sophisticated side to his character. He's a political animal.

"Tarzan was one of those people who'd look you in the eye. Someone I'd trust. He was well informed, pragmatic, a calm facilitator walking a tightrope between the different camps," says a Western diplomat who'd observed him in close quarters.

But hold on, I tell Tarzan. One minute you were a community organizer and the owner of an internet café in north London, and suddenly you're rubbing shoulders with Islamists and presidents and diplomats. What am I missing?

"You see, I was now the leader of the diaspora," he answers casually.

It seems like an extraordinary claim. Typically Tarzan. And indeed, in the overheated, clannish world of Somali politics, plenty of people will tell you it's a bad joke—that Tarzan was a self-promoting imposter, a thuggish clan stooge, a nobody.

But it is clear to many others that he had genuine skills. In London there is no doubt that he'd become heavily involved in diaspora politics, even creating his own campaign group. His critics said it was just a cover for his clan's interests. But he attended and arranged Somali diaspora conferences in places like Stockholm and Leicester, and before long he was able to point to an organized process of gatherings, committees, and votes to back up his assertion of a leadership role. He had become someone who mattered.

This was a time when many Somalis abroad were trying to piece together the broken ruins of their country. With foreign funding, they staged dozens of peace conferences—I attended one of the more successful ones on a sunbaked hilltop in Djibouti—and tried to build something concrete out of a babble of competing interests.

Over time, they elected a transitional government and parliament in exile, complete with ministers and MPs, who ran up huge hotel bills in places like Nairobi, waiting for an opportunity to return. Some of them were corrupt time-wasters or warlords. Others were credible and desperately well intentioned. But overall their efforts were easy to dismiss or even ridicule as external, top-down exercises in wishful thinking. The years dragged by, and there remained an unbridgeable chasm between the worthy aspirations of the diaspora and the ruthless realities of life and power back in Somalia.

But now a new force had risen up from within Somalia. Organically, you might say. From the grassroots. No wonder people were so hopeful about the Islamic Courts.

And yet, toward the end of his first short trip back to Mogadishu, Tarzan caught a worrying glimpse of what might yet go wrong. He took his old friend Asbaro to one side.

In the years since the orphanage Asbaro had moved to Canada and become increasingly devout. Then he brought his family back to Somalia in 1997 and began working for a man named Sheikh Dahir Aweys. Aweys was a fiery, red-bearded Islamist leader who had already been linked to the 1998 U.S. embassy bombings in Nairobi and Dar es Salaam, Tanzania, and another attack in Mombasa. After 9/11 he was added to the U.S. government's list of international terrorists.

Now, Aweys was being promoted to the leadership of the ICU.

"How can you appoint this guy? We want a new face for Somalia. We want to have contact with the international community, but this guy is associated with Al Qaeda and terrorism," Tarzan fumed.

Asbaro looked down at the floor.

"The reason is Al Shabab," he replied quietly. "They don't have respect for anyone except him. So to contain Al Shabab—to control them—we have to make Sheikh Aweys the leader."

Al Shabab was the ICU's militia. Their name means "the youth" in Arabic. While the clerics discussed justice, clan matters, and, eventually, the exercising of political power, Al Shabab was busy confiscating weapons, building up its private army, and waiting for the right moment to unleash a far more radical agenda.

Tarzan's brother Yusuf visited Mogadishu during the same period and also met his old friends in the ICU's leadership. He remembers them as being hopelessly naive. "None of them had any idea about the weighty issues they were tackling. They thought good intentions were enough—that with Allah's help everything will fall into place."

The United States—preoccupied by its new "war on terror"—was watching with alarm. Washington had good reason to fear that Somalia was becoming a haven for international terrorism. But instead of welcoming the new stability in Mogadishu and trying to build on it by reaching out to the moderates in the ICU, the United States took the opposite approach. The CIA had already tried funding Mogadishu's warlords in their fight against the Islamic Courts. When that failed, Washington encouraged and supported neighboring Ethiopia's plans to invade Somalia.

It was coldly logical and—it seemed to Tarzan—utterly mad. The Americans were playing into the hands of the extremists.

Tarzan says he saw the rise of Al Shabab coming. He became closely involved in a succession of tortuous peace negotiations involving Islamists, Ethiopia, Somalia's weak transitional government, and a host of foreign intermediaries. The work involved regular travel back to the region, and to Mogadishu, and slowly pulled him away from the life his family was building in London. He was straddling two worlds.

But the talks were hard. Al Shabab sent their own silent, unsmiling men to keep an eye on the ICU negotiators. It felt like the more moderate officials were being held hostage, that any sign of weakness would be punished. The threats became increasingly explicit. Tarzan called Asbaro, urging him to use his influence within Al Shabab. Asbaro said it was hopeless. The militants did not want a deal, they wanted war.

It came soon enough.

AT THE END OF December 2006, Tarzan answered the phone in London and was told that his older brother Mohamed—the boy his mother had chosen to keep with her in the wilderness all those years ago—had been killed by Ethiopian troops on the western edge of Mogadishu.

"He was a shopkeeper. He left his house and a sniper shot him."

The Ethiopian army had charged through Somalia from the Ogaden, traveling along the same road Tarzan and Yusuf had taken when their aunt brought them to Mogadishu as starving children in 1960.

Ethiopia's invasion was a profoundly divisive moment for Somalia. Some welcomed it as an uncomfortable but necessary intervention—a price worth paying to rid the country of extremists. For others, the idea of Ethiopian troops patrolling Mogadishu was the most profound humiliation, a rallying call to join those fighting a criminal occupation, and an act of unforgiveable treachery by Somali politicians in the transitional government who had invited the Ethiopians in.

Al Shabab's ranks were soon swelled by earnest young men convinced the militants were, for all their faults, the only group prepared to defend Somalia's borders and honor.

Behind the scenes, in negotiations, Tarzan could be as shrewd and calculating as anyone. But not on this issue. When it came to Ethiopia's role in Somalia, he saw red. His brother Yusuf, too. Back in London, Tarzan likened the Ethiopians to Hitler and those Somalis who backed the invasion to "British people who supported the Nazis. We consider them all as traitors."

He led protests outside the American embassy, handing over a petition against U.S. support for Ethiopia to a junior official and grabbing his arm to tell him, "I used to love America. It was the land of freedom and prosperity. I had a map of America above my bed as a child. But today I hate America."

When the president of Somalia's transitional government came to London for medical treatment, Tarzan organized another demonstration outside his Kensington hospital. For some Somalis that was a step too far—you don't harangue a man on his sickbed. But Tarzan was unapologetic—the president was a traitor.

Later, I ask him if his fury was in part, perhaps, a reaction to his brother's death. He brusquely rejects the suggestion, as if grief and principle have no right to share the same space.

AT FIRST, ETHIOPIA'S OFFENSIVE looked like a success. The ICU split apart. The Ethiopians were backed up by a motley collection of Somali government troops and militias, and together they managed to carve out the time, and the space, for something radical to happen. An experiment. You could think of it as a bold but risky heart transplant operation on a frail patient.

The new heart was Somalia's transitional government, artificially created in exile, and now dropped into the festering wound of central Mogadishu. But how to make sure it was not rejected by its host?

The short answer was money. Western nations would spend hundreds of millions of dollars over the coming years to keep the new heart pumping, and above all to pay for an African Union peacekeeping force to protect the transplant from succumbing to the infection of Al Shabab.

But it was a struggle from the start.

Al Shabab was growing in power. Instead of fighting skirmishes against an assortment of warlords and clan militias, it was now involved in something far grander—a holy war against a Christian invader, Ethiopia. What better rallying cry for an ambitious Islamist army?

And sure enough, faced with an increasingly intense guerrilla war, the Ethiopians withdrew their forces from Mogadishu. The foreign peacekeepers that replaced them—mostly from Uganda—were too few in number. Before long, Al Shabab controlled almost all of the capital once more. The transitional government found itself besieged inside Villa Somalia, under mortar and sniper fire, with its back to the ocean.

It began to look as though the transplant operation could not possibly succeed.

In Mogadishu, Al Shabab was at least confronted by a substantial military force. In the countryside its position now seemed almost unchallenged. The group set up checkpoints, recruited accountants, collected taxes and fines, settled legal disputes, and administered its own ruthless justice. Like the Taliban in Afghanistan, it was organized and ambitious. By 2009 it controlled almost the entire bottom third of Somalia, an area not much smaller than the United Kingdom.

IN JULY 2009, I visited the town of Buale, deep in Al Shabab's new heartland. Buale sits on the east bank of Somalia's "other" river, the Juba, perhaps 300 kilometers southwest of Mogadishu.

I sat in the shade of a large acacia tree on the edge of the town, watching a bearded man slip his hand away from the table and his two mobile phones and down, past the arm of his plastic chair, to caress the brown neck and ears of an infant dik–dik, which tolerated the affection for a few seconds and then ambled away across the compound.

"We killed the mother," said the man, briskly turning from the tiny antelope and back toward the unusual visitors seated before him. Around us, half a dozen armed men stood at what seemed like an almost respectful distance, watching closely.

The man staring across the table at me, wearing jeans and sandals and occasionally fondling his wispy beard, was the local commander of Al Shabab.

It was a rare encounter, for both of us.

By now, Al Shabab had already been condemned as a "violent and brutal extremist" terrorist group by the U.S. State Department. It was in the process of becoming even more radical, and was forging formal ties with Al Qaeda.

With remarkable speed, Al Shabab ousted warlords and clan militias from rural Somalia and began imposing an austere, repressive, fundamentally alien but not unwelcome peace.

Football and music and films were banned. Dancing too. Even ringtones were carefully censored. Men were forced to shave their heads and women to wear veils. Adulterers were buried to their necks in sand and stoned to death. Thieves might have a hand or leg hacked off. Such practices, imported from countries like Saudi Arabia, came as a shock to many Somalis. But it was hard to deny their effectiveness. Like the Taliban in Afghanistan, Al Shabab was bringing order to an anarchic nation, and its ranks were now being swelled by a steady influx of foreign jihadists who headed to the Kenyan coast and slipped across the border by boat or on foot.

Al Shabab had its own Twitter account and a keen sense of the importance of its own media profile. But it was not in the habit of meeting Western journalists in the flesh. They were more likely to be seen as targets for ransom or execution than as conduits of information.

Still. Here we were.

The rules were strict. We were to leave our television camera and all other recording and photographic equipment in the car, and no names were to be used. As the commander must have known, he was taking a substantial risk by agreeing to meet with an infidel journalist.

Our conversation was brief.

Despite the absence of a camera, the commander was taking no chances. He straightened his back, jabbed a finger, and stuck to the script. It was a fiery performance. All those who opposed Al Shabab had "sold out" their religion. The foreign militants who were arriving, he claimed, by the hundreds, were most welcome here. Al Shabab operated within a system of strict, fair laws that had brought peace to much of Somalia, and that oppressed no one.

There was no suggestion of a handshake at the end. The commander stood up, and it was immediately clear that we should leave the compound.

Al Shabab sold itself as a single, united movement. In fact it was far more complicated than that. It was an umbrella, beneath which a variety of agendas and groups overlapped and competed. Rival clans, foreign jihadists, patriotic Islamists, more moderate nationalists, courts, businessmen, smugglers, students. And before long, the umbrella expanded to take in disillusioned members of the Somali diaspora—mostly young men struggling to adapt to their new lives in Europe or America and lured by the prospect of returning to Africa and belonging to a worthwhile cause.

IN BRITAIN, AS ELSEWHERE, the authorities reacted with alarm and warned of an "intense struggle" against Al Shabab and its foreign recruitment drive.

One morning, Tarzan's second son, Mohamed, was about to leave his flat in Camden, north London, when the doorbell rang unexpectedly.

"It's the postman," said the man outside, and Mohamed could see through the spyhole that he was holding up a red bag of some sort.

He opened the door.

Mohamed was twenty-five at the time and nothing like his father. For a start, he seemed more devout and much more private, too, a family man whose playful sense of humor was often hidden behind a wary, defensive wall. A very strict person, no trouble at all, thank God, his mother always said.

"Mohamed, I need to speak with you. I'm from the police and this is an emergency. We really need to talk."

It wasn't a postman after all. And he wasn't alone. Inside Mohamed's flat, the policeman introduced a colleague who produced an ID badge and explained that he was from MI5, Britain's domestic security agency. The conversation that followed—according to several accounts Mohamed has given—went something like this:

"Mohamed, you're suspected of being involved in extremist activities. Islamic extremism."

"Where did you get such an idea? Who told you that?"

"I'm not permitted to discuss our sources."

"But I've never done anything extreme. I've never been involved in anything like that."

"It depends what you mean by extremism. Maybe we see things differently." It was the policeman, jumping in.

"Fine, define it then."

"Well, going abroad to study extremist materials, training, and eventually taking your own life for extremist purposes."

Mohamed had been sharp but controlled until that point. Now he lost his temper.

"What! The only reason I went abroad to Egypt was to study Arabic. Now if you consider that to be an extremist activity, then fine, I am an extremist!"

Mohamed was one of at least five young British Somalis, from the same neighborhood in north London, being approached by the security services. At the time, he had not managed to finish his university degree. He was earning a little extra income as a personal fitness trainer, but his main job—alongside some of the other men targeted by M15—was at a local Kentish Town welfare association that worked with disadvantaged young British Somalis.

With his thick beard, muscular build, and guarded demeanor, Mohamed seemed to enjoy confounding other people's expectations—exposing their prejudices.

One night after work he'd traveled across to another neighborhood, Holloway, to attend a diaspora meeting. His father was speaking, as usual, and Mohamed slipped in late, carrying a rucksack, and sat at the back of the room. People immediately started looking around and getting nervous. The man sitting beside Tarzan leaned across and whispered to him, "Look. I think Al Shabab has sent someone tonight." Tarzan saw who he was pointing at and laughed.

The visit by M15 ended on an ambiguous but threatening note. The agent told Mohamed that he needed to cooperate—in other words, that he was being recruited as an informer. His colleagues at the welfare association were told much the same. And there was an unmistakable threat behind the request.

"You travel regularly. If you want to travel more, then I suggest you cooperate as we have very good connections all around the world. Any country that you go to—we can give you problems."

Mohamed didn't refuse outright. Instead he told the visitors that they needed to explain to him exactly what he'd done wrong.

"If you do that, I'll be more than willing to help."

The agent said he couldn't discuss that right now, but how about meeting up again in three days' time?

"Either you tell me what you have against me right now, or I will never agree to anything," he said. The men stood up and on their way out promised to call Mohamed in three days' time. They never did.

The incident left a deep impression on Mohamed. Years later, he's still arguing with his mother about the way the British security services have handled the "Al Shabab issue" within the ethnic Somali community.

"Would you like it if the police suspected something here, at this house, and came and broke in? Came in and checked around? It can cause more enmity. It can push people to join Shabab. Would you like it?" he asks her.

"No problem. They have to find out what is happening," she replies cheerfully. It sounds as though they've had this argument before.

"It's normal," she goes on. "London is a safe place. They break into your house and check. If the people are innocent, the police apologize and say, 'We did this cos of your safety.' People are happy. You don't understand."

"I do. But I would say you can achieve security in a different way. You get rid of that 'us versus them' thing."

⁂

BACK IN MOGADISHU, THE new transitional government was still under siege, clinging onto a handful of districts, its future as precarious as ever. But the growing power of Al Shabab, and its rising profile in places like London, was slowly forcing the international community to play a more active role. After nearly twenty years of misery, enough was enough. The government in Mogadishu would not, and could not, be allowed to fail. It was time for the diaspora to come back and lend a hand.

PART 3

Picking Up the Pieces

2010—2016

"Calamity is capable of wonders."

—EXCERPT FROM "SOCIETY"
BY MOHAMED IBRAHIM WARSAME
"HADRAAWI"

9

A Man with a Plan

"All this is doable."

—MOHAMED ABDULLAHI MOHAMED "FARMAJO"

It was November 2010, and I was crouched behind a low wall perhaps twenty yards from Mogadishu's frontlines.

I heard the fizzling shriek of a bullet passing just above my helmet. It is the most intimate sensation. For that brief, frozen moment, it feels like your head is a giant eggshell and the whole world is coming at you with a hammer.

I shrank deeper inside my flak jacket as the bullet hit a nearby wall. Then another zipped overhead and ricocheted off something metallic with a noise like a high-pitched snarl.

"Run-run-run!"

Behind me, a disconcertingly plump Ugandan soldier was shepherding us through a maze of rubble, broken walls, and sandbagged windows.

We ran, then froze, then ran again across a patch of open ground, sweating and panting under the weight of our body armor and trying to make sense of the noises echoing around us—what was sniper fire, what might just be a warning burst from a machine gun, how to know if that mortar thud was incoming or outgoing.

It was almost noon, a few blocks east of Villa Somalia. Two Somali government soldiers were crouching behind a building to our left and I watched in astonishment as one of them tipped forward in what looked like slow motion.

For a second I thought he'd been hit.

But no, he was praying.

View from ruins of Al-Uruba hotel, Mogadishu, 2010. COURTESY OF THE AUTHOR

Al Shabab's fighters controlled at least half of Mogadishu—the inland half, including the suburbs. That left the transitional government besieged, with its back to the sea, in the older quarter. Still, the militants had been pushed back a couple of city blocks in this sector over the last week, and we were now moving through their old defensive lines.

It would take a special sort of archeologist to pick through the rubble and distinguish between the different eras of destruction in Mogadishu. But a few frantic hours touring the new frontlines were enough for me to see that a sort of weapons inflation was at work— that the freckle-like bullet holes and gashes of the early years were being buried beneath the craters and rubble of a far more devastating age.

Those fighting over each city block appeared to have no vested interest in whether Mogadishu itself survived the ordeal.

For now, the outside world seemed content to sit back and watch the contest. It was business as usual, after all. Foreign governments were more preoccupied with what was going on off the coast of Somalia, where foreign ships were now being threatened by a handful of intrepid gunmen in flimsy fiberglass skiffs. Somali piracy was reaching its peak, with more than 150 ships, including oil tankers, cargo, container, and cruise ships, and many fishing vessels, attacked so far that year.

There were no pirates in Mogadishu. Somalia has Africa's longest coastline, and the pirate gangs had made their bases much further north, in remote areas where local clan militias and kidnappers could operate with impunity.

A few months earlier, I'd driven to the pirate stronghold of Eyl, a dusty little town scattered along a narrow canyon that stretches down toward a blindingly white, sandy beach, not far from the tip of Somalia's "ear." I'd seen the hijacked ships moored offshore and spoken to the men who'd seized them. Far out to sea, an increasingly aggressive international naval armada was now on patrol and spending, evidently, billions of dollars to safeguard the world's shipping lanes. Everyone onshore, from the pirates to the local authorities to the handful of foreign agencies operating in the area, was in broad agreement about one thing. If only the world could show the same determination to help fight the poverty and chaos within Somalia . . .

That thought rattled somewhere in my head as we began working our way further north through Mogadishu, toward an apartment block where Ugandan troops had set up a forward base overlooking Al Shabab's positions. The Ugandans were the major players in the new African Union peacekeeping force, brought in to protect the transitional government now that the Ethiopians had pulled out.

The Ugandans, along with some Burundians, were known as AMISOM. The funding came from overseas and through the UN, but AMISOM gave the impression that African solutions were being found for Africa's problems. Besides, it was cheaper than bringing in a full UN peacekeeping force, and it provided Uganda's government with some useful income and the toughest training for its armed forces.

At times it was impossible to tell if we were walking through or around houses. The roofs had long gone, and holes had been punched through surviving walls to enable the militants to move unseen. A patch of bathroom tiles, a strip of wallpaper, or the occasional thorn tree were often the only clues.

Two mortar rounds crunched into the debris somewhere up ahead. Probably fired by the Ugandans, who were often accused of causing heavy civilian casualties with their casual approach toward targeting. We crouched down in what looked like a freshly dug ditch.

"Trenches," said the Ugandan major, a short, resolutely cheerful man with a neatly trimmed mustache perched on a round face.

Al Shabab had launched a big offensive during the recent month of Ramadan, and the trenches—and some impressively long tunnels— were part of their failed effort to push the Ugandans further back toward the sea.

Most evenings, someone from Al Shabab would call up Major

B–B, as he was known, to interrupt his whisky drinking and threaten him. "See here. Sometimes they text too," said the major, unbuttoning a flap in his camouflaged body armor to show me his mobile phone. The text read YOU WILL BE KILLED IN 3 DAYS.

"The terrorists call me up all the time," he chuckled with something close to pride, explaining that because he was a spokesman for AMISOM, and because "there's an oral culture in Somalia," the militants mistakenly assumed he was rather powerful.

We clambered up a dark stairwell to the top of the apartment block. Two slumbering figures lay curled on a mattress in one corner. Another soldier perched on an office chair, peering down the barrel of a machine gun that poked through a narrow slit in a wall of sandbags. I leaned forward to share his view—a brightly lit hillside covered in the ruins of buildings that had been so comprehensively demolished that it was hard to find a straight edge. Change the colors, and we could almost have been looking out over a forest.

For now, the war felt like a stalemate—a familiar condition for Mogadishu. It was volatile and dangerous, but those with the necessary perspective understood that a deadlock could also be lucrative.

The Ugandans complained that they still had only half the number of men they needed to finish the job; that the Somalis fighting alongside them were unreliable and would often defect, or even call up Al Shabab and arrange to sell them their own guns. But Western diplomats helping to channel international funding to AMISOM suspected that the Ugandan top brass were stealing and reselling their own ammunition and using the airport for other scams.

In other words, the status quo was a little too profitable for anyone to disrupt in a hurry.

The Somali soldiers complained that their own leaders were stealing their government salaries. Many of the men on the frontlines hadn't been paid for months. Maybe it was still true—that for all its faults, the clan was the only thing you could trust.

At night, when the gunfire stopped, the militants would call out across the frontlines, brotherly words now, not insults, drifting over the rubble, urging their fellow Somalis to change sides, to join their fight against an infidel government. Sometimes it worked the other way.

One of the Al Shabab fighters was a slim, soft-spoken twenty-one-year-old called Hanad. He'd joined four years earlier, tempted by the prospect of a job and an income. To begin with, he was told he could have no contact with his family, but, in the chaos of Mogadishu, the rules about mobile phones were harder to enforce, and Hanad had finally called his brother Mohamed. It turned out that Mohamed had joined Somalia's new national army, and was now fighting in the very same sector in Mogadishu.

"He was right there. And I thought that if I fire one more shot, the first person to die would surely be my brother. And if my brother shoots, it will be me who dies. So I changed my mind about what I was doing." Hanad tells me this when I meet him some years later in a government camp for low-ranking Al Shabab defectors in the town of Baidoa. There are high walls, watchtowers, and guards there, looking after perhaps fifty men and women living in tents outside a military base. The security is not to prevent escape but to protect the defectors from Al Shabab reprisals.

It wasn't just Somali soldiers crossing from one side to another in Mogadishu. Although some sections of the frontline were impassable, there were plenty of other routes. Civilians could, within limits, come and go, running errands, visiting different markets or clinics, and hunting for work.

A few days earlier, waiting for the flight into Mogadishu from Nairobi, a tall young Somali man had come striding over to me at the departure gate. He was a journalist I'd met perhaps seven years before. He and his family were still living in Mogadishu, in an area now firmly under Al Shabab control. I asked him if he was still reporting, and instead of replying, he mimed the action of a handsaw, vigorously amputating his own arm.

"Too dangerous. They lash people there. Every day—for the smallest thing."

And so he'd begun working for a foreign aid organization instead.

Better paid but hardly less risky. "Al Shabab call us the hands of the infidel. Their eyes are on us all the time." For a while he'd sent his seven-year-old daughter to a Koranic school as part of an effort to "try to fit in." But one day she came home looking somber and finally explained that their morning class had been taken over by a man who had tried to teach them how to use a pistol. Now she stayed at home, and her father felt a hundred eyes on him every time he set foot outside.

AFTER A NIGHT SLEEPING in a shipping container lined with sandbags back at the AMISOM base beside Mogadishu's airport, I clambered up and inside one of the giant armored trucks the Ugandans used to ferry people around their half of the city. We were heading to Villa Somalia.

The truck roared up the airport road, swinging right at the K4 roundabout, four kilometers from the city center. We'd been warned not to discuss our movements on mobile phones. Al Shabab had been having such success with its roadside bombs that it seemed they might now have the capability to monitor communications. I twisted around to look through a tiny porthole and noticed a single bullet had left a pattern like a spider's web in the glass.

Ten minutes later, we lurched around one last roadblock, then up the short, steep, sandbagged road into Villa Somalia, and emerged from the back of the truck, clothes soaked with sweat beneath our flak jackets and eyes blinking in the bright sunshine of a white-walled courtyard. It was not a place to linger. Al Shabab's nearest positions were only a few blocks to the west, and the Villa was a favorite target for their mortar and rocket teams.

The mood inside the dark reception room appeared oddly relaxed at first. Perhaps a dozen men and women sat on the plump beige sofas that lined the walls. There were carpets, coffee tables, bottled water, and even some plastic roses in a vase. But from time to time an explosion somewhere outside rattled the windows and everyone tried, with varying degrees of success, to pretend not to notice.

Somalia's new government—or much of it—had assembled to meet the media. It was, overwhelmingly, a diaspora cabinet. Most of the earnest figures, rising in turn to greet the sweaty foreign journalist, had only recently returned to Mogadishu from abroad.

The new Women's Affairs minister, Dr. Miriam Qasim, had flown in the week before, after twenty years as a primary school teacher in Birmingham, England. Her family told her she was mad. She spoke of sacrifice, of hard work, and of the possibility of a turning point for Somalia. It was hard not to be impressed.

The bespectacled new prime minister, Mohamed Abdullahi Mohamed, had taken a leave of absence from the State Transportation Department in Buffalo, New York. He was a steady, competent figure whose nickname, "Farmajo"—from *formaggio*, the Italian word for cheese—never seemed quite to fit him. His wife had opposed his abrupt career move, but after nearly a month in the city he was getting used to the sound of bullets hitting the outside of his bedroom wall.

"All this," he said—waving an arm in the general direction of the frontlines—"is doable."

As I moved around the room, chatting with the information minister, then the foreign minister—who insisted there was "an iceberg of normality" lurking beneath the surface of Mogadishu—I could feel my skepticism welling up. All these smart suits and polished shoes, foreign doctorates, and grand ambitions seemed so surreal, so wholly out of context. But you don't even control the city, I found myself saying with a growing edge of shrillness. And if the Ugandans left you'd be overrun in minutes. How can you all sound so optimistic?

At which point someone patted me on my shoulder and I turned around to face one of the AMISOM officials who'd organized the trip to Villa Somalia.

"Have you met the new mayor yet?" he asked.

No, I had not.

⁂

TARZAN WAS STANDING NEAR the door, wearing an open-necked white checked shirt, dark blue trousers, and the relaxed, disarming smile of a man enjoying a rather adventurous summer camping holiday. Nothing like the other politicians on their sofas, keenly aware of the dignity of their positions.

"Ah! I love the BBC," he said almost immediately, with a toothy, eager smile.

We stepped outside and walked around the corner of the building, past the pickup trucks and bodyguards, to look down the hill toward the bright blue sea and the slice of Mogadishu that currently lay under his authority. Something went boom further north, and Tarzan's grin seemed to widen.

In another context, the mayor would have seemed a rather minor player in a villa full of senior ministers. But this was a government without a country—an expression of ambition, rather than of ability, a wobbly alliance of competing clan interests parachuted into one corner of a ruined city. A political heart transplant operation.

In the circumstances, Tarzan was the exception. He had people to govern, needs to meet, plans to implement, and measurable ways to judge success and failure.

"They call this the most dangerous city on the face of the earth. But it's not," he began. Kabul and Baghdad were apparently worse in terms of daily casualties, although I'm not sure where his statistics came from. And if we get five years of peace, Tarzan continued, warming to his theme, then "it will become something like Hong Kong."

Two things quickly became apparent. The first was that Tarzan had a grand strategy for Mogadishu, and it wasn't based on any practical knowledge of how to run a city—he freely acknowledged he knew nothing about the job whatsoever. Rather it was about mobilizing the population—using the skills he'd learned at the orphanage and as an activist both in Mogadishu and London—encouraging them to participate, in cleaning the streets, reporting suspicious activities, and getting businesses to work together. He spoke of a population trapped in darkness for so long that people had forgotten that there was another, better way to live. Tarzan's job was to break some windows and let the light back in.

"Money isn't everything. The only people who can bring security back to Mogadishu are the population here. Not foreign troops. The day people decide they want a stable government, it will happen."

The second thing I began to realize is that Tarzan saw his own public role—his character—as an integral part of that strategy. He couldn't fix the city from behind a desk. He had to be the vocal, visible embodiment of the changes he sought. Amid the chaos, the mayor of Mogadishu had to be larger than life, a fearless, inspirational figurehead, something worth believing in.

It was a convincing performance. But in the months that followed, I slowly came to understand that the truth was a little messier; that at least to begin with, the mayor of Mogadishu saw this new job as an insult, a demotion, a poisoned chalice. A trap.

"Believe me," he said.

⚜

THE FIRST OFFER HAD come in May that year, over lunch in Villa Somalia with the country's new president, Sheikh Sharif Sheikh Ahmed.

"It cannot be. No. It's too risky. It's a mess, and I don't want to get dirty," Tarzan said emphatically.

In recent years he'd come to know Sheikh Sharif well. The former teacher had been a founding member of the Islamic Courts Union and a big winner in the difficult negotiations that had brought more moderate Islamists back into the transitional government in the years following the Ethiopian invasion and the rise of Al Shabab.

"Think about it. We'll talk another time," said the president, who promptly asked the interior minister, then the speaker of parliament, to try talking Tarzan around. Before long, Ali Madobe, Tarzan's old orphanage friend, was on the phone, too. He'd already come back to Mogadishu to try to rebuild a police force from scratch.

It was easy to see that Tarzan might suit the role of mayor. He certainly had the charisma. But clan issues, as usual, mattered, too, and the fact that Tarzan came from a conveniently marginal branch of the giant Hawiye tree—one that carried relatively little divisive baggage from the warlord era—was particularly useful.

"I'll think about it," Tarzan finally conceded.

It wasn't the prospect of moving to Mogadishu that worried him most. He'd already been allocated a seat in the new parliament, based on his clan and his prominence in the diaspora, and he had been coming back to the city for short visits. His real concern was that his political rivals were, at best, sidelining him—that the mayor's job was a high-profile suicide mission.

Back in London, Shamis thought as much and begged him on the phone not to accept it. In fact she told him, point blank, that it was too dangerous. She was scared. Furious. Her youngest son, Abdullahi, heard her arguing on the phone night after night.

"At first I didn't think nothing about him going back. But when I saw her getting so worried I started thinking, too. I don't want my dad to die."

Tarzan arranged to travel north to Somaliland where his three surviving brothers had gathered, and they also agreed that the job would be a bad move, that even if he survived, his reputation would not. Yusuf told him, in no uncertain terms, that "if you go to work in a sewer, you'll end up stinking of filth." But over the following weeks, Tarzan's resolve began to weaken. He spent a few days on his own in Kenya, thinking things over. The president called him again on his mobile phone, and Tarzan said he'd return to Mogadishu to discuss the proposal in more detail.

He had some conditions.

ON HIS FIRST DAY in the job, Tarzan walked into the wood-paneled mayor's office on Via Londra, directly opposite the San Martino Hospital and within earshot—if the windows hadn't been sandbagged—of the ocean. He sat down behind his desk and let out a snort of frustration. The building—previously a courthouse—was empty. Nothing. No records, no paperwork, not even a broom or a wheelbarrow for the entire municipality. A few staff turned up to greet the new arrival, but none had received a salary for months. The place was a joke.

Facing him, on his desk, Tarzan found a letter from the outgoing mayor stating that the municipality had accumulated a debt of ten billion Somali shillings—about four hundred thousand dollars. There was no explanation and no invoices or receipts.

In the small car park outside, Tarzan's cousin Fanah was talking to his security team. It was a small army. Twenty or more young men with aging AK-47s, some with bandoliers of bullets draped around their shoulders, too, and a convoy of pickups parked with noses toward the barriers at the front gate, ready to leave in a hurry.

Tarzan had called Fanah before he took the job to ask if he could look after his safety.

"I have no experience in such things. I don't know whom to trust—not even clan-wise," Tarzan admitted.

Fanah was perfect for the role. He'd never left Mogadishu. He understood the local rules of survival as well as anyone. Even his closest relatives seemed more than a little intimidated by this unflinching, fearless figure.

Fanah agreed to protect Tarzan. He assembled a team of trusted guards—mostly from their Udeejeen clan. Anyone else would sell you out in an instant. And that was it. Tarzan made it clear to his cousin, repeatedly, that he wanted nothing to do with the details of any security arrangements. The mayor could justifiably argue that he had too much else on his plate—that he trusted Fanah and saw no reason to get involved—but I suspect there was more to it. He was constructing a mental barrier between himself and the extraordinary dangers that swirled about him. A way to stay sane.

Then again, maybe there was a more political motive. Mogadishu was a dirty town. Perhaps protecting the mayor might prove to be a dirty business. It made practical sense to keep a clear gap—a space for deniability—between himself and those watching his back.

Tarzan's official line about his personal security involved a Zen-like mantra about submitting to fate. "The hour of my death has been written. I cannot change it," he told everybody, again and again, including his own children, who still mimic the line with an eye-rolling mixture of admiration and despair.

With Shamis it was, inevitably, more complicated. During his first five months as mayor, Tarzan says he did not call home. He claimed he didn't want to worry his wife, but I wonder whether it was also another defense mechanism, a way of keeping the outside world at bay.

Through the second half of 2010 Shamis waited in London. She'd come to love the city. Even the weather. By then, Queen's Crescent— once nicknamed the Murder Mile—had lost its reputation for drugs and gangs. Shamis was now working for a local government advice center, helping Somali children integrate into their schools. But she stopped when Tarzan returned to Mogadishu. The children had grown up. The girls were all thriving, and even the youngest, Abdullahi, now twenty-one, had turned into a cheerfully erratic media studies undergraduate. Shamis stayed at home, bracing herself for an international phone call that would, surely, bring bad news. She was anxious and began to lose weight.

Before he left for Mogadishu, and later, when they settled into more of a routine, Tarzan and Shamis talked about the risks he was taking, and slowly—as couples do—they began to develop a joint position.

"I'm not afraid that you'll die. I'm afraid you'll be badly injured— a head injury," Shamis told him.

"My worry is a bad spinal injury—like I saw at the hospital in

Saudi Arabia. But death—I don't worry about it. I don't want to become old, knowing nothing, becoming a burden for my family," Tarzan told me not long afterward.

It was strange to hear them both talk like that, and I was tempted to dismiss it as something close to bluster—a way of making light of the stresses and dangers in Mogadishu. If anyone asked about the risks—and they always did—they had a ready-made opinion they could trot out and then change the subject.

Over the years I've tried to challenge Tarzan on this issue. How can you be so blasé about your own life? But the more I probe, the more he clings to his position. It is tightly bound up both in his sense of himself as a fundamentally uncomplicated figure—what you see is what you get—and in his faith, in the notion that his life is a gift to be used for a cause.

"I believe very strongly that I will die one day, and that nobody can advance or delay it. So there's no reason to be afraid."

Yusuf backs him up. "Fatalism is misunderstood in the West," he tells me. "In Islam, you do all you can to stay alive. You do your best. But after that, you don't worry. That's my attitude, too."

❦

ON TARZAN'S FIRST NIGHT back in the city Al Shabab fired rockets at his hotel. He was staying at a place called the Nasa Hablod 2, not far from Villa Somalia. The name is literally translated as "Maiden's Breasts," in reference to two famous hills in the north of the country, but I have always thought of it as the Twin Peaks. The rockets crashed into a wall without injuring anyone. It wasn't an unusual occurrence, but it seemed to mark the beginning of a particularly intense, personal relationship between the militants and the mayor.

From the outset, Tarzan made it clear that strengthening security in the parts of the city now controlled by the government was his first priority. Safety first, then cleaning away the garbage, and then bringing back streetlights. In fact they were all linked—it was easy to plant roadside bombs in the garbage, especially on pitch-dark streets. That was his back-of-the-envelope plan, and he launched it in typically abrasive fashion.

"Don't disguise yourselves as women. Don't hide your weapons under your clothes. Come for me in the open and then kill me, if you can!" he declared on a local Somali television channel, staring at the camera like a prizefighter eyeing up his opponent.

It was electrifying. No one could think of another politician who had dared to speak to Al Shabab in that way. It seemed suicidal.

"Shabab should be eliminated on the spot. Mobs should stone them to death," he insisted.

It was time, as Tarzan kept saying, to break the windows and let some light in.

But first, the mayor needed some money. Even just a little. His first official act was to write off his predecessor's unexplained debts. The municipality did not, he declared, owe anyone anything. His second move was to head up to the prime minister's office in Villa Somalia to ask for some cash.

In his earlier job negotiations, Tarzan had told the prime minister that he required 50 percent of the income from Mogadishu's seaport. It was one of his main conditions.

They haggled. The prime minister offered 25 percent, then took him along to see the president, who cut that down to 15 percent.

"Fine," said Tarzan. It would do for starters.

He had two other conditions. The first was about his staff. He knew he couldn't get around the clan issue—that the most powerful sub-clans would each demand and expect to place their people within his office. So, he says, he cut a deal. The president would pick out the necessary clans, but he would leave Tarzan free to select the individuals. Done. The third condition was that the national police and security chiefs would come under his control in Mogadishu—a demand that was easy to agree to but that proved much harder to enforce.

Tarzan walked into the prime minister's offices and headed straight for Abdirizak Fartaag's desk. Another middle-aged returnee from the diaspora—Canada in his case—Fartaag was now running the public finance unit. He looked up and immediately recognized Tarzan from his basketball days.

It was an odd feeling. Fartaag had always thought of Tarzan as a bit of a brute, someone who just "beat the crap out of everyone." The PM had said as much to Fartaag in his own office that week, dismissing the new mayor as a temporary irritant, a thug who would soon be chewed up and spat out.

On the other hand, at least Tarzan wasn't an Islamist like the quiet, unnervingly focused officials who ran the president's office. And he was certainly energetic and brave—all that stuff he'd said to Al Shabab. Maybe he was what Mogadishu needed right now.

Fartaag began writing out a letter requesting $50,000 for the mayor's office. But Tarzan was looming over his shoulder, and before long Tarzan was in his seat, finishing the letter himself and racing out the door to deliver it to the prime minister in person. Typical.

At the time, Fartaag—his nickname meant "one who raises his finger in the air"—still thought the new government was on the right track. More or less. Surely all these educated exiles were risking their lives coming back to Mogadishu for something more than personal gain.

It took him a while to realize what was going on.

"We Somalis are good actors," he would later reflect with a scowl. "We're shallow. We like chaos, not order."

⁂

TARZAN'S ARMED CONVOY SWERVED past the barriers in front of the municipality building, turned to the left, and sped along Via Londra. In the front car, Fanah always chose the route spontaneously and at the very last minute.

It was a Tuesday morning and everything appeared to be in place.

The mayor had spent his first few months in office in a frenzy of activity, haggling with local businessmen about how to get the streets cleaned, reminding them that they'd paid no taxes for two decades and that perhaps it was time to think of the greater good, and cajoling the district commissioners who still wielded so much power in the city and were, in some cases, still little more than warlords.

But today was special. Tarzan was throwing a party for Mogadishu. A Peace Festival. There would be singers and poets and stalls for people to sell samosas and other street food. It would be the first event of its kind in a generation.

Tarzan had asked the police and security forces to guard the venues overnight to prevent Al Shabab planting bombs. Indeed there had already been a threat. In recent weeks the text messages from the militants to the mayor had been getting more frequent and more specific.

WE CAN SEE YOU. YOU ARE IN FRONT OF YOUR HOUSE.

WE ARE FROM YOUR CLAN, SO WE KNOW EVERY MOVE YOU TAKE.

YOUR FLESH WILL FLY INTO THE AIR.

YOU ARE WEARING A KHAKI SHIRT AND SUNGLASSES.

WE KNOW THE ROAD YOU USE TO YOUR OFFICE.

IN TWO MINUTES YOU WILL BE DEAD.

Sometimes they called him up, too, and if he was given the chance Tarzan would try to argue back, demanding they justify their actions—that they explain why, for example, those four women, paid by his administration to collect rubbish, had been killed a few weeks earlier.

"They wanted to feed their families. They were not involved in politics. Not armed. What is your aim? Kill me—I understand that because I'm against you. But why kill the ladies?"

The answer was almost always the same. A brief pause, then more threats.

By nine o'clock in the morning, several hundred people, most of them women wrapped in bright blue, red, and yellow shawls, had already gathered on a large patch of open ground at the foot of the hill leading up to Villa Somalia. There were armed guards at every entrance and a small stage with a canopy for the performers. Two large white banners declared, "We want a clean Mogadishu," and "Mogadishu—don't despise yourself." The weather was mild with a light breeze and a sky crowded with plump clouds.

"The only thing they can use against us is a mortar," Tarzan thought to himself. "But it will not happen, Inshallah."

Suddenly, all heads turned in unison as an unfamiliar noise swept through the open space.

It was a brass band, marching across the dusty ground. Thirty men, in four columns, wore a haphazard assortment of yellow, white, green, and blue uniforms, with sashes and epaulets and big buttons and black hats. There were trumpets, horns, a few trombones, a saxophone, and lots of drums. At the front, brandishing a long swagger stick swathed in deep purple cloth, was the bandleader, his sideburns neatly trimmed, sweat glistening beneath his peaked cap.

It was impossible for the crowds not to grin.

The older women in the crowd stretched their minds back twenty years and began to reminisce. Siad Barre. The word danced around like a butterfly. It was just like Siad Barre's time. The good old days. Tarzan thought of the times he'd spent as an orphan, following the police band around the city.

For the first hour or so he sat in the shade, smiling and watching a succession of poets and folksingers and dancing groups take their turn. He'd been right to do this. He knew it. Some people had complained it was frivolous, too soon, too dangerous. But a month earlier, two men had come into his office to demand the mayor's help in settling a business dispute. They'd been quarreling over the ownership of a piece of land near the orphanage and during their negotiations three bystanders had been shot dead, including a pregnant woman. But the men hadn't even mentioned the victims. They just wanted Tarzan to decide who owed what to whom. He had sat there, listening to them whine, feeling the anger rising in him like a wave, and realizing that this was like a virus infecting the whole city—that people had lost all understanding of the value of a life. He had to show them another way.

Tarzan slipped away from the festival just before noon. He'd received a worrying call on his mobile phone, and he told Fanah to get him and his convoy to the AMISOM compound by the airport as fast as possible. He wasn't exactly sure what was being planned, but he needed to talk to the Ugandan commanders to make sure their troops were ready to intervene.

Bah. Bah. Ba-ba. Tarzan was already on the road when he heard the gunfire starting up. He could tell where the noise was coming from, and he gritted his teeth with a sense of dread.

He asked Fanah to turn their vehicle around, but by the time the convoy got back to the festival, it was nearly all over.

The crowds had vanished. A few plastic chairs lay overturned in the dust. At the far end, near the national theater, two pickup trucks full of soldiers were swerving, then reversing, still trying to work out if there was any more incoming fire to deal with. Out in the open, the body of the bandleader, Abdirizak Osoble, lay in the dirt, with his hat upturned by his side, his swagger stick nowhere to be seen. Blood caked his white uniform and epaulets. There was still the occasional burst of gunfire, but someone was already busy trying to tuck one of the festival banners over him. The wind kept tugging it away.

In all, four civilians died in the attack, and a dozen were injured. Tarzan knew who was to blame. And it wasn't Al Shabab.

⚜

A FEW YEARS BACK, Mohamed Dheere had briefly been Mogadishu's mayor. But the title meant even less in those days, and most people already knew him as something else. A warlord. He was a tall man with a bulky figure that didn't seem quite his own and sleepy eyes that still managed to convey a vague sense of threat. Dheere— the nickname means "tall"—came from the Abgal clan, another powerful branch of the Hawiye. He had his own private army of perhaps four hundred men, the occasional financial support of the CIA, and had earned a reputation as a man with no tolerance for Islamists. He also seemed to loathe the new upstart mayor.

It didn't take long to join the dots. The warning call before the attack had mentioned Dheere, and the security forces recognized his gunmen. Within hours the whole city seemed to know. But would anyone dare to arrest Dheere and his men?

Tarzan charged into the president's office and threatened to resign on the spot if nothing were done.

"The government should have a monopoly on violence," he insisted. Dheere should not be considered "untouchable." This was a chance to send a message to all the warlords that change was coming.

Two days later, after much haggling and several false starts, Dheere and four members of his militia were indeed arrested. A photograph was released to the public showing Dheere with his wrists bound in front of him with a plastic cord. It felt like a big moment for Mogadishu, as if the whole city had passed some sort of test.

In reality, it was nothing of the sort.

I met Dheere a few months later, soon after his release from prison. He'd been detained for forty days until a judge ruled there was no evidence against him.

Three armed guards peered down from their watchtowers above a long gray wall as I hammered at a giant metal gate. Another man, with an AK-47 slung casually over his right shoulder, finally opened a small door within the gate and beckoned me in with a cursory nod. It certainly felt like a prison. But in fact it was Mohamed Dheere's house—a large, gloomy villa near the old Russian embassy in the center of Mogadishu. Four more guards sat in the courtyard in some shade and looked up to glare at me as I walked toward the front door.

"It was justice. And fair," Dheere told me, running a large, weary hand over his chin and mustache. He did not look well. It was late afternoon, just after siesta time, and he'd been meeting with a group of clan elders in the cavernous hall downstairs. After about half an hour, he climbed a rickety stairway to join me on an upstairs terrace that caught the afternoon breeze.

It was, he declared, all Tarzan's fault.

The new mayor was an Islamic extremist, Dheere insisted. After all, Tarzan used to work as an advisor for the Islamic Courts Union—and half of the ICU went on to join Al Shabab. Besides, he knew the mayor was in conflict with "some other guys" in another clan who were after a position in his administration. So it was clear that the mayor should never have gone ahead with the festival in the first place. The blood was on Tarzan's hands.

More to the point, having been chained up and branded a criminal, his dignity and reputation damaged, Dheere now wanted compensation. It was all about the rules, you see. His big hands began to play with two old mobile phones.

"I'm demanding ten million dollars," he said, holding my eye. "The government must pay."

Three months later, after what was described as a long illness, Dheere died.

"This is a city of sharks," Tarzan said with a grunt of contempt. There had been efforts to bring the two men together, to reconcile. They were the same age. One day Dheere had even turned up at the mayor's office without an invitation. Tarzan promptly got into his convoy and left without meeting him. Rumors circulated suggesting that Dheere was innocent after all, that Tarzan had either staged the attack or pinned the blame on his rival because he saw him as too big a threat. Nothing was ever resolved.

"Mohamed Dheere was jealous of me," says Tarzan. "When he was mayor he did nothing for the city. Then he realized a better person had come. Some people don't want change—they want the chaos to stay."

And the chaos was, indeed, hard to scrape off the streets of Mogadishu. The mayor was like a pinball to be flicked and pushed from one crisis to the next.

LATE ONE FRIDAY AFTERNOON in June 2011, Tarzan was standing on the back of a truck trying to address a crowd of angry protestors. Trying to stop things from getting even more out of hand. He'd been mayor for a year now. There were already tires burning on the street nearby. The transitional government was in crisis. It was always in crisis—a house of cards balancing on the backs of rival clans who seemed preoccupied with carving up the best jobs rather than doing anything with them. And now Farmajo, the new prime minister and a member of former dictator Siad Barre's clan, had been ousted. His supporters were seething.

Standing beside Tarzan on the truck was a man who could almost have been mistaken for his brother. The same features, perhaps slightly better assembled. He was taller than the mayor, and a little more suave, with the same gray beard and mustache and quick, thoughtful eyes.

Abdishakur Sheikh Hassan Farah had grown up in the orphanage, too, but a couple of years below Tarzan. They were friends now, but back then Tarzan had always thought of him as the crybaby in his dormitory.

"If you hit him, he'd always cry and run after you going, 'haaah . . . haaah,' all the time, so you don't even like to beat him."

They nicknamed him "Af-qalooc"—crooked mouth.

Abdishakur had become a successful businessman in Dubai. He had no experience in politics, but his clan had called him back to take up "their" post of interior minister. And he turned out to be unexpectedly good at it. Honest, competent, tough, and, it seemed, not overtly biased toward his clan. He, Tarzan, and Ali Madobe, who'd become chief of police, felt that the security of Mogadishu now lay in their hands.

"We three—we are all orphans. If we cannot make this city safe, no one will be blamed but us," Tarzan told them over lunch.

But now the city was in uproar. Demonstrators had tried to storm at least two of the hotels where Somali government officials and members of parliament were staying. Guards had shot into the crowds.

The death toll was rising and the fate of the transitional government seemed uncertain. Abdishakur and Tarzan finished their impromptu speeches, clambered down from the back of the truck, got into their respective convoys, and went their separate ways.

About an hour later, Tarzan called Abdishakur on the phone to get an update on the security situation. The minister was at home. They talked for a while, but as they were speaking, Tarzan heard someone else come into the room to greet Abdishakur.

"Salam Alaikum." Peace be with you. Tarzan heard his friend greet the visitor, and so he said a quick goodbye into the phone and hung up.

It must have been another half an hour before he heard the news.

For the last few weeks one of Abdishakur's teenaged relatives—a cousin's daughter, but they all thought of her as a niece—had been staying at his heavily guarded home. Haboon wanted to study medicine abroad, and her uncle was trying to help arrange it as a favor to her father, who was working in Dubai. The minister's guards were always strict about searching everyone who came to see him. Even relatives. After all, five transitional government ministers had already been killed. But they saw Haboon every day, and they began to relax.

"It was a lady who exploded," said the voice on the phone.

Tarzan listened in horror. At first, the news was confusing. Someone said Abdishakur was still alive, that he was even talking. Another friend called to say he'd been taken to the Medina Hospital. No, he was at the Banadir Hospital. Within an hour, it was confirmed that he'd died of his injuries.

How, and when, did Al Shabab recruit Haboon? Was it easy to convince her to turn her back on everything she'd been raised to believe? To kill her own relative? Was she threatened? Did she hesitate? Her family has chosen to remain silent. All we're left with is the image of a teenaged girl, climbing the stairs, a bomb hidden under her robes, intent on squandering two lives.

"It hurts me. It really hurts me," says Tarzan now. "It affected me really, psychologically, more than any other death."

It's a rare admission, and of course it doesn't last long. He won't go into details, and when I ask him if Abdishakur's death made him more nervous about his own security, the door slams shut.

"A death like that? It will be great if I die like that."

His brother Yusuf was visiting Mogadishu at around the same time and saw the sorrow, rigid on Tarzan's face.

"I don't remember him grieving about any other death like that," he remembers.

By now, anyone living in Mogadishu was familiar with all manner of atrocities. But this killing felt different. The use of such a close relative. And one so young. Inevitably, perhaps, some people reacted by making jokes. They would laugh if a relative approached and say, "Don't come near! I don't want you to blow me up!"

"Black humor." Yusuf shrugs. "It's a way of coping, of dealing with it."

But the minister's death was another grim milestone. Chillingly intimate in its execution, it changed people's behavior in their own homes. And in a city of raw nerves, it incubated a whole new set of suspicions.

Wild Dogs

"What I see, I speak. I don't hide it."

—MOHAMUD "TARZAN" NUR

IT MUST HAVE BEEN A mortar. I woke with a start to the sound of windows rattling. A few seconds later I heard a heavy thud from the northern edges of Mogadishu. Now I was wide awake, lying on an old mattress beneath my mosquito net and contemplating the three disconcertingly fresh-looking bullet holes in the wall above my bed.

It was eleven at night, and less than a month since the minister had been blown up by his niece.

A few days earlier, a famine had been declared in two regions in southern Somalia. The experts had been warning for months that this might happen. The annual Gu rains had failed again, and much of the country had now been bone-dry for more than two years.

Already, tens of thousands of desperate families were on the move, trudging either west toward the long, straight Kenyan border or east toward the coast, and Mogadishu.

Outside my window, the generators had finally been switched off and the city seemed to lie, sprawled and expectant, in the darkness. There was a rattle of automatic fire just a few streets away, and my mind stretched out for a reassuring explanation. A teenager showing off to friends, perhaps. Or a sleepy guard, startled by shadows.

For the first time in several years, I was staying outside the giant UN and African Union compound on the beach beside Mogadishu's airport, with its high fences, watchtowers, reinforced bunkers, sirens, and endless green sandbagged walls. Being "embedded" within a

Armed escort, Mogadishu, 2011. COURTESY OF THE AUTHOR

huge, highly bureaucratic fortress offered—or appeared to offer—
better protection for visiting journalists but far less access to the city.
And so, in order to get a closer look at the famine, I'd made hurried
arrangements with a well-connected local charity known as Saacid,
which means "to help" in Somali.

"Don't worry," said the wiry, confident young man who'd greeted
me in the cavernous old arrivals hall at the airport that morning. "We
will keep you safe."

Bashir Mahmoud ran Saacid's food program in Mogadishu,
which, he told me, involved distributing eighty thousand meals a day
to all sixteen districts in the city, including those still controlled by Al
Shabab.

The job required a steady nerve and impeccable contacts.

"It's difficult, but possible," Bashir said with a grin, climbing into
the front passenger seat. He pulled out his phone and called ahead to
alert the eight guards waiting for us in another pickup outside the airport entrance. We drove together up the hill toward the K4 roundabout, and as we swung right toward the narrow gates of a small
hotel, I looked through the tinted glass and saw a crowd of perhaps
thirty people squatting forlornly in the dust outside.

"New arrivals," said Bashir.

The gates squealed shut behind us and shouting immediately
erupted in the hotel courtyard. Some sort of argument between security guards—ours and the hotel's. Within seconds, two men were
pointing guns at each other's heads. More shouting. Then they both
seemed to reconsider, turning nonchalantly away as if nothing had
happened. Just another squall. As we finished unloading the car and
walked inside, Tarzan's phrase jangled in my head—"city of sharks."

The famine itself was on its way to Mogadishu. The new arrivals
on the roadside in front of the hotel were part of a far larger influx—
thousands heading to the city in search of food and water. But the city
was in no shape to help everyone. Within days, it would be official.
Mogadishu and two nearby regions would also be declared famine
zones.

The weather was part of the problem. But droughts alone do not cause famine. It requires human intervention of the most stubborn and callous sort to push a population over the brink. And it was no coincidence that by far the worst-affected regions were firmly under the control of Al Shabab.

Later that day, Bashir took me to a makeshift camp on the southern edge of the city. A place called Badbaado, or Camp Salvation. Thirty thousand people were already crowded inside the flimsiest homemade tents—scraps of cloth and cardboard crudely stitched together. Outside the emergency feeding station, a queue of women waited in the sun, their thin shadows swaying on the side of an old shipping container. One woman was holding silent, fly-covered twins in her arms and was eventually nudged to the front of the line, where the infants—paper-thin skin stretched tight over jutting bones—were carefully lowered into a sling to be weighed.

A few days earlier, I'd seen similar scenes in Dadaab—the cluster of vast refugee camps over the border inside Kenya. More than a thousand new arrivals were turning up there each day. They were ushered into long lines, marked out by sticks and strips of tape, in the blazing sun, and told to wait to be processed. It felt industrial. Like some giant sheep dip. And what struck me there was the same silence I noticed in Mogadishu. The silence of tough, resilient people with no sense of entitlement and no expectation of help. Some of them had arrived by truck, clutching a few possessions. Others had walked for weeks.

When I think of Dadaab now, the first image that comes to mind is not of dying children, or a tearful Kenyan nurse struggling to find a baby's vein into which she might connect a saline drip, but rather of the drive we made one morning, up toward the Somali border. We'd been traveling for nearly an hour on a rutted track that meandered through a sandy, desolate wilderness when I glanced into the wing mirror and saw the dogs.

There were twelve of them. African wild dogs—a distinct, rare, endangered species of carnivorous pack hunters, with mottled brown, white, and red coats, sharp teeth, and big, rounded ears.

They jogged confidently behind our car, ears alert, long front legs biting into the sand in a steady gait that seemed to require no effort. Like hyenas.

It was mesmerizing.

And for the five minutes or so that it lasted, I couldn't shake the sense that this was more than simple curiosity—that we were the prey, that the dogs had done this sort of thing before, patiently stalking other groups that had dared to cross through their barren territory, waiting for the weakest to fall behind.

⁕⁑⁂

I THOUGHT OF THE African wild dogs a few days later, in Mogadishu's Camp Salvation, as I tried to speak to some of the new arrivals.

There seemed to be gunmen everywhere—a bristling, bewildering assortment of militias, our own security, police, and soldiers. Five men squatted in the shade of an acacia tree, weapons balanced on their knees. Another group started shouting at the women in the queue—the line wasn't straight enough for them. A truck arrived and the soldiers onboard stared with raw, undisguised interest at a new tent beside the feeding station, where donations of food and other supplies had been stacked.

Before long, Bashir's antennae began to twitch with alarm. "Too many guns. Time to go," he said, and we got back in our car to leave.

It was clear from those families I'd managed to speak with that almost everyone in the camp had come from territory controlled by Al Shabab. It had been the same in Dadaab. I remembered my trip to Buale and the Al Shabab commander I'd met with his pet dik-dik.

The declaration of famine seemed to have caught the militants off guard. They tried to play it down. They called it a test from God. They harassed and killed aid workers and continued to ban or obstruct most foreign aid organizations. They asked for help from fellow Muslims. They tried, aggressively, to prevent civilians from fleeing. They insisted that, God willing, the rains would soon come and all would be well.

But before long, an exodus was under way.

I thought of the dogs again when I spoke to a couple of government officials in Mogadishu that week. They couldn't say it on the record, but in truth, they couldn't believe their luck. The famine, they whispered cheerfully, was "an opportunity," even "a blessing." Not only was it discrediting Al Shabab, but it was luring away their civilian populations—the militants' source of new recruits and income—and bringing them over to government territory. And that, in turn, would force the outside world to pump more aid into places like Mogadishu, into the government's hands.

I felt a jolt of outrage at the cynicism of it all. But I shouldn't have been surprised. It was, in a sense, just business as usual—a struggle for power and resources in a land without rules. The starving civilians flooding into Mogadishu were simply a new set of props to be herded into place by the men with guns.

⁂

TARZAN WAS ABROAD WHEN the famine was declared, and he rushed back to Mogadishu a few days later.

It was the windy season, the Hagaa, when the monsoon winds stir the Indian Ocean clockwise, bringing cooler waters up the coast of Somalia from the south, whipping sand across the parched countryside, and, sometimes, nudging a few rain clouds toward Mogadishu.

One morning soon after his return, Tarzan went to visit some of the new arrivals camped out in the skeleton-like ruins of the old cathedral. Human turds floated in the middle of the giant puddles. A woman sat in the entrance of her homemade tent, cradling a sickly child on her lap and trying, with her free hand, to relight a tiny clay cooking stove.

It had been raining heavily in the city for the past hour. Already, the low-lying areas near the coast were starting to flood. Imagine it. The irony of a flood in the middle of a famine was lost on no one.

Tarzan looked up at the cathedral. The corner of its one remaining tower—now just a few blocks balanced on top of one another—still jutted, improbably, into the sky. The roof was gone, and large chunks of white stone littered the ground. But the nave was more or less intact—a procession of elegant columns and arches leading into the gloom, and the air was cooler inside. The scuffing footsteps of Tarzan's armed guards echoed quietly across the stone floor.

"This is a disaster," Tarzan thought. "I won't allow it."

Over the past fortnight, hundreds of families had set up camp in the neighborhood. The only available space was in the ruins and in the cathedral's grounds. The familiar makeshift tents were packed tightly together here. There were no toilets, no clean water, and precious little food. A group of young boys chased each other through the mud. A cholera outbreak seemed almost inevitable.

Tarzan describes all this to me in a fierce torrent of indignation. When he remembers the children "playing in an open space with floating human feces," his eyes glisten with tears.

In the fight against the famine in Mogadishu, the mayor describes himself as being at the center of the whirlwind, a frenzy of activity, an organizer—demanding land on the edge of the city, setting up camps for the displaced, begging the public for donations, bullying local truck drivers into transporting thousands of families out of the city and into the camps. And all the time, fighting against the petty clan interests of his critics, against the rumors that he was only helping his own clan, and against an incompetent central government that promised help but contributed almost nothing.

"The government appointed five ministers to deal with the famine. Five ministers! They promised half a million dollars for the camp, but never paid. Their dignitaries all came there to take credit, to have their photos taken. The military were nearby but they're always thugs. They rape at night."

Tarzan doles the blame out like a generous orderly at a soup kitchen confronted with a long queue. It is the politician in him, and it fits a pattern. He often struggles to volunteer praise for anyone but himself.

"What I see, I speak. I don't hide it."

⁂

ONE AFTERNOON, TARZAN DECIDED to make an unannounced visit to one of Saacid's food distribution points—a makeshift kitchen perhaps a mile north of the K4 roundabout and close to the frontlines. Stew and rice were being cooked in large, dark, steaming pots. Three dogs sat in the dirt nearby, as if considering their strategy.

Saacid's operation seemed remarkable. I'd already visited some of the kitchens with Bashir. Here was a Somali charity that was doing something concrete, taking some of the vast stockpiles of UN food, milling the grain, cooking meals, and delivering them across the city.

But Tarzan was less impressed. The food being served was, he declared, "not fit for dogs." More to the point, he claimed, it was all a scam—that in reality the food was being quietly sold off as animal feed, and the grain was ending up openly on sale in the city's markets, still in its original World Food Programme bags.

Tarzan had clashed with Saacid before, accusing them of corruption over a contract to clear rubbish from the city's streets. Then, as now, the organization vigorously protested its innocence. I found myself siding with Bashir. Could it really be possible, as another well-placed source later told me, that 80 percent of the food aid they were supposed to be distributing in Mogadishu was actually being stolen?

I was ready to believe that corners were being cut, commanders and warlords paid off, in order to get the food to the needy. But surely that was just the price of getting things done, of cutting through the red tape and ending the famine?

Then again, I was in a difficult position to judge. I liked Bashir, and perhaps more to the point, I was depending on him and his guards to keep me alive.

This was Mogadishu, after all. And as the drought continued, it became increasingly clear that it wasn't just the politicians who were viewing the famine as an "opportunity."

There were the militias, of course, who prowled around Camp Salvation, looking for unguarded, or poorly guarded, food convoys. There were riots, gunfights, and deaths. But there were also far more sophisticated scams by businessmen who took advantage, as they'd always done, of a weak government and an international community still trying to organize things at arm's length, from Kenya.

"Bogus camps! Everywhere!" Tarzan fumes again. He'd inspected half a dozen around Mogadishu. "No fires in the huts, nobody used the latrines. No trace of life. Bogus!" And to maintain the illusion of credibility—at least when the camps were being evaluated—genuine famine victims were shunted around at gunpoint to sit, and queue, and be counted. Like hostages.

The United Nations Security Council commissioned its own investigations, which concluded much the same, and worse. Some serious allegations were leveled against Saacid. Again, it defended its actions vigorously. But it was not alone in facing criticism. From the moment foreign aid arrived at Mogadishu's port, it was, the UN experts concluded, being siphoned off, illegally taxed, and distributed to local groups that went to enormous—you could almost say impressive—lengths to manipulate the entire process and hide their deceit.

"A pretty sick society, basically," one of Tarzan's deputies summed it up with a sad shrug.

⁂

THERE IS NO DOUBT that the famine exposed Somalia's faults and failures more starkly than perhaps anything else since the country's collapse two decades earlier. By some estimates, it killed more than a quarter of a million people, most of them children.

But the Somalis were not the only ones to blame. The outside world was too slow, and too political, in its response. The UN, understandably concerned about safety, kept its staff in Nairobi, Kenya, and let smaller local organizations like Saacid to do much of the hard work.

Then there were the Americans, with what many felt was a fastidious, squeamish, legalistic, immoral obsession with ensuring not a single drop of outside help—no bags of grain, no tents, no emergency rations—fell into the hands of Al Shabab.

But imposing such strict rules on the aid operation seemed, at best, impractically naive. Many considered it an act of monstrous cynicism. Surely, the best thing to do was to relax the rules, focus on the needs, and flood the whole place with cash and grain in order to bring the prices down and save lives. But the Americans were the biggest donors, and many foreign aid organizations privately, and sometimes publicly, fumed that Washington was proving to be an even bigger obstacle to fighting the famine than the Islamists.

⁂

AND THEN, IN THE middle of the famine, the entire equation in Mogadishu changed.

Sometime after midnight, on August 6, 2011, Tarzan's mobile phone rang by his bedside at the Nasa Hablod 2 hotel, rousing him from a deep sleep. He listened, grunted, turned over, and thought nothing more of it. Another rumor. Wishful thinking.

The rumor had been brought to life a few hours earlier by some soldiers on the frontlines. Sentry after sentry began reporting the same thing. No one was returning fire anymore or even answering them when they shouted out in the dark. No insults, no entreaties. It took a while to piece together all the information across the city, and longer still for a few soldiers to edge forward and make sure. But before the sun had even appeared above the rim of the Indian Ocean the following morning, all doubt had vanished.

Quickly, and without warning or fanfare, Al Shabab had pulled

out of Mogadishu, its fighters slipping away from the frontlines overnight, quietly abandoning the ruins and trenches and tunnels that
they'd held onto with such furious determination. The group's admin-
istrators, commanders, and tax collectors had likewise disappeared—
either leaving the city or melting into it.

Several people in the nearby market town of Afgoye, further
inland, had peered out of their windows during the night to see the
convoys race past—trucks packed with fighters and smaller pickups
with blacked-out windows—heading into the vast countryside of
southern Somalia where Al Shabab still held sway.

Tarzan rose early the next morning, called Fanah to get him to
bring his guards and convoy around to the hotel, and was soon driving
north through the city, crossing the old frontlines and heading into
districts and suburbs that were suddenly his to administer. He needed
to see this for himself. But he also felt the politician's instinct to
introduce himself to the rest of the city's population, to reassure them,
to give them a taste of his own confidence.

His mind was racing. He'd been mayor of Mogadishu for more
than a year now, but until that morning, peering through the tinted
glass in the backseat of his own armored convoy as he sped from one
district to the next, it hadn't felt real. He'd been trying to survive, not
to govern.

Not that the population was exactly celebrating yet.

In the claustrophobic, dusty streets of the giant Bakara market—
for years the financial stronghold of Al Shabab—the small stallhold-
ers and the wealthier businessmen with their mobile phone shops,
money exchanges, and electrical goods stores quietly sipped their tea
and wondered who would fill this strange power vacuum. A warlord,
perhaps? Or the feeble government? How soon would Al Shabab be
back with its suicide attacks and roadside bombs? How many spies had
they left behind? And more to the point, would business prosper or
suffer even more now that the stern Islamists had gone and the old
ways—of clan and corruption—seemed poised to return?

Twenty years of disappointment had bred a wariness that could not simply be shrugged off.

Still, in some neighborhoods, crowds did gather behind high walls, in courtyards and in local government offices, to welcome the militants' departure, and to listen to an increasingly hoarse but energized Tarzan.

"This is your victory," he shouted. It wasn't just the African troops, the Ugandans and Burundians with their guns and mortars. It was the public who had rejected Al Shabab's evil ideology. "You made this possible."

It was good to hear it said. Maybe there was even a hint of truth to it—in recent months more businesses had been lured across the frontlines to Tarzan's side of the city, reducing Al Shabab's opportunity for raising funds through taxation.

But the simpler fact was that, in Mogadishu, Al Shabab had bitten off more than it could chew. Militarily, it was, at heart, a guerrilla organization. But somehow it had allowed itself to get lured into fighting—and funding—a conventional war, holding and administering half of Somalia's biggest city. And it was struggling. Its enemy had international backing and far more troops and ammunition. Al Shabab could always buy more weaponry from corrupt government sources, but it had been losing too many men on the battlefield. More importantly, internal rifts were threatening to tear the militant group apart. Besides, there were other frontlines to protect against new factions, warlords, and self-declared administrations, which were starting to chip away at the edges of Al Shabab's territory in other parts of southern Somalia. And although the organization had recently sworn allegiance to Al Qaeda, there was evidence that some of the group's foreign fighters were now drifting away to new, more tempting conflicts in places like Libya and Syria.

And, of course, there was the famine, which imposed new financial burdens and constraints on Al Shabab and its revenues. Something had to give. And Mogadishu was the obvious choice.

THE CHALLENGE NOW, FOR Tarzan and for Somalia's government, was to prove that they were a better alternative, that Al Shabab's departure was a blessing that would not be squandered.

Leaving Mogadishu, I remember driving to the airport and swinging, counterclockwise, around the K4 roundabout. Something began fluttering beneath my rib cage, and I found myself shrinking back into my seat, as if that would make me safer. The roundabout always had that effect. It was a choke point. Everything slowed down at K4, as trucks and cows and carts and armed convoys and motorbikes tried to push their way through the traffic, jostling for access to one of the dusty, beyond-potholed roads leading either east into the city center, south to the airport, north toward the old frontlines, or west toward Afgoye.

Inevitably, it had become a favorite target for Al Shabab, and for all the other political assassinations and revenge attacks and score-settling that were invariably blamed on the Islamists, too. Black stains on the roundabout's hard-worn tarmac still marked out a couple of the more spectacular explosions. There would be many more in the years ahead. But the wreckage would always be dragged away within an hour or so—there was no sense in making K4's traffic wait even longer.

As our guards leapt off the pickup in front of us, waving furiously at a man sitting on a homemade cart, with two car wheels beneath him and an indifferent donkey in front, I leaned forward for a moment and looked through the darkly tinted window.

Coming up the airport road was a small convoy of white trucks. I could just make out a bright red flag with a white star and crescent on the front vehicle. It was the Turks.

Turkey—ambitious, business-minded, and Muslim—was poised to shake up, and to shame, the international aid effort for Somalia by abruptly striding into the country as if no threat existed, as if other foreign aid agencies had been cowering beneath the emperor's new clothes. It was the start of a dramatic humanitarian intervention, and slowly, it would help to change the way the outside world perceived Mogadishu. With hundreds of Turks working and living in the city, it would become a lot harder for diplomats and aid workers to justify living in Nairobi and flying in for a few hours.

Suddenly there was a piercing, unfamiliar noise outside the car window.

Fffwoooeeeeeeeef.

It wasn't a car horn. As we nudged forward, past the donkey and around the big concrete block in the center of the roundabout, I saw where it was coming from. Wading into the traffic, in a clean white shirt and beret, was a traffic policeman.

It seemed absurd. Unthinkable. Ordinarily I'd have jumped out to talk to him, but we had a plane to catch and security was an issue. So we drove on. But I can picture him now, through the rear window.

The famine wasn't over. Al Shabab remained an existential threat. But here was a middle-aged man—someone who must have been able to remember how smoothly this roundabout had functioned two decades ago—charging out into the chaos, waving his arms at the traffic, convinced that in this city of brandished guns and quick tempers, the time had come for someone to try their luck with a whistle.

Believe Me

"Mogadishu's bangin', man!"

—HASSAN MOHAMED

I T FELT GOOD TO BE bored.

I was sitting in the back corner of the mayor's office, stifling a yawn and wallowing in the sheer ordinariness of what was going on around a long, varnished wooden table that took up almost the entire room.

Six men were squeezed along each side, talking, in turn, in measured tones. At the head, behind his own desk, which was pressed up tight against the top edge of the long table, like a rather cramped wedding banquet, sat Tarzan. He was wearing an open-necked pink shirt and seemed to have put on a little weight. He looked supremely relaxed.

"Just two hundred dollars?" he asked the men, with just a hint of incredulity. "Even the biggest companies, the telecom companies, they should pay the same?"

A gray-haired man coughed and explained that yes, that was "global practice," that "everyone" did it like that. The others nodded. They were businessmen, representatives of Mogadishu's Chamber of Commerce, and the topic under discussion was a plan to begin licensing the city's businesses—a necessary step toward reviving a formal tax system that would, for the first time in two decades, involve giving money to the local administration rather than paying protection to the men with guns.

"We must collect taxes to build the nation," said Tarzan, a touch pompously. I wondered whether he was talking, at least in part, for my benefit, offering up a sound bite for a wider audience.

Fisherman carrying shark, Mogadishu, 2015. COURTESY OF BECKY LIPSCOMBE

"For now we depend on outside help, but with the business community's support we can fund our own basic services," he declared. More slow nods around the table.

Tarzan's program manager, a relentlessly upbeat young returnee from Texas, Abdirashid Salah, had kindly offered to translate for me, whispering in my ear over the wheezing drone of the room's solitary, ancient air conditioner. He'd left Mogadishu in 1992, finding his way to the United States via Kenya and South Africa.

I'd heard stories of official translators trying, patriotically, to clean up the language of the various thugs and warlords who sometimes gathered and swore and threatened around the mayor's table. No topic was too small to trigger a row. On one occasion, the city's sixteen district commissioners had all assembled for a meeting, only for three of them to break off into a fierce, seemingly dangerous squabble over the biscuits. There were not enough to go around.

Before the year was over, two of the Chamber of Commerce's senior officials sitting at the table would be murdered, presumably by Al Shabab. But today was all smiles and humdrum negotiations. Abdirashid whispered something to me about a deal involving five different categories for licensing, and then he fell silent. I could tell he wasn't leaving out any swear words; he was just trying to spare me the boring bits.

And it seemed to me, in that instant, that humdrum was a pretty good milestone for Mogadishu, a sign of progress and of something close to normality in a city that had once forgotten the meaning of the word.

Tarzan stood up wordlessly and disappeared behind a large curtain that appeared to lead into a separate office beside his desk. The conversation at the table stopped. He emerged a few minutes later and sat down again as if nothing had happened. He did the same thing several times over the next hour, and—although he later explained that he either went to pray, to discuss something with an aide, or to relieve himself—it struck me as an overtly theatrical flourish. It was the behavior of a man who was aware of the power he now exercised and was more than comfortable in displaying it.

The Chamber of Commerce delegation left. Next up was a group of women who wanted to organize another festival, to mark the first anniversary of Al Shabab's withdrawal from the city.

"Agreed."

"Next?"

At about noon, Tarzan went behind the curtain, returned almost instantly, and came over to greet me. We walked out together, through a tiny reception room packed with more officials and civilians clamoring for a few moments of the mayor's time, past a middle-aged guard seated at the entrance to the building who was carefully rearranging a giant bandolier of bullets around his neck like an actress with a mink stole, and outside to Fanah, Tarzan's cousin, who was standing in impenetrable silence, as usual, beside his car.

"I want you to meet a friend," Tarzan said to me with a grin, as we got into the backseat.

⁂

WE SPED THROUGH THE narrow dirt lanes of Hamar Weyne with seven armed guards in the "technical" battlewagon ahead of us—one guard manning a huge anti-aircraft gun on a tripod, pointing over the driver's cabin—and ten more in the pickup behind, a jumble of legs hanging over the sides.

"More guns these days?" I asked.

"We don't want anyone to intimidate us," Tarzan said with another big smile. He had recently begun carrying his own gun. A small black pistol.

"Belgian, I think," he said.

Someone—presumably Al Shabab—had tried to blow up his car with a roadside bomb a few months earlier, but by chance he'd just been dropped off at home. The explosion was weak and had only lightly injured the driver. There also had been a separate hotel attack, again just after he'd left.

We turned a corner and passed a huge, whitewashed building.

"The mall," said Tarzan. "It's been unused for twenty-one years. We're trying to rehabilitate it."

He was talking fast now, pointing out old landmarks amid the rubble and confidently rattling off plans and projects. He pointed to the new drain covers by the side of a freshly tarmacked road and then gestured toward some new streetlights.

"This is a big change. Believe me."

For months, Tarzan had been trying to bully local businesses into providing lighting for some of the city's dark, dangerous roads in order to improve security and lengthen trading hours. But he wasn't having

Tarzan clearing garbage, Mogadishu, 2011. COURTESY OF ABDIRASHID SALAH

much success. Now, though, Norway and Britain were funding a new scheme to put solar-powered lights along all of Mogadishu's main arteries. And the first results were already transformational.

Some nights, the main road from K4 to the parliament would be clogged with children, from end to end, in a succession of floodlit, impromptu, five-a-side football matches. Girls as well as boys. It was a message to Al Shabab—we are taking our city back. Mogadishu had seen nothing like it since the time of Siad Barre, and the spectacle was enough to make some people weep. This was what Tarzan meant when he talked about changing people's mentality, repairing the psychological damage of war.

It wasn't just the European donors who had taken a shine to Tarzan. The Americans, the Turks, everyone seemed to be knocking on the mayor's door these days, now that the city was united under one administration.

He offered something tangible. Or at least he seemed to. Instead of red tape and backhanders, Tarzan, with his boundless energy, offered an open door and quick results.

And speed was essential.

A more experienced administrator might have taken things slowly, building up the city's institutional capacity, strengthening the bureaucracy—and indeed there would be a time for that in the years ahead. But Tarzan seemed gripped by a furious sense of urgency, by the need to behave, you could say, like an army surgeon rather than a physiotherapist.

"Time is running out. We have to build people's confidence. We have to provide services. The day people ask, 'What's the difference between the government and Al Shabab?' That day we are dead."

And so Tarzan let the Norwegians arrange the streetlights. He let the Turks fix the roads. He bypassed what he still considered the hopelessly inept bureaucracy of the UN. He was a facilitator, a catalyst, a hustler, a symbol. And if that meant he shamelessly took the credit for other people's work and investment, so much the better. After all, people needed to believe in him. That was part of the plan.

TARZAN WAS BUSY SCOFFING at several government ministers—at their pathetic work ethic, at their long lunch breaks, at the pitiful way they begged foreign donors for minor items like office furniture and computers—when the convoy swung to the right, crossed the open patch of ground where the mayor's Peace Festival had come under fire a year and a half earlier, and stopped sharply in front of a small, freshly painted building opposite the national theater.

"This is my friend's restaurant," Tarzan said.

It didn't look like much at first. The Village restaurant was more like a shack, squeezed onto a patch of ground between the main road and a large, refurbished office block, with an open kitchen beneath a bright green corrugated roof and a dozen plastic tables on the curb outside.

I'd heard the place was more popular toward dusk, when the ocean breeze began nudging aside the day's heat. But today a dozen men and a handful of women were sitting at tables in the shade of a big tree, sipping cappuccinos and waiting for lunch to arrive.

Ahmed Jama walked out from his kitchen and ushered us toward a table. He was a bald, scrawny forty-six-year-old, with a beak-like nose and an earnest, gentle manner. His politeness seemed like a rebuke, or a challenge, to the city around him. He reminded me of the British-Somali athlete Mo Farah, who was poised to win the 5,000 meters at the 2012 London Olympics a couple of days later.

"Tea, coffee, some lunch? We got barbequed shark, some lovely stews, grilled lamb, spaghetti?" Ahmed spoke quietly, with a thick London accent.

I noticed some fresh-looking scars and burn marks on his face. He followed my eyes and gestured with a nod, across the road, toward the refurbished national theater. Five months earlier he'd attended a ceremony inside. A woman sitting a few rows behind him had detonated a bomb strapped around her waist. Ten people were killed, including Wiish, the basketball referee who had objected so strongly to Oscar

Robertson's dribbling style. Al Shabab was quick to claim responsibility.

"If I'm killed, then I'm killed," Ahmed said with a shrug. I was beginning to see why he and Tarzan were friends.

Ahmed Jama, Mogadishu, 2013. COURTESY OF XAN RICE

Ahmed also came from a poor family and abandoned Mogadishu to find work in the 1980s, before Somalia collapsed. He went to Kenya, Uganda, Sudan, Tanzania, and finally—after saving enough money to buy an air ticket and a false passport—to London. He was given temporary residency in the U.K., got married, stumbled into cooking almost by accident, trained as a chef, and by 2006 had his own Somali restaurant in Hammersmith, catering to an enthusiastic diaspora still eager for a taste of home.

"But then I said to myself, 'One person can change something. I can do something for Somalia.' So I decide to come back here, with my heart, and a clean mind. To be a man of hope.'"

He left his wife and three young children and flew back to Mogadishu. It was a bold, bizarre, and, to my mind, typically Somali decision. Another nomad move. The sort of drastic uprooting that only someone who had thrown his luck to the wind before seemed likely to attempt. And this was in 2008, long before the famine, before Tarzan's return, before Al Shabab had even pushed out the Ethiopian army.

Ahmed started with a coffee shop. Then a restaurant. Then a small hotel. Soon he added another, bigger place called Village Sports, blasting out music and football matches within earshot of Al Shabab's frontline and catering to the growing crowd of diaspora Somalis who were starting to venture back to Mogadishu, testing the water at first, seeing if it was worth coming back for good. Before long, Ahmed was employing more than a hundred people.

"I miss London. I miss my friends. I miss Arsenal. We live by Queens Park Rangers in White City. But I'm an Arsenal fan," he told me, sitting at our table now. But he had no plans to leave Mogadishu. He and Tarzan were gripped by the same sense of mission, of pride, and of purpose.

"We're not coming back here for the money. Me, the mayor, we're looking to change the city, to change the mentality, to show people how we lived abroad as Somalis—not as different clans. To show them a different way of life," Ahmed said, his eyes holding mine.

The flip side of that plan was to convince other Somalis in the diaspora to follow his example. To show them that Mogadishu was on the road to recovery.

"There's a lot of work to be done here. You need patience. Rome wasn't built in a day," Ahmed said.

"So it's time the diaspora came home?"

"Absolutely. And it's happening already. The flights from London are full! Soon it's going to be like Shepherds Bush here," he insisted.

He was talking about the wealthier diaspora, mostly making brief visits from Europe and America. But before long, tens of thousands of poorer Somalis would weigh up the odds and start making the long trek home from their crowded refugee camps in Kenya.

Unlike Tarzan, Ahmed chose not to have any personal security. There were guards outside his restaurants, and the gate to Village Sports already bore the scars of a couple of suicide attacks. He admitted to paying bribes—essentially protection money—to the government security and intelligence services. But he drove himself around the city on his own, unarmed.

"I'm not a politician. I don't have anything against anyone. So even if I see the Shabab, I'll try to show them a different way—to show them how human beings can live together."

He was busy training new chefs and trying to encourage his guests to eat more seafood. Somalis preferred camel or goat meat, but the old fish market had just been reopened down by the lighthouse, and the small boats were bringing in an impressive catch. I went down there one afternoon—the fishermen tended to come ashore around 3 p.m.—and watched, half-hypnotized, as one man carried a large hammerhead shark up from the beach on his head, then threw it down on the dark concrete floor of the market. Three scrawny kittens, and a swarm of flies, immediately gathered by the spreading pool of blood.

A couple of days later, I met Ahmed and his family at Village Sports. He'd finally persuaded his wife, Amina, to come over from London with their boys.

"She's shy," Ahmed said when Amina hurried away. "And she's never been keen about this. She's still not keen. I just kept pushing her, asking her to give me more time. Still, she's here now."

A few weeks later, the Village restaurant was attacked. I was back in Johannesburg and called Ahmed the following morning.

"How are you?" he asked. Even now, he couldn't shake off that instinctive politeness.

"Me? Fine. But you? What happened?"

"There were two suiciders," he said quietly. "It was a bit unexpected."

Ahmed had left the restaurant perhaps ten minutes before it all happened—at around quarter past six the night before. He had some errands to run. One attacker began shooting at the diners outside. As usual, there was a mixed crowd of politicians, journalists, and businessmen sitting at tables by the roadside. The other gunman then ran inside, behind the kitchen, toward a smaller dining area, where he threw a grenade and detonated his suicide belt.

"Five of my staff have been killed. But ask me more questions. It's OK."

In all, fourteen people were killed. Al Shabab claimed responsibility. But perhaps the most remarkable thing about the attack was the way Ahmed responded. The idea of quitting never appeared to have crossed his mind. Almost immediately, he and his colleagues began clearing up the mess.

It was straightforward enough outside, but inside the restaurant, the suicide bomber's remains now coated the walls and ceiling. The team used shovels and trowels, and eventually brooms. Then they began to repaint. It took three, four, sometimes five coats to cover up the blood. A little over a fortnight later, the Village restaurant reopened. Tarzan was there to mark the occasion.

IT SAYS A LOT about Mogadishu that Shamis can't quite remember if she heard about that particular attack. After a while the individual blasts and incidents all seemed to blur into each other.

But the important thing was that Shamis had finally come back to Mogadishu to join Tarzan. She'd tried once before, toward the end of 2011, staying at the Nasa Hablod 2 hotel with him. But she'd hated it. One evening, two mortars had exploded in the courtyard, and the next day she told Tarzan that she wanted "to go home." She meant to London. Her visit had lasted five days.

This time, Tarzan found a house to rent. It was just behind the national theater, up the slope toward the State House, and within earshot of the Village restaurant. There was a big, well-guarded barrier at the bottom of the road, and another at the entrance to their cul-de-sac. They were within the security bubble of the presidential compound—often breached but still much safer than any other options around the city.

Shamis was not back for good. That was never the plan—she had far too many ties to London. All six children were now grown up, but they lived close by, and their lives were still closely entwined.

Abdullahi was finishing his degree and living in the family flat. Ayan had her two daughters to care for and was about to meet and marry an African American truck driver on a visit to Baltimore.

"A lot of people assumed that my dad wouldn't allow it," she tells me with a grin. "And I was like, 'Er, he's not going to care as long as he's a good person—a Muslim, and a good person.' A lot of Somalis are not like that. Somalis tend to be racist within themselves, so marrying a complete outsider . . .'"

"Yeah," Abdullahi chips in, "it's like they won't even marry a Somali from a different tribe. I wouldn't care—any race. It doesn't even have to be a Somali girl."

Through different academic routes, Ayan, Mimi, and Muna had all ended up finding full-time jobs at the nearby Whittington Hospital, Ayan and Mimi in customer care and Muna as a health advisor. After struggling to make ends meet as a fitness coach and community worker, Mohamed was looking to study physiotherapy at a university.

So Shamis was in no mood to abandon Queens Crescent altogether. She would stay in Mogadishu for a few months at a time. That was the agreement.

She talks of it now as a sense of duty. And love. She wanted to be with her husband. But for Tarzan, I wonder if there was an element of politics in it, too. He didn't want to be seen as another diaspora dilettante with one foot in London and a British passport in his back

Shamis and Tarzan. COURTESY OF THE NUR FAMILY

pocket, ready to scarper when the going got tough. Bringing his wife to live in Mogadishu with him was a sign of commitment. They were lucky the children were already grown up.

But Mogadishu held few attractions for Shamis. The shared dangers and drama inherent in everyday life in the city brought them closer together. But they began to argue, too, about how little time he spent with her, about how long he was going to keep doing this; after all, they'd both worked hard for years. Weren't they supposed to be thinking about drifting toward retirement now? Shamis asked. Why didn't he warn her he wanted to be a politician before they married?

She could hardly even leave the house.

"It's not easy. I miss the freedom. I miss taking the bus, going for a walk. So it's tough. Really tough."

The murder of Tarzan's friend, the interior minister, Abdishakur, by his own young niece still weighed heavily on people's minds. One morning soon after she'd arrived, Shamis found herself sitting at an aunt's house and being overwhelmed with panic. Another guest had just arrived. It was a man wearing a thick beard with a shawl over his head.

"Is he Al Shabab?" Shamis hissed when he left the room for a moment.

"Of course not."

"Then why is he dressing like that? Maybe he's gone out to tell someone that I'm here. Maybe they'll kill me when I leave."

Nothing of the sort happened. But still, it was almost impossible not to become paranoid. Most days she just stayed in their house, preparing food and trying not to pick up the phone every few minutes to call Tarzan and check that he was safe.

I CAUGHT UP WITH Shamis again, back in London on one of her trips home. It was a dark winter's evening and she was in the flat, bustling around nervously as she prepared to come out to Somalia again. Her granddaughters—Ayan's children, eight-year-old Malia and five-year-old Maya—were in the sitting room watching *Scooby-Doo*. Her sons, Abdullahi and Mohamed, popped in later to say goodbye and started teasing Shamis about Tarzan, speculating about whether he might take a second wife in Mogadishu.

"He wouldn't dare," Shamis laughed. But she had heard rumors that some families were making inquiries, maybe even nudging younger nieces and sisters forward.

"If he takes another, I will leave. He knows that. I'm not going to be a second wife. Why should I? All these years we live together and he goes and takes another, a small girl? Those people are crazy. Did I do a bad thing? No. And he's not like that, anyway."

"It's not right. I don't want him to," said Abdullahi, turning serious, too.

Mohamed, the family provocateur, shrugged. "It's human nature. But the truth is that Dad's quite shy. And he's too old now."

On my way out, Shamis came to the top of the stairs in the apartment block to say goodbye. It was starting to drizzle on the street outside. She told me she'd lost eleven pounds in the last few weeks. She seemed suddenly coy, like that young girl holding hands with Tarzan in a café in Mogadishu all those years ago.

"I want to be an hourglass figure before I go back to him," she said with a small smile, her hands drifting self-consciously toward her hips.

By then, their oldest son, Ahmed, had already gone out to live in Mogadishu, to make a new start after his divorce. He remarried a local woman almost immediately. Before long, like other diaspora families who shrugged aside the risks in order to reunite with their far-flung relatives, Shamis was making plans to bring Abdullahi and the granddaughters out to visit the following summer.

"It was really fun!" Malia told me in London after that first trip. It was another cold afternoon, and she and Maya were skipping back from school to their granny's flat for tea.

"We went to the beach some days. Lido beach. It's beautiful! We got to collect seashells from the sand." The girls wandered off into the sitting room to watch *The Great British Bake Off*.

"They like it in Mogadishu because they have space," Shamis said. "They live in a small flat here in London, and their downstairs neighbor is always shouting at them to be quiet."

Abdullahi, now a twenty-three-year-old unemployed graduate, found the whole experience of visiting Somalia much more uncomfortable. Everything seemed to amplify his sense of not belonging. Even the language. He spoke Somali, but it was rusty, so he'd get the sentence structure wrong—saying "I'm watching TV," when in Somali it should be "TV I'm watching."

He got spooked the very first time he went out in the car in Mogadishu, with guards, to get an ice cream. Another car was following them and they had to race to get away from it. Luckily nothing happened. But still. A few days later, he was at his parents' house, alone with his nieces, when Al Shabab launched a series of attacks around the city. It sounded like someone was driving down the road throwing out bombs.

Abdullahi tried to talk to guys his age in the neighborhood. But it was like they were on a different wavelength. One day a local man in his late twenties was killed by accident. His friend hadn't realized there was a bullet in the chamber of the gun he was fooling around with. Twenty minutes after it happened, Abdullahi ventured outside.

"Wasn't that your friend?" he asked a group of men standing on the street near the spot where it had happened. The police had just come to take away the body, plus the guy who pulled the trigger. The others were goofing around, laughing, joking. Sure they were upset, they said. But so what? Stuff like that just happens here.

Abdullahi didn't leave the house for a week after that. "It was crazy. Crazy. I swear to God I just slept all day." He felt like he couldn't trust anyone at all—especially those who'd never been abroad. And the stuff about the interior minister's niece—people were still "freaking out" about that.

Toward the end of the holiday, Abdullahi accompanied Tarzan to Villa Somalia for Friday prayers. There was a big crowd. The president was there, and Abdullahi felt both proud of his dad and a little out of his depth. He stood at the back, declining to join his father in his usual prayer spot.

It was only when people started to get up to leave that Abdullahi finally found space on the floor to begin his own prayers. He was standing, focused, about to kneel down, and he began saying "Allahu Akb . . ."

At which point it felt like the entire room jumped on top of him. It was the president's bodyguards. They were all over him. Pinning his arms. One guy had his hand on Abdullahi's throat. And Abdullahi was fighting back. He found himself screaming and swearing at the men—in English, which seemed embarrassing in retrospect. "Fuck you. Fuck you." Stuff like that.

Finally someone who knew him, one of Tarzan's friends, pushed his way to the center of the group and told the guards who Abdullahi was.

"He looks like Al Shabab," one of the guards retorted. "Look at the way he's dressed. Jeans. And he's skinny. And that haircut—short at the sides, long on top—that's how Al Shabab cut their hair."

Abdullahi left Mogadishu soon after that.

A few months later, back in London, he told me about the incident. He could laugh about it now. But what was really interesting was his mother's reaction.

"They nearly killed him that day!" Shamis said, as if it were a big joke.

At first it reminded me of the way many Africans use laughter to cover either fear or embarrassment. But then she started turning it all against Abdullahi, chiding him for staying in the house the whole time in Mogadishu. "He didn't go out! Not at all. He was not brave." And it got more pointed. Shamis compared him to her oldest son, Ahmed, the one they nicknamed "Kill Me" for his casual approach to danger.

"Ahmed is very brave. Like his dad," she said.

"I don't call it brave. I call it stupid," Abdullahi shot back.

It was a strange, awkward moment. Shamis seemed to be behaving out of character. She made me think of some caricature of a patriotic mother, grimly sending her sons out to battle and ridiculing any sign of weakness.

But that was unfair.

I was sitting at a table in the Sir Robert Peel pub, on the corner of Queens Crescent, typing up my notes on a laptop a few hours later, when I remembered something else Shamis had said to me back in Mogadishu. She was talking about the sense of being marooned between two identities, about how she felt like a second-class citizen in both the U.K. and Somalia. Here in London people still picked at her accent, even other immigrants did—she'd had a row with an Egyptian man in the market just the other day. And back in Mogadishu, she was marked out as "diaspora," as someone with a foreign passport.

And I realized that sense of ambivalence must be how she felt about courage, too.

On the one hand, she had to believe in what Tarzan was doing, in the risks he was taking in Mogadishu. And if her sons were prepared to share those risks, then maybe that would help to shore up her own conviction that it was all worthwhile. On the other hand, she was a protective mother of six Londoners, of children who had never even heard a gunshot, had forgotten most of their parent's language, and barely understood Tarzan and Shamis's commitment to their messed-up homeland.

No wonder Shamis sometimes swerved erratically from one extreme to the other.

By now, the mood in Mogadishu was definitely changing. The city was still dangerous, but Tarzan's message of optimism was starting to catch on. He couldn't take all the credit—much as he may have wanted to—but his name was on the lips of many members of the Somali diaspora as they booked their air tickets and began to flood back to take a look.

Some came to visit relatives, or reclaim a property, or to straighten out a troublesome teenager who didn't appreciate how lucky he was living in Toronto, Columbus, Minneapolis, San Diego, Seattle, Stockholm, Nairobi, Bristol, Birmingham, or wherever. Sometimes it was to help—doctors and teachers looking to share the skills they'd learned abroad. And sometimes, it was just to see if there was money to be made in a city on the upswing.

I met dozens of them over the next year or two. The women, often young, were particularly bold and inspiring. An indignant London student who was chased out of Mogadishu within days by an uncle who thought she'd come back to steal his clan's seat in parliament. An irrepressible human rights activist from Dublin who spent her days shaming and haranguing government ministers about their failure to tackle female genital mutilation and rape. A holidaying divorcée from rural North Dakota, eating fresh lobster by the beach and relishing the heat. A teenaged boy from Wembley who was so afraid of Al Shabab he couldn't even say their name, but kept declaring, "Mogadishu's bangin', man!" An estate agent from the English city of Luton with grand plans for a compound of luxury villas in the dunes north of the city.

In fact the estate agent, a man nicknamed Martello, after the Italian for "hammer," later emailed me a letter that his twelve-year-old son, Akram, had written to his teacher, back home in Luton, after spending the summer holiday with his father.

"Dear Ms Raffee," he wrote, "Somalia is a very different place now. I went to the beach several times and play football with my friends. The threat and influence of Al Shabab is very minimal, although they are still out there. A new government is in place now, although it is very weak and broke. With my dad I met with the mayor of Mogadishu, who allowed me to sit on his chair in front of his senior officers even though he doesn't allow anyone else to do so. He told everyone in the room that I will be a future mayor of this city. I hope you will come and visit us to see the beautiful beaches and the education system here. My dad will provide you with accommodation and security during your stay."

The diaspora's stubborn, defiant optimism seemed unshakeable.

ONE MORNING IN MAY 2013, I arranged to visit a grand, sturdy villa just a few blocks inland from the old lighthouse and the fish market. It was built by the Italians in 1919 and had recently been patched up and painted in the blue and white colors of the Somali flag. It looked wonderful and entirely out of context, surrounded by ruins, like a wedding cake in a butcher's shop. I walked up the cracked marble steps, pushed open a huge wooden door, and entered a cool, dark atrium.

I was there to correct something.

Journalists tend to be drawn toward conflict in places like Somalia. It makes for the strongest headlines, the most dramatic stories, and easily the best pictures. Besides, it's often just plain hard, and wrong, to ignore that sort of stuff. But after years of seeing their country labeled as a "failed state," Somalis were getting tired of people like me focusing, exclusively it seemed, on the negatives. What about the "iceberg of normality," that the foreign minister had told me about when I first met him and Tarzan in Villa Somalia three years earlier?

The Somali Central Bank was that iceberg. Or at least a symbol of it.

The building and its contents represented everything the outside world had ignored about the country for two decades—the ingenuity, the resilience, and the resourcefulness of a nation whose economy had somehow managed not only to weather the endless storms but even to thrive. It seemed impossible, but the statistics were beyond doubt. Without the constraints of a central government, the local economy was doing just fine. Somalia's mobile phone networks were among the cheapest in the world. The power grid in Mogadishu was an eccentric monument to unfettered capitalism. The livestock trade was booming. Customary law and clan elders kept things more or less in check. In many spheres, Somalia was doing better than at least half the continent, fueled in part by a spectacularly steady, generous flow of cash from relatives abroad, who sent some $1.6 billion in remittances back home each year.

And the miracle that underpinned this improbable success story sat on long shelves, in clammy, musty piles, in a giant vault in the basement of Somalia's central bank.

"Look how fragile they are," said Abukar Dahir, picking up a bundle of faded, crumbling Somali banknotes.

"What's the exchange rate?" I asked him.

"This morning it's approximately 17,800 shillings to the dollar."

Abukar Dahir outside Central Bank, Mogadishu, 2012. COURTESY OF THE AUTHOR

Thirty years ago, Abukar's father had been the head of the bank's foreign exchange department. He died weeks before his son was born and two years before the family fled abroad. Five months ago, at the age of twenty-five, Abukar came back to Mogadishu from west London to take up a job as one of the bank's senior policy advisors.

If Abukar's name sounds familiar, it's because I mentioned him at the start of this book. A few months after our first meeting at the bank, he found himself trapped along with Tarzan in Villa Somalia's mosque during an Al Shabab attack.

We left the airless vault and headed back upstairs to the marble-floored lobby of the bank. Abukar was sporting a blue suit jacket, checked shirt, thick eyebrows, and Lenin-like goatee. He'd studied law in London and then moved into banking. But here he was, now, helping to rebuild a central bank from scratch and not even trying to hide his glee.

"I'm so proud. This is something that happens once in a hundred years," he gushed in a voice that matched his youthful, gangly appearance.

The bank itself had closed down in 1991, along with everything else, and stayed shut for the next twenty years. But to the consternation of most economists, the Somali shilling persisted, like the bumblebee that had never been told its wings were too small to conform to the rules of aerodynamics.

"These are forgeries," said Abukar, taking me over to the desk of an elderly gentleman, with bright orange hennaed hair, who was counting a pile of thousand-shilling notes.

"And yet, they're legal. Or rather, they're accepted by the public."

No new, legal Somali banknotes had been issued since 1991. And because paper notes rip and disintegrate and get lost, you'd expect the currency to vanish almost entirely within a decade. Instead, on four separate occasions, different regional administrations and warlords had printed their own, forged notes.

"So this old one is genuine. But this one's a fake," Abukar said gleefully, picking up a note with a picture of a fisherman mending his net.

Rather than rejecting the forgeries, the Somali public simply nodded and went off to spend them in the market. What else were they to do in their surreal world, untethered from the usual rules? Sure, they used U.S. dollars now for bigger purchases, but the survival of the shilling reinforced Somalia's sense of itself as something resilient and unbreakable.

Abukar was good company, sharp and eloquent. Having overcome an early bout of nerves when he nearly refused to get off the plane in Mogadishu, he now appeared wildly optimistic about the city's future. When I asked him about security, he pushed back. "Sure, I've been scared here. But I've been scared in London, New York, Stockholm. Besides, there's almost no crime here. Just Al Shabab. And there is a kind of beauty in all this rubble."

I knew what he meant about the beauty. It was as if the city was coexisting with its history. A living museum. It had the effect of making you constantly imagine the future, too—of what these ruins would look like when they'd finally been restored.

Abukar led me upstairs to see the bank's prized possession. In a glass case, in a locked room, sat a small computer. It was a brand new SWIFT machine—a precious link to the outside world, finally and officially reconnecting Somalia to the global banking payment network. Abukar was grinning again. The next priority, he declared, was to start tracking down the Somali state's money, lost for a generation in forgotten bank accounts around the world when President Siad Barre's government collapsed in 1991 and its foreign assets were frozen.

Like so many other members of the diaspora I've met, Abukar had led a disjointed life. He grew up in Sweden but moved to London when he was fifteen. A few years after that, his mother woke him up with a jolt in the middle of the night. They'd both agreed to the plan beforehand. They wanted to find out which was his first language— Swedish, Somali, or English.

Abukar blinked in surprise at his mother's face and said, without thinking, "Blimey."

In Mogadishu, it was fun trying to guess which Somalis had been living in which foreign countries, not just by their accents but by the habits they'd picked up. "We Somalis are adaptable. We've all been forced to reinvent ourselves," Abukar told me.

It was almost like a new set of clans. The Americans are "a bit more outgoing, they like to push things harder. They're not so interested in consensus." But the Scandinavian Somalis are the opposite, "endlessly trying to bring everyone on board." The British are somewhere in between.

Abukar had left his British Somali fiancée back in London. It was putting a lot of pressure on their relationship, and he wasn't sure how long he'd be staying in Mogadishu. But for now, he was hooked. I saw him on subsequent visits, and before long he'd moved into a brand new flat just behind Ahmed Jama's Village Sports restaurant. He had high-speed internet, a gang of friends, and weekend trips an hour down the coast to Ahmed's latest venture—a small resort on a lovely, isolated cove called Jazeera beach.

I began to wonder if the strain would ever start to show.

Abukar was getting phone calls from Al Shabab. Usually they just threatened him. "I'll slit your throat." But sometimes the same people would call up a day later, and he'd end up having long chats with guys who sounded about his own age. One was called Ali. Another said his name had once been Michael. They had thick Cockney or Birmingham accents and wanted to talk about how they missed KFC and football.

"You get desensitized," Abukar told me one evening, when I asked how he was coping. "It's fascinating how humans can adapt to different circumstances." *Fascinating* . . . The word seemed too cold. It sounded like he was trying to bottle it up, to build a mental wall between himself and the dangers around him. By now, he'd lost a number of friends and been caught up in four near-miss attacks, including a huge bomb blast on the airport road, immediately outside a hotel where he'd been meeting some American treasury officials.

"It's amazing how different people react. Some freeze—the shock takes over." But not Abukar. He felt he was starting to get used to it. After the windows shattered and the shock wave threw him off his feet, he barricaded the doors shut and helped his colleagues hide under a bed, telling them he feared that the militants were about to storm the hotel.

"Mentally, I'm very strong," he insisted. "I feel I can manage it. It's not boring here. And that adrenaline keeps you afloat."

FROM TIME TO TIME, Tarzan left Mogadishu on official business. One of his earliest trips was to Casablanca for a gathering of mayors from the United States and the Arab world. A networking opportunity for rich cities and powerful leaders. When it was his turn to speak, Tarzan suggested that it was the duty of wealthier cities, like Chicago, Amman, and Riyadh, to lift up their poorer relations. He peered around the conference hall.

"Does anybody want to become Mogadishu's sister city?" he asked.

No one raised a hand.

Tarzan laughs at the memory. "Not a single person! Ha!" But the moment clearly stung him. "Arabs—that's usually their attitude. If you're bigger or better than them, then they lick your arse. But if you're poor, they step on your head."

But London was different.

In 2012 Tarzan traveled to Britain as part of an official government delegation to attend a huge international conference specifically aimed at raising funds for Somalia and helping the government chart the path ahead. The following year, a second, even grander conference took place in London.

Both events came across as cheerfully chaotic and half-frantic scrambles—a mixture of pledges, pomposity, frank talk, and backroom bargaining. But the second conference, in particular, felt like a special moment for Somalia, almost like a coming-out party for a government that was finally reconnecting—like that SWIFT machine in Mogadishu's central bank—with the outside world.

In terms of the pecking order, Tarzan was a rather peripheral figure, comprehensively outflanked by dozens of presidents, prime ministers, and so on. But toward the end of the event, there was a special gathering for Somali officials, and for the diaspora, in Westminster's imposing, historic Great Hall, across the road from the Houses of Parliament.

Is it possible to pin down the precise high point of any politician's career?

Tarzan walked into the Great Hall and up toward a podium framed by huge organ pipes. There must have been more than two thousand British Somalis packed inside the chamber, their bright dresses and flags coating the baroque interior like some dazzling wallpaper spreading up into the steep galleries and toward the vast, domed ceiling. Winston Churchill, Gandhi, and Martin Luther King, Jr., had all given speeches from the same spot.

No one seems sure of the exact size of Britain's ethnic Somali population. But it's grown to well over a quarter of a million. Most families retain strong links to Somalia, and some have begun venturing back—a foot in each country—although again, the numbers are hard to pin down. But there's no doubt that Tarzan has played a pioneering role, testing the water and urging others to follow his lead, a heckling, inspiring, antagonizing figure.

As Tarzan came into view, the place erupted into a giant, collective roar of approval. Here he was. A London boy. Maybe even a Somali hero. A man who had helped people to believe in Mogadishu once again.

"Tarzan! Tarzan! Tarzan! Tarzan!" It was like a football crowd.

Tarzan grinned. How could he not? A year earlier, he'd attended a similar event in London and the same thing had happened. He knew he was a powerful public speaker—even his enemies conceded that. "I speak from my heart, and people can sense it," he says. At one point, the year before, he'd begged the crowd to come back home to Mogadishu. Come back to the beach. Back to the Lido.

"Lido! Lido! Lido!" They went wild.

But this year was different. Somalia's transitional government had officially been replaced by a new and marginally more representative body. His old ally Sheikh Sharif was no longer president, and the new man did not enjoy sharing a stage with Tarzan. His agitated expression and his aides had already made that very clear. So when someone introduced Tarzan as "our next president," he wondered if he was being set up—if someone was trying to create more friction between him and the new president. It was not improbable.

Not that it stopped him from giving a speech. Instead of begging the crowd to come home to the Lido, this year he picked another beach—Jazeera—where Ahmed Jama's new resort had opened.

"Jazeera! Jazeera! Jazeera!" The crowd lapped it up again.

But then Tarzan looked across at the president and his team, and realized he better keep it short. Somali politics were dangerous enough already. The British ambassador to Somalia, Matt Baugh, was sitting in the chamber, watching the drama unfold.

"I've never seen anyone get such a raucous reception," he told me later. He'd come to know Tarzan in Mogadishu and sensed a politician of growing clout and shrewdness, someone who seemed able to reach out beyond clan.

"There's no way that room was full of Tarzan's own supporters. What I think they were seeing was a Somali who was fighting on behalf of other Somalis."

The ambassador stopped for a moment, as if picturing the scene again.

"He was like a rock star."

Mogadishu Mud

"Where did all the money go?"

—ABDIRIZAK FARTAAG

I‍T DIDN'T LAST LONG—THE whole rock star thing.

Indeed, some would say it was never a "thing" at all, and that a few heartfelt cheers in London, or Stockholm, or Minnesota translated into precious little back in Somalia.

Either way, toward the end of 2013, the public mood seemed to be swinging against Tarzan. I say "seemed" because it's not easy to measure popularity, or anything else, in Mogadishu—a city that remained too chaotic and dangerous to hold proper one man, one vote elections.

Still, that was the perception. That after three years in office, the mayor was losing momentum on several fronts.

One morning, a young gardener who worked up at Villa Somalia but did a little extra sweeping around Tarzan and Shamis's house, too, blurted something out without thinking.

"We hate the diaspora. Hate them," he said vehemently to Shamis. For a moment, he had completely forgotten that she was one of them. Not that Shamis was surprised by the vitriol; the growing backlash against the diaspora was becoming hard to ignore. People had started calling them *"dayuus-baro"*—a clever bit of Somali wordplay that implied they were here to spread immorality and indecency.

Shamis was not the sort of person to keep quiet.

"If it wasn't for the diaspora you wouldn't even be alive," she told the gardener angrily. "We've been sending money all these years to support the country, to stop people dying. So why do you hate us?"

"I don't know," he mumbled, but then summed it up rather neatly.

"Because you left us here. We were the ones who suffered. Now they come back and it's like they're hijacking the city. They want all the jobs."

Shamis left it at that. But she was seething. It took her straight back to the old days, to being a teenager in Mogadishu, growing up with members of the Beizani—the urban elite—and looking down on the clannish nomads who had brought their ugly prejudices into the city and ended up ruining everything. Besides, look at what happened to those who had stayed behind in Somalia. Twenty years of war had twisted them out of shape.

"These people are so traumatized," she told me later. "It's like they're in a coma. Every one of them should be in hospital. They kill, they do anything, and they don't care. Maybe Mogadishu is already a mental hospital, and it's making me crazy."

⁂

SOMALIA WAS NOT THE first country to experience that acid jolt of mutual resentment—the inevitable tension between those who left and those who stayed behind. But there was a particular intensity to the relationship in Mogadishu—it was partly about clans, inevitably. But it was also because of the speed with which people had first fled from Somalia and then charged back in two decades later.

On one side there were the returnees with their education, money, worldly experience, impatience, good intentions, and condescension. On the other side, there was a city swamped with poorly educated, unemployed, mostly young, often religiously conservative Somalis, wrestling with their own insecurities and wary of the sophisticated outsiders coming back to patronize and to sideline.

Tarzan didn't always get the tone right. His years in Britain had reshaped him, too. He expected too much, too quickly. He was always telling people about the former mayor of London, Ken Livingstone, and about the urban regeneration around King's Cross railway station. Sometimes Shamis would watch him giving a speech or an interview on Somali television and would try to put him right when he came home.

"You're confusing them," she told Tarzan. He sprinkled too many English words into his Somali. And he talked about complicated issues too much, and always about London. "These people come from the countryside. They don't understand any of this. They have no experience of government, of Western ways. All they know is chaos. So you have to talk to them in a way they can understand."

Sometimes, when I saw Shamis and Tarzan discussing politics together, I'd get a glimpse of how I imagined it must have been between them when they first became a couple. The well-heeled girl strolling along the beachfront after siesta time, doing la passeggiata, and holding hands with her rough, penniless, street-fighting boyfriend.

He just needed a little polish.

But it wasn't just about the mayor's job anymore. These days there was a much larger project hovering in the background.

TARZAN HAS NEVER HIDDEN from me his ambition to become president of Somalia—one day. It's always seemed like a logical progression to him. He drops it into the conversation without any sense of awkwardness. Very un-British, you might say. And over time, I got the sense from Shamis that she had also bought into that dream—that for all her fears and frustrations and the talk about retirement and feeling imprisoned in Mogadishu, her husband's confidence had rubbed off on her, and she believed he could, and indeed should, become president.

She sometimes joked about being first lady.

"That's the only way I'm going back to Mogadishu again," she laughed, or half-laughed. She was sitting on the sofa in the London flat—at home after another three months in Somalia. Her grandchildren would be charging up the stairs any minute now for afternoon tea. Then she looked down at her hands, and I caught another glimpse of her confusion.

It was easy for Tarzan. Everything seemed black and white, with me or against me, for him. The day of his death has been written. All of that. But Shamis was still torn between two worlds.

Surely, after all, it would be worth it if Tarzan became president.

But what were the chances of that happening? After three years as mayor, Tarzan had made plenty of enemies, and the diaspora issue was only one of many clouds now blowing in across Mogadishu, casting a dark shadow on his reputation as a man of action and of principle.

The rumors and the allegations against him had begun almost as soon as he took office, and he'd shrugged them off in his usual gruff manner. But they were starting to pile up and—as far as one could tell—were gaining traction.

The mayor was, people said, a murderer. Or at least he'd ordered his tight-lipped cousin and security chief, Fanah, to get rid of a local journalist who'd criticized him. Fanah had even been detained, for a time.

There was Tarzan's fight with the former mayor and warlord Mohamed Dheere, who had sent gunmen to disrupt the Peace Festival. Or had Tarzan arranged the whole drama himself to discredit a rival? The enmity between the two men was notorious.

The mayor was a crook, people insisted, taking backhanders from property developers who were carving up the city before people could return to claim their homes. He was in cahoots with other diaspora businessmen in the Chamber of Commerce, too. The mayor's bodyguards and aides behaved like a private militia, demanding bribes and fighting gun battles to protect his business interests.

And for all his bluster, the orphan boy was really a clannist who was deliberately ensuring that other clans that had been forced out of

Mogadishu during the street battles of 1991 never got the chance to reclaim their homes and challenge the Hawiye's stranglehold on the city. That's what was going on during the famine, they said. Tarzan was clearing displaced families from Mogadishu's streets according to clan, not need.

So what was the usual Mogadishu mud—the gossip stirred by rivals, the barbs hurled by other clans, the noise that filled the vacuum—and what was true?

Whenever I brought the issues up with Tarzan, he insisted it was all a giant smear campaign. He said, for instance, that he'd handed his cousin, Fanah, over to the police and told them, "If you can prove he organized the murder of that journalist, then kill him." But after a month, the police had come up with nothing.

I've mentioned before the difficulty of pinning facts down in a country that had lost so many of the conventional instruments by which we usually try to establish the truth. The courts were weak, corrupted, and used for settling scores. The police faced similar challenges. The opaque clans still protected their own. Foreign governments could do little more than stand on the sidelines and guess. Somalia's government was riddled with corruption and consumed by its own internal wars. Mogadishu's journalists were often courageous and outspoken, but they were facing enormous pressures and were being murdered— by Al Shabab and no doubt by other vested interests—with chilling regularity.

Over the years I've spoken to a number of people who've leveled serious allegations against Tarzan.

Some have argued that in comparison with the corruption elsewhere in government, the mayor was an impressively modest offender. One of his biggest admirers wondered whether involvement in a little corruption was simply the price of exercising power in a city like Mogadishu, a place without credible institutions to fall back on. And that Tarzan was under such immense pressure, cutting deals and bulldozing his way through obstacles, that at some point he simply lost the ability to maneuver and became part of the problem.

Most of these claims and allegations have come from people who've quickly admitted they were getting their information and their speculation secondhand, at best. However, two sources in Mogadishu have come tantalizingly close to spilling the beans on Tarzan. Both are well positioned and, to my mind, credible voices—not rivals with axes to grind. One claimed that Tarzan's cousin Fanah, working with someone senior in the mayor's office, operated a small extortion racket, shaking down businesses for bribes. The other source said that Tarzan used his influence to direct big municipal contracts—often funded by British or American aid money—toward his friends and family, who allegedly set up fake "shadow" companies to siphon off the funds.

Both sources gave me a few more details but then got cold feet. They said they were afraid for their own safety. That Tarzan might work out who they were.

"There's a dark side to him," one source told me by phone. "In Mogadishu, they just kill people—silence them—and blame Al Shabab. That's how people do business here."

I hung up and sat back in my chair at our house in Johannesburg, wondering whether the man I'd been talking to was being paranoid or entirely logical.

I thought of Tarzan in his orphanage, pouring boiling water over a sleeping bully or rubbing Congo's face in the dirt. The tough child had grown into a tougher man. But did it then follow that he was capable of murder? Corruption was another matter. But either way, I had no absolute proof of anything.

"I'm not saying he's perfect," Tarzan's brother Yusuf told me when I called him at home in Indiana. He was in bed, resting bruised muscles after a long mountain bike ride. "I'm sure when you're in a system like that there may be temptations. There may be gray areas. But I know he had opportunities to steal, and he turned them down." He scoffed at the idea his brother could be a killer.

Still, Yusuf was hardly an objective witness. And so, late one afternoon, I found myself in an upmarket café, inside a crowded shopping mall in Nairobi, Kenya, waiting to meet Somalia's most famous, most despised, anti-corruption whistleblower.

⁂

ABDIRIZAK FARTAAG IS A Canadian Somali who returned to Mogadishu in 2009 and worked in the prime minister's office in charge of public finances. He was the man who had authorized Tarzan's first official check in 2010.

In 2011, Fartaag was quietly relieved of his duties. He left Somalia in a hurry and proceeded to publish, in forensic detail, allegations of grotesque corruption that he said he'd uncovered during the years he'd worked at the heart of government. His allegations were breathtaking. Hundreds of millions of dollars had, he claimed, been systematically pocketed by officials at the very highest levels.

And he wasn't just making vague allegations. In the tax year of 2009–10, he said that precisely $72,725,000 in foreign bilateral assistance had been "stolen."

No wonder Fartaag was now receiving death threats.

When I first contacted him by email and told him what I was writing about, he wrote back almost immediately and with refreshing frankness. His email was full of words in capital letters and highlighted text, and it reminded me, in its indignation and its brusque certainties—though not its content—of the way Tarzan talks.

"Why [is] a thug like Tarzan . . . news worthy? It's amazing how people . . . with no pedigree of government assume these offices with the sole purpose of enriching themselves while playing clan politics to remain in power. All the hope and aspirations of 3 years ago seem like a fart in the wind."

No punches pulled. And Fartaag's email roared on, capturing the essence of something I'd heard from many other Somalis, particularly in the diaspora. "Why isn't positive news being reported from Somalia?" he demanded, and then proceeded to give me a list of worthy, well-known doctors and human rights workers—"the true heroes of Somalia"—whom I should be writing about instead.

I could well understand his frustration. Still, I could also see a certain irony. Here was a man who had risked his life to expose massive government corruption demanding that outsiders focus on the good news instead.

Fartaag walked into the Nairobi café nodding and smiling at a few other Somalis sitting at nearby tables. He was wearing a white shirt with dark brown stripes, and his tousled gray-black hair sat toward the back of his scalp, leaving a large forehead exposed above his metal-rimmed glasses.

He sat down and systematically unveiled his qualities, like a doctor setting out his implements. Charm first, then a probing intelligence, followed by skepticism, blistering indignation, self-doubt, contempt for lazy conformity, and finally a wry, half-amused sense of gloom.

"Frankly speaking, everybody was corrupt," Fartaag said of his time in Somalia's transitional government.

"Everybody?"

"Everybody." He grimaced and tapped the side of his head.

"Up here . . . We're mentally poor. Just a bunch of nomads."

Fartaag described how the president or prime minister would routinely come back from trips to one of the Gulf states carrying briefcases full of cash. Sometimes $1 million. Sometimes up to $5 million. Sudan's government would send $2 million every month.

"And it was your job to keep track of it?" I asked.

"It was my job. It was hell. At the beginning . . . I don't want to give myself excuses, but at the beginning I did not understand exactly what was going on."

He described taking two black suitcases containing $5 million to the central bank. The deposit was formally acknowledged, but without mentioning where the cash had come from. From time to time, an official would take the suitcases out and disappear with them.

Fartaag in Nairobi, Kenya, 2014. COURTESY OF THE AUTHOR

Fartaag's description chimed with an anecdote I'd heard from another source, about the way blocks of cash would, it was claimed, be handed out during governmental cabinet meetings. On one occasion a minister allegedly accused a top official of pocketing nearly $1 million from the suitcase before the money was shared out. There was a huge row, but in the end, everyone took his or her stake.

You could interpret such a scene, charitably, as business as usual—a clan-based government, in a system shorn of any credible bureaucracy, dividing the wealth between those same clans in an open way that encouraged a degree of trust. Or you could see it as a Mafia-like move to establish collective guilt and to make it harder for anyone to blow the whistle.

Over time, Fartaag said, he came to understand that the corruption was an uncontrollable force. And he was clear about where the bulk of the blame lay: the diaspora.

"Everyone who came there had one thing in mind. How to rob the system," he claimed.

***

AT WHICH POINT, I raised the topic of Tarzan.

It was a strange, uncomfortable moment for me. In some ways I was ready to hear the worst about him, to find out that he was, after all, no different from any other corrupt politician, spoiled by the temptations of working in such an opaque system and fueled, perhaps, by a sense of entitlement—after all, he was risking his life, surely he deserved to profit somewhere along the line, too.

But I was also worried. The more I'd learned about Tarzan's life, and about his family—all those hours together at their modest council flat in London, in Mogadishu, and on the phone—the more inclined I'd become to believe him and Shamis, and Yusuf.

Given what he'd already said, I was expecting Fartaag to be blunt and damning. What I wasn't anticipating was his own discomfort—his own reluctance to topple a statue.

Fartaag began with the "facts." Before Tarzan had taken over, the mayor's office had been "idle and dysfunctional." There were no records of any government funding. When Tarzan arrived in 2010, his office received $50,000 from the prime minister's office, but the accountant general never declared it. Soon afterward, $1.5 million was reportedly allocated to the mayor's office by the Ministry of Finance, but in an annual statement, only $682,504 was declared. In other words, in Tarzan's first few months in the job, over $800,000 appeared to have gone missing.

Conclusive? No. The Finance Ministry was, itself, profoundly corrupt and was blocking the government's auditors at every step. Fartaag had discovered large-scale misappropriations in almost every corner of government.

But still.

"Where did the money go?" Fartaag asked. And what about the subsequent income the mayor's office received as a share of the revenue from Mogadishu's seaport?

"What has been done with that 15 percent share?"

Fartaag let the question hang in the air for a while. He had no answer to it.

"Show me the documents," he said, as if Tarzan was at the table with us. "Just show me. Allow me to vouch for your books."

And it was only now that Fartaag's frustration became tinged with something more melancholy, with a sense of having been let down.

"I don't know if I'm being unfair here. But I was expecting someone like him, someone who has lived in England—the beacon of democracy—to do the right things. He could have established a committee and said, 'This is what I get—15 percent from the port. This is not my money. I'm going to go to England and get external auditors and I'm going to open my books. If you find anything wrong, expose me.'"

Fartaag ran a hand through his hair. I could see him picturing how things might have been.

"Oh, oh, that guy would have been a hero! He had all the possibilities to do the right things. He never did them. All these years I was hoping he would come to me and say, 'Fartaag, you're wrong,' and show me the documents."

And now I could see his anger returning, along with something close to self-loathing.

"We're all useless. Mediocre." He spat the words out. The diaspora were weak, greedy, and divided. The Islamists in the government were strong, driven, but utterly ignorant of Mogadishu's culture and history.

"It's really sad. Really sad. I try to be fair to Tarzan. He's not the only one. We've given a bad name to the diaspora. Each and every one of us is pathetic."

Fartaag's thoughts began to ricochet. How could Somalia be

fixed? The UN were "rubbish," but maybe Britain and America could get together and set up some sort of "soft colony," putting their own officials in to oversee each ministry. He began criticizing Somalia's new president, a quiet professor named Hassan Sheikh, who had chosen to stay in the country during the wars, working for several international aid organizations. Some believed the president was now beholden to Islamists.

"Honestly speaking, I still prefer Tarzan to Hassan Sheikh," Fartaag said abruptly.

The comment came out of the blue—as if he couldn't get the mayor out of his head.

"You mean you'd vote for Tarzan, after all you've said about him?"

"I swear to God, I would vote for Tarzan. Because . . . Now I'm going to contradict myself." Fartaag paused for a moment to collect his thoughts. He wanted to make it clear that he could only support Tarzan if he could prove he hadn't stolen any money. But still, by saying that, he was now admitting it was a possibility.

"The guy has guts. He's lived abroad. He's enlightened. He's someone I could . . . I could . . . I could . . . I could accept to be at the helm of the government."

It was dark by the time I walked outside. I caught a cab by the petrol station across the road and we crawled off into Nairobi's traffic. I sat in the front seat, trying to work out what I'd just learned. Fartaag's vivid, self-flagellating sense of disillusionment rang true. Somalia had lived by its own set of rules for so long that corruption seemed almost hardwired—like a logical, functioning system rather than an aberration. But where did that leave Tarzan? Again, Fartaag's own furious ambivalence seemed to make sense. Maybe it was as close as anyone could get to the truth. It would be several months before I would sit down with Tarzan in London and try to get some answers.

All this time, Mogadishu continued to grapple with its own feverish contradictions. Impromptu cement block factories were popping up in empty courtyards to cater to a housing boom. New universities and dozens of small private schools were opening up.

Modern hotels, too. But Al Shabab seemed more active than ever, launching a string of bloody assaults on government buildings and hotels and taking the blame for the hit-and-run assassinations that erupted almost daily on the city's increasingly traffic-clogged roads.

※◎◎◎※

In 2013 Abukar Dahir was still at the central bank and still finding the whole experience of life in Mogadishu weirdly addictive.

Anywhere else, he reckoned, would be a ghost town, but Somalis had developed thicker skin.

"People don't give a fuck! They're like, 'What, am I going to flee for a fifth or sixth time? And live in the bushes? Fuck that! If I'm going to die, let me be shot here!'"

But Abukar was struggling with his job. He'd installed a card entry system at the bank to check who was actually turning up to work. There were lots of "ghost" employees who drew a salary but did nothing else. Not surprisingly, there was some push-back against this young, cocky outsider who wanted to shake everything up.

But that wasn't the real problem.

A UN investigation had alleged massive corruption at the bank. Thirteen million dollars had reportedly gone missing. And in Nairobi, Fartaag weighed in, too, writing his own report that described the place as operating "more like an ATM rather than a public financial institution."

Abukar was outraged. He and the bank's governor flew to Nairobi to confront the authors of the UN report. None of them, he complained, had even deigned to step foot in the bank or to make any attempt to contact senior officials there before publishing their allegations. It was another example of hypocritical foreigners sitting in Nairobi, pretending to understand what was going on in Somalia.

"It was ridiculous, fictitious stuff," Abukar told me indignantly. "Every single dollar they claimed was stolen—I accounted for all of it. Not a single dollar was missing."

But either way, it didn't look good. The governor was fired (although he was later brought back into government) and Abukar jumped ship, moving to a new job as an advisor in the Foreign Ministry. Once again, he found himself helping to reconnect Somalia to the world, this time helping to figure out where to open, or re-open, embassies. I met him when one of his work trips took him through London. He liked to walk the city's streets—to shake off the claustrophobia of Mogadishu—and we meandered south from the British Library, down toward Oxford Street and beyond. He wore a blue puffer jacket and a baseball hat. He seemed to have lost weight.

Abukar had never been a big fan of Tarzan. Too loud. Too crude. But watching him at work in Mogadishu these past few years, he'd come to appreciate that maybe those qualities had a role to play.

"He's not the most technocratic guy. He's not someone who understands civil service reform, or how to build up local government. But maybe he was a perfect fit. Mogadishu needed a pioneer, a rookie, a rough, hard man. Someone to hold public rallies and talk about sensitive issues. Someone to pull the masses out of despair."

But the past tense was telling. Abukar felt that Tarzan's moment had come and gone. He'd played his galvanizing role and now the city needed someone different—an administrator.

We turned north again, up Tottenham Court Road, and Abukar began telling me about a recent incident that had turned a lot of young diaspora Somalis against Tarzan. It concerned Mogadishu's Lido beach. On Fridays, in particular, the beach had become a focal point for thousands of young people. A whole industry had built up along the shoreline, with traders setting up makeshift stalls to rent out inner tubes and life jackets by the hour. At low tide, the long, sandy beach was perhaps 50 meters wide. At high tide the crowds retreated onto the rocks.

"What Tarzan did was a bit sad," Abukar went on. The diaspora youth had few qualms about holding hands in public. Boys and girls had even been spotted swimming together and kissing. But Tarzan had objected. He'd made it clear he felt that the diaspora were becoming a bad influence and that they needed to leave their foreign habits abroad.

Abukar's theory was that Tarzan was making a cynical appeal to conservative forces within Mogadishu.

"It was his desperation to win support. He was talking about people from abroad coming with bad influences. Well, hey, where did you come from? Who are you to criticize us? Right? So I totally lost respect for him on that. He's a sellout, if I can use that word."

But Tarzan saw it very differently. He'd urged the diaspora to come home, to reclaim Lido beach after all these years. But at the same time, he could feel the friction growing between the locals and the diaspora, and he feared that the beach would become a flash point.

"The diaspora bring alcohol and women. Especially at night. So as mayor I have to mediate. If a group of religious people takes the law in their own hands, there will be a conflict. So I have to prevent that."

Tarzan's answer made some sense to me. But perhaps that wasn't the point anymore. He was losing momentum as mayor. The knives were out. He simply had too many enemies.

<hr>

It was February 21, 2014. The day Al Shabab tried to kill the president in Villa Somalia's mosque. The day Abukar Dahir had listened over the phone to his friend being shot, and Tarzan had remained on his knees in prayer, unaware that the gunfire was coming through the windows.

Shamis stood outside the gate at home, waiting for news. She had convinced herself that Tarzan was dead, that he was the target. It was a moment she'd played through her head many times over the past few years.

But suddenly she caught sight of his car turning into the cul-de-sac. Fanah was driving. And now she could make out Tarzan in the passenger seat, his hand raised in greeting. The car's tires had been shredded by bullets or perhaps a grenade, and the metal wheel rims clawed their way over the potholes.

"Thank you, God," she said, as they embraced on the street. For once he seemed dazed. She looked down and saw his dusty socks and missing shoes.

"Never go back there. Never go back to that mosque. Please."

What she really meant was, let's leave Mogadishu. Both of us. Immediately.

Six days later, Tarzan was sacked.

He heard the news on a local television station. It was not unexpected. A couple of weeks earlier, the president had called him up and offered him a new position in his cabinet.

"What position?" Tarzan asked.

"Deputy minister."

"I'm sorry, I don't want it. I can't do anything in cabinet. I know the way it works. I have lots of plans, and initiatives. A deputy minister can't do anything."

The conversation had ended awkwardly, and Tarzan knew his days were numbered. The day after the Villa Somalia attack, he had another meeting with the president. This time he was offered the prestigious post of ambassador to Washington, D.C. He turned it down again.

"Can I ask you why?" the president said.

"That is my own decision. Even if you offered me a full minister's job, I would not accept it."

Tarzan heard nothing more until the following week, when the president went on television to announce that the mayor was, indeed, being moved to a new position—deputy minister for sports and youth.

I called Tarzan up that evening. "Yes, it's true," he said calmly. "I was not told, but it was expected." He didn't have time to talk for long. I could almost hear his brain grinding through a new strategy. The next day he called a news conference of his own in Mogadishu and declared that he'd never been consulted, that the news had come as a surprise, that he was turning the new post down, and that he was re-signing.

At home that night, Shamis could hardly stop grinning.

"You're very lucky. You did the job. You didn't die, and you didn't get harmed. Now we have to go back to London," she told him.

But she could already see it was no use.

"I will take some time to cool off," he said. "Then I will go back to work."

⁂

On my next trip to Mogadishu, I managed to arrange an interview with President Hassan Sheikh. Maybe "arrange" is too formal a word. The president was leaving Mogadishu for a few days, and as was the custom, half the cabinet and various other officials and their entourages had descended on the international airport in the hope of catching a few moments with him in the VIP lounge. Me too.

The scene outside was chaotic. A scrum of officials, soldiers, and uniformed and plainclothes security guards waited at the side entrance to the new, unfinished airport building. Lots of guns. A morning rainstorm had left big puddles in the dirt. The president's armored convoy swept in and he was bundled inside, a move that triggered an angry shoving match as everyone else tried to follow him. There was no sign of a guest list. Officials who'd managed to talk their way past the security guards at the door simply leaned back outside and tried to drag in their colleagues and guards, and their guns. It was a useful reminder that Somalia's government—superficially polished now with its emailed press releases, foreign advisors, and ambitious policy documents—was still a chaotic work in progress and, at times, little more than a temporary alignment of rival factions.

Inside the glass-walled VIP lounge, the air conditioners did not appear to be working. It was sweltering. My shirt was soaked by the time I was ushered forward toward an armchair where the president was busy taking leave of an army general still kneeling on the floor in front of him. Sheikh was a soft-spoken man with a rounded face, and he managed to look impossibly cool despite his heavy jacket and tie.

There wasn't much time. We talked briefly about the fight against Al Shabab. "Someone who wants to die . . . you hardly know how to stop them," he said wearily. Toward the end, I mentioned Tarzan. Why was he sacked?

"Well, Tarzan, he has been doing quite a good job, but . . ." The president's voice trailed off for a moment. "Er . . . The major reason that he left is that here in Somalia we are dealing with perceptions. Not so much the realities. So it's about internal politics. Because he's not a bad guy. I never said he's a bad guy."

As he stood up, he smiled and then muttered something about needing to get rid of "the baggage of the past."

A couple of days later, I went around to visit Tarzan at his home and told him what the president had said.

"Ha! Haah! I enjoy it. Yes, I enjoy it . . ." He was chuckling to himself. But I detected no sarcasm, no bitterness. It was more like a chess player acknowledging his opponent's tactical skill but still confident of his own superior strategy.

"Still, I have the right to be ambitious." Tarzan was talking about the presidency.

"I want this country to be fix-ed. I can do it."

Lido Beach

"A change will come."

—MOHAMUD "TARZAN" NUR

I<small>T'S</small> <small>FOUR IN THE AFTERNOON,</small> and the streetlights along Queen's Crescent are already starting to flicker into life, nudging portions of the gloom aside.

"Let's cook!" Tarzan shouts down the hall to Abdullahi, who recently lost his job and has spent the day in the flat, lounging on his bed with his headphones on.

"I'll cook for the children, Abdullahi. When are they coming?"

Tarzan stands by the kitchen stove in a checked shirt, sarong, and bare feet, emptying a tin of tomatoes into a frying pan. Shamis is away this week, at their apartment in Dubai.

"I'm learning," he says cheerfully. "My wife spoils me. Treats me like a king."

It will be spaghetti again tonight. Soon the tomatoes are sizzling, and the sounds of shouts and giggles float up the stairs from the front door.

"*Awowe! Awowe!*" Before they've even reached the kitchen, Malia and Maya, now seven and ten, are calling out the Somali word for "grandfather."

"I love you." Tarzan greets them with a simple statement of fact, then a hug, and tells them to go and say their prayers while he finishes cooking.

"More tea?" he says to me. I'm sitting behind him at the kitchen table with my back to the window and the darkening silhouette of London's skyline, waiting for the right moment to begin.

Lido beach, Mogadishu, 2015. <small>COURTESY OF BECKY LIPSCOMBE</small>

It's been five years since I first met Tarzan in a crowded room in Mogadishu's Villa Somalia, and perhaps three years since I first began to consider writing a book about his life. It's a strange relationship to have with someone. He agreed to the book idea immediately and apparently casually. Plenty of foreign journalists were interviewing him in those days, popping into Mogadishu to talk to the man with the "most dangerous job in the world." It was all good exposure for an ambitious politician.

But a book is a much longer project, and it requires a degree of trust and cooperation I was not entirely sure how to sustain. Besides, there was the constant and very real possibility that, on any given day in Mogadishu, he would be killed. We'd shared a near miss, once, when he'd been called out to settle a dispute at an army checkpoint on the edge of the city and a roadside bomb had detonated, killing eight soldiers a minute or so after we'd both left the area.

I had warned Tarzan that I would not be airbrushing out any dirt I found out about him.

Still, as he leaves the sauce bubbling on the gas stove and turns to join me at the kitchen table, I'm wondering how he'll react now, whether things will get awkward.

I tell him that I've got a series of questions—about alleged corruption, about his life story, about a lie that he's told me. I've asked him about some allegations before, but I'm also aware that I've been saving this moment, biding my time, waiting until I've got as much material as I think I need for the book, worried this could be the end of our relationship.

Tarzan leans back in his chair and says, "Fine! Fine."

He sounds pleased and impatient, like a restaurant guest being told the oysters are on their way. And I realize, almost immediately, that I already know how this is going to go, that he is not the sort of man to be cornered, or intimidated, by mere questions.

He scoffs at Fartaag's insinuations.

"I have nothing to hide. Nothing to hide. Whatever he says is suspicious. Fartaag was with the prime minister. I'm the only politician in Somalia who can stand in front of the public and say, 'Ask me any question you want. I don't care how rude, how confrontational. You'll get an answer.'"

And he proceeds to talk about the municipality's accounts. How the government's auditor general checked and approved them every year. How his rivals—corrupt rivals—tried to undermine him with rumors. How no one can actually point to a specific incident. How, by the end of his term, he'd set up a computerized accounting system that rendered fraud impossible. How he'd left a tidy sum in the municipality's accounts for his successor. And besides, he said, coming back to Fartaag's question about getting foreign auditors in:

"How could we afford to pay for PWC or Ernst and Young? Do they work for free?"

I ask him about the land deals. The claims that he was taking kickbacks and money abroad in suitcases. What about the apartment in Dubai?

Tarzan sits forward now. There's finally a hint of indignation in his voice as he begins listing his property and business interests: a share in the old internet café here in London, a share of another business in Birmingham, the Mogadishu villa he built for his mother from the money he was earning in Saudi Arabia, and another one that he finished in 1986 but never lived in. Then there's a big chunk of land—150 by 350 meters—on a main road leading out of Mogadishu that he ended up selling for half a million dollars. In 2004 he bought an apartment in Cairo. "Property was cheap at that time, and there was no hope for Somalia." He mentions another "cheap" piece of land in Mogadishu, bought more recently, but he doesn't want to say where it is in case the government "misappropriates" it. The apartment in Dubai is rented, and Shamis is "really struggling" with the shop she's opened there.

It all comes out in a torrent, and when he's done, he sits back in his chair.

"I was a businessman before I got into politics. This is the apartment I've lived in since 1993. That's the couch I bought before I became mayor. This is the kitchen that the council just renovated. I still pay rent here. So when people accuse me of corruption, I won't waste my breath defending myself."

And yet it's obvious that Tarzan can't quite leave it at that.

His children—fiercely protective of their father—have been getting grief on social media. Mimi, the youngest daughter, was accused of getting Tarzan to buy her a new car with stolen money. Abdullahi posted holiday snaps from Dubai on Instagram and got asked if his dad was buying more villas.

"I used to get really angry. But now it's just funny. I know my dad better than anyone. He knows what will happen on judgment day. Know what I'm saying?" Abdullahi asks.

But how do you disprove the allegations and the rumors in a place like Somalia? And perhaps more significantly, how does it affect people to live in a society where the very concept of uncontested truth seems to have been utterly eroded? It was like his brothers warned him when they told him not to take the job. You'll smell of the sewer. Tarzan compares it to an Ebola outbreak. A city like Mogadishu is so contaminated that any politician quickly becomes tainted and suspect. In the end, you can never convince everyone. That's the price of admission. It's also rather convenient.

The girls come in to fetch their spaghetti and take the bowls, carefully, into the sitting room to eat in front of the television. Abdullahi wanders in again, headphones still on, and tells Tarzan about getting made redundant from his part-time hospital job.

"You're smart," Tarzan replies. "Volunteer. Don't ask for money first. Volunteer."

When Adbullahi drifts back to his room, I turn the conversation, warily, to the story of Tarzan's birth. I'm more apprehensive about this than I am about the corruption allegations. I know for certain that he's lied to me about being born in room 18 at the San Martino hospital.

Tarzan looks up. Then he grins. He offers two explanations. And I suggest a third.

The first one begins with his accent. For some reason he's never quite shaken off the rural lilt that marks out those who've grown up in the wilderness of the Ogaden. So when he became mayor of Mogadishu, people—particularly from other clans—started whispering that he wasn't really a local, and that he didn't "belong" in the city. Tarzan took it as a challenge and an insult. It was like being called "bastard" all those years ago at the orphanage. And so he constructed an elaborate story.

"The Martino hospital was by the ocean. So I said, 'Anyone who is born closer to the ocean is more Mogadishu than me. But anyone born further inland than me is not from Mogadishu!' I even invented room 18. So with that argument, I silenced the argument. No one can challenge me."

"So you're saying, 'It could be true, in theory'?"

"Yes, it could be true! Believe me! The facts themselves have no value."

No value. It was the cornered orphan, lashing out. Undaunted, threatening, and effective.

The second explanation is really just an extension of the first. Like so many Somalis of his generation, Tarzan has no idea exactly when or where he was born. So why not invent your own story?

Perhaps it's not really a lie at all. Just a different way of looking at identity—as a suit one chooses rather than something imposed. While Tarzan is trying to articulate that thought, he talks about his own offspring.

"I don't know how to put this exactly, but my children, they have the right to say they're Londoners."

I think I understand him. It feels like the dilemma of the modern nomad. What happens to your roots when you move? And I immediately think of Shamis, ruefully describing herself as a second-class citizen in two countries and wondering why anyone should be trapped by the accident of birth.

"But what about your mother?" I ask Tarzan. I've been thinking that maybe the story about her coming to Mogadishu to give birth was, at least in part, his way of feeling closer to her.

Tarzan brushes that theory aside. "She had no role in it."

The remaining tomatoes, for our dinner, are starting to burn, and Tarzan gets up to stir in some more water from the kettle. His mind is still back at the orphanage.

"I'm not ashamed of my difficulties there. I used to borrow clothes. Nothing was mine. Did I tell you that I had insects in the bed? So you scratch yourself. One night I couldn't sleep so I went outside to where they'd been digging a well, and I buried myself in the sand. I slept there. This is a part of my life. I'm proud of it. It's not my father who made me. It's me.

"I'm the Tarzan."

He's heading back to Mogadishu first thing the next day, stopping off en route in Abu Dhabi for a conference, then Dubai for a few days to see Shamis. We say our goodbyes, and I head off down the hill toward Camden. It's morbid, but I can never help wondering whether I'll see him again or whether his luck will run out before our next meeting. I know he ponders much the same every time he takes leave of his children in London. I find myself checking his Facebook profile several times a day. He's become very active online, and I get the sense he's worried about falling off the public radar now that he's no longer mayor. He's set up a new political party, the Social Justice Party, as part of his campaign to become president, and he's always jumping at every hint of a media interview, or a plane ticket to visit diaspora groups in Sweden, or Holland, or anywhere else. But he's a political outsider once again, worried about funding, scratching at the door.

※⊙☾

THE NEXT MORNING IS cool and windy. It drizzles for a few hours, but by lunchtime London is looking freshly scrubbed and self-assured, as I stand outside Moorgate Underground station, in the financial district, waiting for Abukar Dahir to arrive.

He's an hour late—stuck in the Swedish embassy trying to renew a passport—but we quickly fall into our usual rhythm, striding fast through the city, south toward the Thames, across Southwark Bridge, and then down onto the crowded embankment, heading west.

Abukar has always seemed more pensive in London than in Mogadishu. And today he has more than usual on his mind. He's just decided he doesn't want to go back to Somalia anymore. He's done with it. And the realization has dislodged something—nudged the boulder away from the cave entrance.

"I try to make myself busy. But it creeps up, in a funny way. It's not guilt, but when I'm having a very good day, it comes back to haunt me," he says, hunting for the words to describe the weight in his chest.

It feels like familiar territory. I've covered many wars in the twenty-five years I've been working as a foreign correspondent and have seen and learned something of the damage such experiences can inflict. I ask him if he feels like he's abandoned his post. He pauses and looks toward the river. We've just passed the Globe Theatre, and we're walking through a block of shade cast by the Tate Modern art gallery's high tower.

"That's the question. It's difficult to answer. And do I really even want to get an answer?"

He starts talking about his first trip back to Mogadishu. Too scared, at first, to get off the plane but fueled by a sense of mission—almost like he was seeking redemption.

"If I knew what I know now, would I still have done it?" he asks himself, probingly. He hasn't decided yet.

Abukar has been having troubled dreams, often when he's heard of another friend being killed. There was a guy from the Somali diaspora living in Poland, a builder, who left his family and went back recently. His business was just starting to pick up in Mogadishu when it happened. And there was a girl. Abukar has mentioned her to me before but skated over some of the details.

"It was during a rough period between me and my fiancée. I got to know this girl, Sahra, and she was very nice. On Friday morning we were supposed to go to Lido beach. But the night before, she was taking her little brother to hospital, walking past the K4 roundabout.

"We heard the explosion. And I thought nothing more about it. But later, I called her, and phoned, and phoned. And the next morning we drove round to pick her up from her home, to go to the beach, but she wasn't there. We all went to the beach anyway.

"So it turns out there was this Qatar delegation coming from Villa Somalia, and Al Shabab was targeting the convoy. She was standing right next to the cars. She was blown to bits, with her little brother. Splattered on the wall." Abukar is almost whispering now, and I have to lean in as we walk, to catch what he's saying.

"That was . . . It was like somebody just ripped me apart. That somebody can be killed, just like that. And you know, it means you don't want to get attached to people. You're just so scared all the time to lose someone."

We've just passed the National Theatre and we cross the river again, heading toward Whitehall and into the parks around Buckingham Palace.

For years, Abukar told anyone who would listen that Mogadishu was on the mend. Like Shamis, he felt stronger knowing he was making a difference, that it was worthwhile. It's not that he's lost all hope now. "But at the same time I realized I was losing everything that was important in my life." He means his fiancée. His family back in London. He never told his mother what he was going through. Seeing the severed heads of suicide bombers. What it felt like to have someone else's blood on you.

Instead he began to develop his own rules about how to stay alive. Never go to Lido beach on a Friday. Never go out between noon and 2 p.m. when all the security guards take their lunch break. Avoid restaurants. Never get cocky about safety. And if you're flying out of

Mogadishu, go to the airport first thing in the morning and just wait there.

Finally, he decided to leave for good.

And now it all feels surreal, almost like it never happened. It's made him wonder about his Somali-ness, and about how much it's linked to geography. He feels more British than anything else now, and he's even thinking about giving up his Somali citizenship altogether.

"It's still hard, speaking about this. All these fears build up. They have such a profound effect on you, but I don't even understand it yet."

But he knows one thing for sure now. "I came back in the nick of time."

※☼☼

For once, Mogadishu is buried in rain clouds. On our first attempt at landing, the plane overshoots the runway, swings sharply to the right over a slate-gray sea, and roars back up into the whiteness. A few minutes later we're safely down and taxiing across a flooded apron toward the newly completed airport terminal—a sharp-edged, expensive-looking, giant shoebox of a building and a powerful statement of confidence. Another milestone for Somalia.

As we all queue up quietly in the air-conditioned arrival hall, I think back to all those angry, sweaty scrums—for bags, for immigration, for bribes—that used to mark the start and end of any trip to Mogadishu. How quickly we adapt to our surroundings.

But outside, it's back to the usual routine. Five armed guards waiting in our escort car. Rain-drenched Ugandan troops manning the barricades. Tight chicanes formed by white concrete slabs to slow down any suicide bombers. And then we're out onto the tarmacked airport road, heading into the city.

"These'll take forty-seven rounds before they start to crack," the British private security guard in the passenger seat says, tapping the window. It seems ludicrously precise.

I can't get hold of Tarzan at first. So instead, I head up to see

Ahmed Jama at his Village Sports restaurant. The rain has stopped now, and the traffic is moving smoothly around the K4 roundabout. As we head up a side road, I scan the walls for new adverts. They're something of a Mogadishu specialty—bright, detailed, hand-painted pictures covering every inch of the outside walls of shops, depicting exactly what they're selling inside, from cereal and toilet paper to car parts and computers. I was once told they were a sign of failure—a response to the fact that generations of Somalis can no longer read. But they strike me now as a celebration of commerce and a happy tradition. They also can be

Advertising, Mogadishu, 2015. COURTESY OF BECKY LIPSCOMBE

surprisingly graphic. The pictures outside some private clinics show childbirth and other available "procedures" in eye-watering detail.

I find Ahmed in his outdoor kitchen, wielding a frying pan, and talking to two young members of staff. I can smell wood smoke and something spicy. There's swordfish steak on the menu today, and samosas, spaghetti, omelets, camel stew, and fresh doughnuts.

As usual, Ahmed is full of plans. He's building a new restaurant inside the military camp at the airport, and another in Hobyo, an ancient port city up the coast where his grandparents came from, a place more famous these days for its pirates.

"I'll be opening that one next year, if I'm still alive. Ha."

The sentiment is familiar. But the tone has changed. Ahmed sounds weary, like someone going through the motions. He looks it, too. Big bags under his eyes. He's survived six attacks now, some by Al Shabab, and others, he's sure, from business rivals.

"We never give up," he says. But then he lets out a sigh. "There's always hope. Always hope. But we can't keep running. It looks like this government is a bad one. The problem is still corruption."

I ask him if he's still in touch with Tarzan, and something flickers across his face.

"I don't see Tarzan. I don't go with him. He made some good money, so . . ."

"What are you hinting at?" I ask, surprised.

"I'm hinting because . . . we know what he's done. If you want the truth, ask him."

"But you were friends, right?" I had no idea they'd fallen out.

"We were friends. We came here to change something, but if you ask people about Tarzan, they'll tell you who he really was."

That's all he wants to say on the subject. But then he asks me why I'm writing a book about Tarzan. And I think I know what he's getting at. In recent years a number of Somalis have asked me the same question. Although it's not really a question at all. It's a rebuke. It's like Fartaag said in his email—why can't you write about "the true heroes of Somalia"?

I give my usual, neutral, and, I hope, honest answer—that it was chance, convenience, and curiosity that led me to Tarzan. That I wasn't looking for a hero, per se, but rather someone willing to share an interesting life story that seemed to follow Somalia's own turbulent path, or at least to intersect with it from time to time in startling ways.

Ahmed offers a curt laugh. "Well, good luck to him."

We say our goodbyes, and I get back into the car, thinking about the indignation that I've provoked from other Somalis. It's not just that some people don't like Tarzan. It's not just about clans either. It's something more abstract and profound. Somalia doesn't get much outside attention, and when it does, it always seems to be of the wrong sort.

I've come to picture it like this. It's as if Somalia has been buried for a generation, with foreigners like me standing on its grave carving the words "failed" or "pirate" or "terrorist state" on the headstone, and ignoring all the grieving, exiled relatives standing to one side, trying to point out that Somalia isn't actually dead, that it's finally coming back to life, and that the next words to be written—on a celebration banner, not a tombstone—should, at last, be their own words, or at the very least, should be words that they can all agree on, all be proud of.

But what would those words be, I wonder. And after all this time, is agreement even feasible?

TARZAN IS SITTING BAREFOOT and alone on his porch, sipping tea with a dash of Somali honey, and fidgeting with his two mobile phones.

He seems unusually subdued, and it soon becomes clear why. He's feeling trapped. It's like he's under house arrest. When he was mayor, the government and his clan were responsible for providing security. But now he's on his own. He has to pay for everything. And even his

Tarzan at home in Mogadishu, 2015. COURTESY OF THE AUTHOR

cousin Fanah has found a new job running one of the city's bigger police stations.

Tarzan hardly ever goes out now. And frustration has quickly turned to resentment.

"If I was a simple citizen I could enjoy my freedom. But I compromised my security to come and work as mayor. And I did a good job—everyone knows I did a good job. Now the government is supposed to protect me and pay my income. But they don't protect me," he says bitterly.

And that leads into an angry outburst about the president. It's odd. Within the space of a minute, Tarzan can be the cautious diplomat, declining to criticize individuals by name. Seconds later, he's singling out senior officials and accusing them of corruption—of openly selling off public land to the highest bidder.

"A change will come," he warns darkly. He means when he becomes president.

But the political process isn't working in his favor right now. And I wonder if it ever will. Tarzan is convinced he has a chance to win a one man, one vote presidential election in Somalia. He's always believed that. But not for the first time, those in power seem to be finding reasons to keep the electoral process limited to the votes of a few carefully chosen clan and regional representatives.

We sit in silence for a moment, sipping our tea, and I listen out for gunshots. I realize that I haven't heard a single one since I arrived. It's hardly scientific, but it sounds like progress.

It seems like the right moment to ask Tarzan about what happened with Ahmed Jama—about why they fell out.

"He's a very strange character. A very bad character. Impulsive. Lonely. He cannot cope," Tarzan declares abruptly.

Then he goes off on a tangent, and it's almost like he's declaring his creed. As familiar as I've become with his clear-cut worldview, his certainties, and his confidence, I'm caught off guard.

"Anyone against me is a bad person," he says.

"Anyone? Really?"

"Let me repeat. Whoever is on my side is in the right. Whoever is against me is wrong. People hate me for the wrong reasons—they're people who are highly corrupted, and those with a strong clan mentality. But people love me for the right reasons."

I can hear, in that voice, the angry orphan challenging any boy who dares to mock him, and the hard-skinned adult carving a path through a forest of enemies. But it is a little unnerving, too.

IT'S PAST FOUR IN the afternoon when Tarzan and I set off for a drive around town. He seems keen to get out of the house, and between us we now have ten armed guards to watch our backs.

We turn out of the cul-de-sac, down the hill toward the barrier beside the national theater, and swing to the left. Tarzan is in tour-guide mode. There's the spot where Shamis's old school used to sit—the place he first met her. That used to be the Chinese embassy. This was Casa Italia, the old Italian club. Then the Shabelle Hotel. A night-club. The banana export agency. The Juba Hotel.

We pass near the Central Hotel, too, and I think of an email I recently received from its owner manager. Ahmed Hussein came back from Sheffield, England, two years ago, inspired, at least in part, by Tarzan. But the hotel has recently endured two major suicide attacks, and now Ahmed has decided to cut his losses.

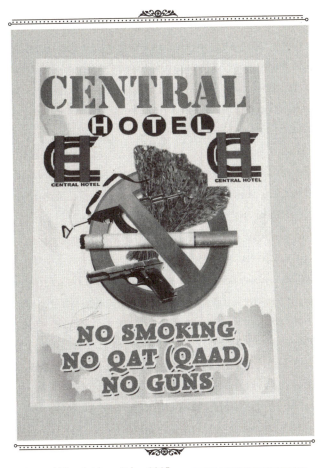

Central Hotel, Mogadishu, 2015. COURTESY OF BECKY LIPSCOMBE

In his email, he said the only customers he could get to fill his hotel were government officials. But that leads to two problems—attacks from Al Shabab and the fact that "the government does not pay. I therefore concluded that there are no business opportunities unless you are connected with corrupt officials, or equally corrupted Al Shabab."

We turn a corner, and Tarzan peers through the armored glass.

"There used to be an Italian butcher somewhere here," he says, pointing at another spectacular pile of rubble. Even now, for all the new building work going on, you're seldom far from the ruins in Mogadishu.

Tarzan starts telling me a story. One I'd never heard before—about a close relative who had joined Al Shabab.

Hussein was Tarzan's cousin, his father's brother's son. He'd been living for many years in America and was tall, handsome, and devout. But Hussein had surprised his family, first by becoming a fashion model, and then by abruptly leaving the United States for Mogadishu, where he briefly visited his mother before disappearing. He had, it seemed, gone to join Al Shabab.

Tarzan says he received a warning phone call at some point in 2012. CIA officials in Mogadishu had apparently tipped off Somalia's security services, believing that Hussein might be planning to use his family connections to get close to the mayor.

"If you see him, if he comes close to my house, shoot him," Tarzan promptly told his security guards.

But Al Shabab was suspicious of Hussein. The group assumed he was working for the CIA and treated him accordingly. After several months, he decided to escape, and with the help of another disillusioned diaspora recruit, he hid in a lorry packed with bananas and made it back to his relatives in Mogadishu. Five days later, an American drone killed Al Shabab's leader, Ahmed Godane—reinforcing the suspicion that Hussein was, indeed, a spy and a traitor.

"So now he's hiding in Mogadishu. He's wanted, dead or alive, by Al Shabab," says Tarzan. The whole story is making him chuckle. "He's a weak man, a chicken, so scared. He has no life right now. NO LIFE!"

Tarzan went to see him recently.

"I told him, 'You're the most foolish person I've ever met.'"

"Did you ask him if he planned to kill you?"

"Yes. He said, 'No, never.' But I cannot trust him."

Our convoy stops outside the old basketball stadium—the scene of all those teenaged dramas and of the exhibition match with Oscar Robertson and Kareem Abdul-Jabbar. There's a big sign over the gate now that reads "Wiish Stadium." The place has been renamed in honor of Wiish, the referee who sent Oscar Robertson off for dribbling the ball "incorrectly."

A dozen girls are training on the outdoor court. There are new floodlights and a couple of advertisements painted on the stands. The next-door building, three stories high and riddled with bullet and shell holes, looms over one end.

Tarzan spots an old friend, someone who was once on the national team, and begins reminiscing. The man, who has been coaching the girls' team, sees me and promptly declares, "We need Tarzan to become president of Somalia! Truly, he was good as mayor. We saw improvements."

"But what about his faults?" I ask.

"Well, he's sometimes nervous." I think he means excitable. "And when he doesn't get what he wants, he becomes angry and makes mistakes. Just like when he was playing basketball!" Tarzan is right next to us, grinning.

We leave soon afterward and drive around the corner to an orphanage that Tarzan and Shamis recently set up. Eighty boys are sitting silently beside a sandy football pitch. Tarzan seems to relax before my eyes. He makes a point of shaking each boy's hand, and then asks the man in charge, Shamis's half-brother, Abdi, why they're just sitting idly.

"They were waiting to pray? But that's in half an hour. They should be playing, exercising. It's most important for them at this age." He turns to me. "Abdi doesn't understand this. He didn't grow up in an orphanage."

We can't stay for long. And not only for security reasons. Tarzan has just had a phone call about a possible gathering in the city. A rally, of sorts. It's a rare chance for him to address a local crowd and I can sense his excitement. But as we're getting back into our cars he gets another call. The crowd is too small. It's not worth the risk. I suggest we go to one of the cafés on Lido beach instead, but he's not keen on public places.

"I have to protect myself. If I spend an hour in a hotel, someone will call Al Shabab and say, 'Tarzan is here.'"

⁂

IT'S LATE AFTERNOON NOW and the sun is starting to sink through a clear blue sky behind the city. We drive to Tarzan's house to drop him off and then head back toward Lido beach. We park on a sand-covered road nearby and walk down toward the surf.

It's nearly high tide, and the crowds are pressed up close to the rocks on a narrowing strip of sand. I can hear the screams and the laughter, and I think I can already make out a few accents—kids from Wembley and Minnesota, back for the holidays, plunging into the waves.

I stop to talk to an earnest middle-aged man, perched on a home-made wooden lifeguard's chair, but I'm interrupted, abruptly, by an angry man brandishing a grenade. Perhaps "brandishing" is the wrong word. I only notice the grenade after a few seconds. He's holding it clenched in his left hand, like a purse. From his behavior, I'm pretty sure he's been chewing khat. He's some sort of district security official, and he wants me to leave. The presence of foreigners might, he says, attract Al Shabab. I've been through similar drills before, and I make a call to someone senior in the government—an old London friend of Tarzan's, as it happens—and hand the phone over to the grenade-man.

Ten minutes later, I'm sitting in the shade, on the terrace of the Lido Seafood restaurant, drinking a large glass of fresh fruit juice. It's Friday, and the place is packed with well-to-do Somalis, men and

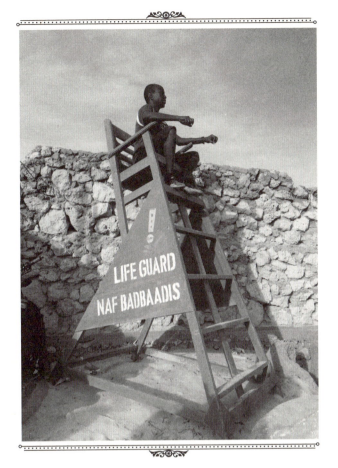

Lifeguard, Lido beach, Mogadishu, 2015.
COURTESY OF BECKY LIPSCOMBE

women, locals and diaspora, in elegant suits and long dresses, mingling and chatting.

I think about Shamis, still in Dubai, trying to make a success of her dress shop. I called her the other day and she sounded overjoyed. She told me Tarzan had promised her that this would be his last year, his last attempt, to get somewhere in Somali politics.

"He said, 'Give me a chance. If we're not successful, I'll stop.' And we'll never go back to it, ever," she added, firmly. But I wonder if she really believes it. Tarzan's brother Yusuf certainly doesn't.

"It's in his blood! In his veins! He's not going anywhere. If she thinks he's going to retire, she's deluding herself."

But Yusuf wonders if his brother has the flexibility to rise to the very top, or whether he's too stubborn to make the necessary deals in an increasingly crowded political arena full of people "without principles or qualms."

And what of Somalia's own future?

Yusuf used to talk enthusiastically about coming back "home" to Mogadishu in retirement. Maybe even of getting some extra-plump wheels for his mountain bike so he could pedal around in the sand, herding camels back in "our home area" in the countryside. But now he's not so sure.

Like Yusuf, I've always bristled against grand predictions—a favorite hobby of foreigners throughout Africa, anxious to pin their epitaphs to Zimbabwe, South Africa, Nigeria, Mali, or Kenya. The continent is either doomed to fail or rising like a phoenix.

Somalia has slowly begun to make measurable progress. It now has an army and a government. Piracy has almost stopped, Al Shabab controls much less territory, there is oil offshore, a flourishing livestock industry, and a talented and wealthy diaspora.

And yet, the politics are still dangerously messy, fueled by the greed of unaccountable politicians, the fragility of opaque institutions, the enduring menace of Al Shabab, and the questionable ambitions of some regional leaders and of Somalia's neighbors, Kenya and Ethiopia.

This may no longer be a "failed state," but the jigsaw is still in pieces.

"I take a long-term view," says Yusuf, looking for an optimistic vantage point. But Tarzan is resolutely gloomy, convinced that "we're not heading in a good way, believe me," and that the decision to carve out powerful new federal states within Somalia will lead the country back toward clan conflict and civil war.

I look out across Lido beach toward the Indian Ocean. A few fishing boats are bobbing in the surf, and above them, a slim jet is roaring northward. In a few months' time, Al Shabab's fighters will attack this same terrace from the road and the beach, killing twenty people.

But right now, on a blissfully clear evening, with lobster on the menu and a cheerful, even raucous crowd of Somalis gathered from every corner of the earth, it feels like the worst must surely be over, like pessimism would be a crime. It feels like a homecoming.

A NOTE ON SPELLING

Tarzan, Tarsan, or perhaps even Tarsame . . . ?

Like so many things in Somalia, the language itself is rich, complicated, constantly evolving, heavily influenced by colonialism, and energetically contested. Not unlike English.

Although Somalia uses the Roman alphabet, it has no appetite for the letter *z*. So many people—including the man himself—say "Tarsan," not "Tarzan." Tar-san has the added (but little known) allure of meaning "one who contributes good." But I've stuck with the *z* because I think it captures the spirit of the nickname most clearly for a wider audience. And I've done the same elsewhere, using Mogadishu, for instance, rather than opting for the old Italian spelling, Mogadiscio, or the Somali—Muqdisho.

Where possible, I've tried to be faithful to the wishes of the person, or the relative, or the organization involved. Sometimes Somalis actively prefer the Italian or the English to the Somali—so Mohamud, not Mohamoud, and Habeba, not Xabiiba. Sometimes it's very much the other way around.

There is, in other words, plenty of thought, but no great consistency, in the application of spelling "rules" in this book. To those who find reason to take offense, I sincerely apologize.

Incidentally, Tarzan's brother told me an intriguing story about how President Siad Barre may have been influenced in his choice of the Latin script for Somalia's new alphabet. Apparently the military dictator was on a state visit to China, and met Chairman Mao, who allegedly told him that "if he could start again" he would choose the Latin alphabet for China.

ACKNOWLEDGEMENTS

Not long after I wrote the last sentence of this book, I received a text message alerting me to a brutal attack, by Al Shabab, that was under way at Lido beach in Mogadishu. News and speculation surged across the internet, and not for the first time, I felt the tug of collective dread that so many Somalis experience on such occasions. Who was there? How many hurt? Anyone I know . . . ?

This time, my colleague Mohamed Moalimuu was among the injured. Thankfully he has recovered well. But I wanted to start these acknowledgements by paying tribute to the courage of so many Somali journalists, and by thanking those, like Moalimuu, who have been so generous with their time and their advice over the years.

I've been traveling to Somalia since 2000, and I know this list will be woefully incomplete, and, as I look through it now, disconcertingly male. But in Mogadishu and beyond, I'm hugely grateful to Ali Mohamed Haji, Ajoos Sanura, Eng. Yarisow, Hussein Moalim, Abdirashid Hashi, Abdirashid Salah, President Hassan Sheikh Mohammed, Daud Aweis, Sharif Hassan Sheikh Aden, Deeq Yusuf, Abdulkareem Jama, Mohamed Abdullahi Mohamed "Farmajo," Naleye Abdirizak, Bashir Mohamoud, Mohamed Fanah, Maryan Qasim, Ahmed Ismail Hussein, Major General Fred Mugisha, General Ali Madobe, General Bashir Mohamed Jama, Mohammed Farole, Ismail Mohamed Omar, Faiza Hassan, Omar "Ringo" Osman, Abdi

Farah Shirdon, Mohammed Martello, Iman Icar, Ahmed Adan, Jabril Abdulle, Abdusalam Omer, Mohamed Farah Siad, Yusuf Garaad Omar, Liban Egal, Mohammed "John" Hassan, Mohammed Yahye, and many more.

I wish I knew their names, but the men with guns rarely seem to talk much. Over the years I've been well guarded by dozens of Somalis—in Mogadishu, Buale, Afgoye, Dolo, Dusamareb, Baidoa, Garowe, Bosaso, Hargesia, Berbera, and on two visits to the "pirate town" of Eyl—and I thank them all. Thanks also to all those who have provided logistical support: beds, convoys, helicopters, meals, medicine, a snorkel and goggles to explore the shallows beside Mogadishu's runway, frontline tours, impeccable advice, and a great deal more besides—Bashir Yusuf Osman, Major Barigye Ba-Hoku, David Snelson, Alisha Ryu, Richard Bailey, Justin Marozzi, Stephen Harley, Ciro Ugrin, Cassandra Nelson, Patrick Loots, Abdirizak Jama, Alan Cole, and many others.

Somalis have reason to be wary of outsiders with hidden agendas. I've deliberately sought to steer away from quoting many foreigners in this book. But I must thank a good number of people for kindly sharing their memories, expertise, and advice, including Matt Bryden, Tim Randall, Ben Parker, Denise Brown, Matt Baugh, Jeremy Varcoe, Colin Wood, Neil Wigan, Sarah Lee, Mick Farrant, Kareem Abdul-Jabbar, Oscar Robertson, Ibrahim Mohamoud, Rasnah Warah, Fredricka Whitfield, Ben Foot, John Prendergast, Keith Biddle, Dino Mahtani, Tony Burns, Mark Bowden, Matt Leslie, Nick Pyle, Peter Smerdon, Steve Turner, Bronwen Morrison, and Johan Ripas.

I have barely scratched the surface of Somalia's vast diaspora. But I've encountered some extraordinary people—generous, passionate, opinionated, and, no doubt, poised to continue setting me straight. Hussein Mao Khaireh "Gabyow," Samiya Lerew, Bashir Omar Qaman, Abdirizak Adan Muhumed, Abdirizak Fartaag, Adam Matan, Duran Farah, Jamal Osman, Musse Sheikh, Abdirashid Duale, Annarita Puglielli, Kadigia Mohammed, Mohammed Adow, Rashid

Ali, Ayan Mahamoud, Ilham Gassar, Ibrahim Isse, Awa Abdi, Mohammed Ibrahim Shire, Lino Marano, Abukar Awale, Idil Osman, Mohammed Hussein Abukar—thank you all.

My many trips to Somalia have been undertaken for the BBC, and I've been lucky enough to work with some of the organization's finest. Phil Davies, Tara Neil, Christian Parkinson, Kate Forbes, Stuart Phillips, Barnaby Mitchell, and Becky Lipscombe, thanks for everything. Also to Karen Peek, who watched our backs from London, and Africa editors Sally Hodgkinson, Peter Burdin, and Jonathan Chapman. In 2005, my friend and BBC colleague Kate Peyton was murdered in Mogadishu. Her infectious energy and optimism remain an inspiration. I'd like to thank foreign editors Jon Williams and Andrew Roy for backing me in my desire to continue returning to the country, and the many other editors, like Hugh Levinson, who've understood Somalia's significance.

There are some wonderful books about Somalia, and wonderful authors, too. The unmatchable, prolific Nuruddin Farah has been generous with his time, cooking, and encouragement—thanks for encouraging me to "milk the cow." Johnny Steinberg's *A Man of Good Hope* is a magnificent, stirring read. My BBC colleague Mary Harper's book *Getting Somalia Wrong?* is an incisive, invaluable guide to the country. Sir Richard Burton's *First Footsteps in East Africa* and Gerald Hanley's *Warriors* are essential reading. I shall never forget watching Ladan Osman perform her bewitching poetry in London. Ali Jimale Ahmed kindly hosted me in New York. Warsan Shire and Mohamed Ibrahim Warsame "Hadraawi" are the richest, most compelling voices of their generations. Thanks to Richard Dowden for his generous advice—and his chapter on Somalia in *Africa: Altered States, Ordinary Miracles*. James Fergusson's *The World's Most Dangerous Place* is a terrific work of reportage and analysis. The journalism of Tristan McConnell, Katrina Manson, Jeffrey Gettleman, Peter Greste, and others has been extraordinary. Many writers and editors have been generous with their advice, including Tim Butcher, J. M. Ledgard—who reminded me about the dik-dik—Alex Perry, Michela Wrong, Jon Lee Anderson, Xan Rice, Cressida Leyshon, Aiden Hartley, Barnaby Phillips, and Giles Foden.

Abukar Dahir requires a special mention and profound thanks for his time, courage, and good company. The same goes for the irrepressible Ahmed Jama.

Above all, I must thank the Nurs. Tarzan and Shamis have been unfailingly generous, frank, and patient with a project that has rumbled on for years, and which they have never sought to control or censor. Their children, in particular Abdullahi, Ayan, Ahmed, and Mohammed, have followed their parents' example.

In the United States, Yusuf Nur has been extraordinarily kind. This book no doubt contains errors, but it would have been riddled with many more were it not for Yusuf's steady, fastidious, enthusiastic support.

Thanks to my agent, Rebecca Carter, and her great team at London's Janklow and Nesbitt, and to Elisabeth Dyssegaard and her wonderful colleagues at St. Martin's Press in New York, for their constant encouragement and wise counsel. The same goes for Michael Dwyer and his energetic team at Hurst, and to Terry Morris at Pan Macmillan in South Africa.

Lastly, I must thank my boys, Alex, Sam, and Dexter, for their love and wit; our cat, for failing in his numerous attempts to delete each chapter; and my wife, Jenny, who has never urged me not to get on a plane, and whose humor and wisdom make all the difference in the world.